A Silence of Mockingbirds

—THE MEMOIR OF A MURDER—

BY KAREN SPEARS ZACHARIAS

A Silence of Mockingbirds

—THE MEMOIR OF A MURDER—

BY KAREN SPEARS ZACHARIAS

MACADAM CAGE

MacAdam/Cage
155 Sansome Street, Suite 550
San Francisco, CA 94104
www.macadamcage.com

Library of Congress Cataloging-in-Publication Data
Zacharias, Karen Spears.
A silence of mockingbirds : the memoir of a murder / by Karen Spears Zacharias.
p. cm.
ISBN 978-1-59692-375-1 (hardcover)
1. Murder—Oregon—Case studies. I. Title.
HV6533.O7Z33 2012
364.152'3092—dc23
2012000748

Book design by Dorothy Carico Smith.

Printed in the United States of America.

First edition.

10 9 8 7 6 5 4 3 2 1

With great love for
Karly Isabelle Ruth Sheehan
&
David Sheehan

Once a mockingbird stakes out its territory, it will defend that territory against all intruders, including animals much larger than itself. The size or type of opponent does not seem to matter, but the bird is not always successful in driving away the intruder.

—Texas Parks & Wildlife Department

CHAPTER ONE

THE ENVELOPE ON MY DESK is addressed to Inmate 16002306. Inside is a letter of request. It is not the first one I've sent, and I don't expect it will be the last. I am tempted to mail one every day until I get what I want: a face-to-face interview.

In the military, the enlisted are most often referred to by their last names, not their serial numbers. I don't know what the appropriate protocol is inside the slammer when referring to an inmate. Do they call him by his first name or his last name? Or do they call out to him— Hey, Baby Killer!—the way so many protestors did to those American soldiers who were fortunate enough to return home from Vietnam?

I don't know Shawn Wesley Field personally. I only know what I've learned about him from plowing through thousands of pages of court documents, or from talking to others who've known him, or from listening to the audio tapes of the police interrogations.

It is uncharacteristic of David Sheehan to speak unkindly about anyone, even when it is justified. David refuses to speak Inmate 16002306's name. He refers to him as a monster. There's no question that David has earned the right to call Shawn Field any name he damn well pleases. There's not a jury in this land that would have convicted

David of murder if he had taken a baseball bat and beaten the life out of Shawn.

Born and bred in Ireland, David Sheehan displays few of the archetypical behaviors often attributed to the Irish. He's neither loud nor boisterous. While he enjoys a good party, he doesn't need to be the center of attention. He's humble, soft-spoken, kindhearted and a hard worker.

It was his job with Hewlett-Packard (HP) that lured him to America. He came straight out of Kenmare, County Kerry, Ireland. In 1996, David, an engineer, joined about two hundred other Irish, employees of HP and their families, who came to Corvallis for training at HP's campus.

It was not, however, his first trip to America. That took place when David was only six years old. Even then, his mother suspected the day would come when her oldest would leave Ireland and make a new home across wide waters. David was a boy born to adventure, always lining up his cars along the fireplace and imagining the journeys that awaited. But no child or adult imagines the sort of terrors the grown-up David would encounter in Oregon.

David Sheehan is the father of three-year-old Karly Sheehan, who was murdered by Inmate 16002306, Shawn Wesley Field.

Located west of Oregon's main north-south drag, Interstate 5, Corvallis literally means "heart of the valley." In 1845, Joe Avery staked out his own emerald plot at the junction where Mary's River slips into the Willamette. For a short time, the city served as the capital of the Oregon Territory.

Corvallis is the proud home of Oregon State University. There are more highly educated people per capita living in Corvallis than any other city in the state. You hear it often in the post office, at the library, or at the local bakery. Everyone's said it and it is true: Corvallis is a good place to raise kids.

This college town became my first home in Oregon. A transfer student from Berry College in Rome, Georgia, I came to Corvallis in 1975 to attend Oregon State University. My family had made the move west a year earlier.

The community of Corvallis wrapped my eighteen-year-old self in an OSU orange-and-black blanket and drew me in close. It was as a student of Professor Thurston Doler that I first found my voice. It was while sitting in the pouring rain cheering on the Beavers, and in the pews of First Baptist Church singing songs from a hymnal, that I made lifelong friends. It was under the tutelage of Corvallis High School's Rick Wallace that I learned the skills I would need to teach. It was in the springtime that I first fell in love with the boy who would become the man I still love. And many years later, because I knew Corvallis to be a good community where a wounded girl could heal, I would urge Sarah Brill to move there and to seek her education at Oregon State University.

In October, maples drop their golden parchments into the Willamette River, where they are carried downstream, letters for the beavers. Fog rises up from the still water as some unseen coxswain calls out strokes for OSU's crew team. In June, the town's pace slows. Dozens of bone-white blossoms unfurl on the magnolias in the campus quad, like sunbathers seeking an early tan. Students squirrel away grocery-store boxes filled with belongings—textbooks, puffy down coats—as they prepare for summer jobs on Alaska fishing boats or driving hay trucks on their uncles' Eastern Oregon farms.

Downtown on the courthouse square, roses pink as cotton candy cushion the flat white-plastered brick. From her perch above the entry stands Themis, Goddess of Justice, the quavering balance in her hands. The eight-foot-tall statue is not wearing the traditional blindfold. There's a clock tower above the lady, and directly above high noon or midnight is the word "OF." It is part of a longer statement—THE FLIGHT OF TIME—etched into the sides of the four-sided clock tower.

It was here at the Benton County Courthouse, through the heavy doors, past the security checkpoint, and up a musty oil-polished stairwell that Judge Janet Holcomb presided over the trial of *State vs. Shawn Wesley Field*. Shawn was charged with twenty-three counts for the June 3, 2005, murder of three-year-old Karla "Karly" Isabelle Ruth Sheehan, the daughter of David Sheehan and Sarah Brill Sheehan.

The prosecution's opening statements were made on September 25, 2006. The defense made its closing statement on Halloween. The trial was contentious, fraught with mind-numbing details and a cast of characters that would confound even CNN's Nancy Grace.

Addressing Karly's killer during the sentencing phase, Judge Holcomb also issued an admonishment to the citizens of Corvallis:

> As a community we have to do some deep soul-searching about how, or if, we might have responded sooner. Might there have been an intervention that could have saved this child's life? I don't know. But after hearing all the evidence it seems there was a continuum of failure after the first hint that there was something terribly, terribly wrong.

That failure is something former District Attorney Scott Heiser said will burden him forever. "This homicide was preventable and we in the system failed, and I'll carry that around for the rest of my life."

Ruefully, he adds, "I was the chief law enforcement officer for the county. It was my task-force team. I'm not going to point fingers at one of my staffers. We set protocol and we didn't follow it."

There's plenty of blame and guilt to go around in the case of the death of Karly Sheehan. Like Scott Heiser, I've got my own burden to bear. More than one person had the opportunity to make a different choice, a choice that may have saved a sweet child's life.

Still, as far as the prosecutor was concerned, only one person is responsible for the death of Karly. That man is Shawn Wesley Field. But some people—jurors, investigators, medical professionals, bartenders, and community members, me included—wonder if there isn't another person who ought to be sitting in a prison cell for Karly's death.

In his closing remarks to the jury, Clark Willes, co-counsel for the defense, said, "The facts tell you something happened with Sarah Sheehan, and she has not been honest with you. The fact is every time she turned around, she did not tell police, she did not tell authorities, and she did not tell Children's Services what really happened."

Only three people really know what happened at 2652 Northwest Aspen Street that bright June morning.

One of them is dead.

One of them is in prison.

And one of them blames me.

CHAPTER TWO

I CLICK THE ICON ON my laptop—the one on the desktop marked "Field/ Sheehan 911"—and I hear her alternately gasping, screaming and crying. On first listen, it sounds exactly like what you'd think such a call would sound like: a woman in shock.

A full forty-five seconds passed before seasoned dispatcher Andy Thompson could make out the nature of the call.

Forty-five seconds. The time it takes to plant a tulip bulb, to steep a cup of weak tea, to floss one's teeth, or to draw one's last breath. For emergency personnel like Thompson, forty-five seconds can seem like the implacable drip of water torture, the danger and risk growing with each passing pause. He later told Corvallis Police Sergeant Evan Fieman that the caller was screaming so hysterically he couldn't understand her.

"911. What's your emergency?" Thompson asked.

"OH MY GOD! OH MY GOD! OH MY GOD!" came a female voice.

"I need you to calm down. Where are you?"

Inaudible, hysterical crying.

"HELLO? I need you to stop crying."

"Tww…*gasp*…Tww…*sob*. Northwest Aspen Strrrreeeeetttt!"

"I can't understand you."

"Twenty-six-fifty-two. Twenty-six-fifty-two Northwest Aspen Street. Twenty-six-fifty-two Northwest Aspen Street. Aspen Street. Twenty-six-fifty-two Aspen Street."

"Twenty-six-fifty-two Aspen?" Thompson repeated back.

"Yes. Yes. Northwest. Right across from Hoover."

"What's the problem?" Thompson asked flatly, trying unsuccessfully to calm the caller.

"Karla! Karla! Come back! Karla! Come baaaack!"

"I need you to calm down," Dispatcher Thompson said sternly, authoritatively. "What's the problem?"

"Karla. Please hurry. I don't know what to do."

"What—is—the—problem?" Thompson repeated his question. "I need you to calm down. What's the problem?"

"SHE'S NOT BREATHING!" the woman screamed.

Records place the call at 1:53 p.m. Friday, June 3, 2005.

The caller was Sarah Brill Sheehan.

David's ex-wife.

Karly's mother.

My daughter.

To clarify: Sarah was not my my daughter in the literal sense, or even in the adopted sense, but in that way people choose others as "family." For a precious time in our lives, I chose Sarah and she chose me.

She had in every way imaginable been a part of our family. During a very unsettled time in her life, Sarah slept under our roof, ate at our table, did her homework at the kitchen island, and sat curled up next to me on the couch as I read to her from *Nappy Hair*, a book I'd bought to help celebrate Sarah: *Everybody is talking about little Brenda's hair—the nappiest, the curliest, the twistiest hair in the whole family. And by the time Uncle Mordecia's done celebrating, everyone's going to want hair just like hers.*

Sarah loved the book, as did my other three daughters. They would beg me to read it over and over and over again. And I would, over the echoes of laughter that the story and the telling of it evoked.

But *that* Sarah, the girl whom I had loved so well, had long been lost to me, and I to her. I am reminded of that every time I click on that 911 call on my laptop and hear the screams of a woman I don't recognize.

I'm a former cop reporter. I spent years tracking the daily logs of the Oregon State Police, Pendleton and Hermiston Police, and the Umatilla County Sheriff's office. I followed the petty thefts, the domestic brawls, the barking dogs, the drunk drivers, the disorderly conducts, the car wrecks, and the sex abuse cases. On rare occasions, there were murders, kidnappings, and at least one shootout.

I know that criminal activity isn't just law enforcement's headache and taxpayers' burden; it is somebody's nightmare. A worried father. A distraught mother. A praying sister. A brokenhearted brother. A frightened wife. A desperate husband.

I'd interviewed these folks and I'd included their quotes in the stories I wrote about how their loved ones ended up imprisoned—or worse, dead.

Just up the road from where I live now is a family who misses the young son they lost to alcohol poisoning. The parents allege that a friend's father plied their son with vodka. An investigation was conducted but no charges were brought.

Down the road in the opposite direction is the school where two young girls won awards for scholarly achievements. The older of the girls crouched in the aisles of a convenience store the night her daddy, in a standoff with police, was shot dead. The younger girl was born after their father died.

In a trailer not three miles from here lives a one-armed woman named Karen whose son was charged with and convicted of a murder-for-hire plot. He'd paid to have his ex-wife murdered. Her two-year-old quadruplets were discovered naked and smeared in their mama's blood.

She was lying on the kitchen floor in her Florida home, shot in the face, her throat sliced like a deer.

And thirty miles down the road from where I sit typing is the prison that has become home to Shawn Wesley Field. I've been inside the doors of Eastern Oregon Correctional Institution. I interviewed female inmates about how difficult it is to be away from their children during the holidays. I talked to the inmates who work in the woodshop crafting items that are sold to raise funds for the American Cancer Society. I've heard the convoluted tales of how women became victims of domestic violence, then went on to endanger their own children through their own crime sprees.

I get it.

There's more than one face behind every crime and there is more than one heartache behind every headline.

I never expected the face, or the voice, behind the crime to be anyone I knew. And I certainly never expected the heartache behind the headline to belong to anyone I loved.

CHAPTER THREE

THAT'S NOT TO SAY THAT I didn't have some premonition. The minute Sarah told me she was leaving David, I knew. I knew. I knew. Deep down in the volcanic depths of my soul, I knew that her decision was going to put Karly at risk, but I never thought for one minute that it would result in Karly's death.

I'm not sure how I knew that other than personal experience. Raised by a single mother, I understand how hard a job single parenting can be. My mother didn't choose to raise three children on her own. My father was killed in Vietnam.

His absence created chaos, some of which continues to this day. I grew up imagining, perhaps daydreaming, about all the ways in which my life might have been different had Daddy been around. If Sarah divorced David, I feared Karly could be burdened with that same nagging loneliness.

More importantly, I worried that if Sarah ended up with custody, Karly would grow up ignored, pushed aside, neglected.

In 1987, when we moved to Pendleton with our four young children, We attended the Free Methodist Church. It was there that we first met

Gene and Carol Brill, Sarah's parents.

Gene is retired now, but when Sarah was growing up, he worked as a lab technician for Interpath Laboratories. Carol worked with special-need students at Sunridge Middle School in Pendleton. Active people, Gene and Carol both love the outdoors, boating, hiking, and such. They've adhered to an industrious and disciplined work ethic. They host Bible study fellowships in their home. With his salt-and-pepper beard, lanky stride, and calm demeanor, Gene has the aura of a beloved professor. Carol's white hair has a kink to it and she moves in an overly energetic manner. She talks fast and passionately, sometimes with an edge, like someone desperate to make a point, lest she be misunderstood.

Although friendly with one another in the way churchgoing people often are, we did not socialize with the Brill family. I must have seen Sarah during our years at the Free Methodist Church, at Vacation Bible School, during Easter or Christmas programs, or while picking up our own kids following Sunday School classes. I must have known Sarah as Gene and Carol's adopted daughter. People of color stand out in a town where less than ten percent of the population is anything but white. However, the first time I actually recall meeting Sarah, she was a fresh-faced girl in high school, and I was a substitute teacher.

I liked her from the start. Sarah was sassy, part of the reason she was attending Helix High, a small rural school on the edge of a farming community not far from Pendleton. Sarah wasn't an at-risk student, but she was doing her damndest to earn that designation.

Sarah was stunning in a Halle Berry way. She had the same sugared-caramel complexion, and the small-waisted, lean build of an athlete. Sarah was a standout runner in high school. She tilted her head when she smiled, the coy manner of girls who are told all their lives that they are *so pretty*, and who desperately need others to think so.

Not only was she beautiful on the outside, Sarah possessed an engaging personality. She came across as someone who loved life deeply. Her laughter was light, airy, uplifting—like bubbles blown from a plastic stick. She was keen of mind, sharp of wit, and had an earthy, soft-spoken style that forced others to be better listeners. Believing Sarah could easily make a misstep, I was inclined to not only hear what she said, but all that she didn't say.

It was Carol who first told me of the troubled relationship they shared. We were standing in the hallway at Sunridge Middle School when Carol mentioned something about Sarah giving her fits. It was hardly an unusual thing for a parent to say and I probably would not have remembered it had it not been for my friendship with Sarah. When Sarah's erratic behavior reached a point where it couldn't be dealt with at home, the Brills sent Sarah off to a boarding school for troubled teens. It was one of many steps they took to try and help Sarah. They feared that without intervention, Sarah's troubling behaviors might turn into a pattern for life.

Gene and Carol adopted Sarah when she was an infant. They also had two biological children, Doug and Kimberly. During the time I knew her best, Sarah had a close relationship with her father and her brother but not with her mother or her sister.

An attentive mother, Carol was cautious about Sarah's manipulative personality. Theirs was a strained relationship. Carol attributed a lot of Sarah's problematic behavior to her attention deficit disorder and to abandonment issues, the result of having been adopted.

During the writing of this book, Carol asked me to read the book *Primal Wound.*

"It explains Sarah," she said.

The book's author, Nancy Verrier, is herself the mother of two children, one of whom is adopted. The book is a testimonial, part experiential and part theory. The overarching message, however, is that the connection between the birth mother and her biological child is so profound that when disrupted it creates a "primal or narcissistic wound" in that child.

Verrier suggests that this wound will manifest itself in a variety of ways: a profound sense of loss, basic mistrust and/or anxiety, emotional and behavioral problems making it difficult to maintain healthy relationships with others and leading to self-esteem issues. Critics of Verrier's theory decry its victim mentality. Her proponents insist that acknowledging this primal wound is the first step toward healing it.

Having never raised an adopted child myself, I respect Carol's insights on Sarah. Narcissism remains the most commonly held assessment of Sarah by people familiar with her. Police and attorneys alike use the term to describe her, as do those who, at one time, considered themselves some of Sarah's dearest friends.

People like me.

On a chilling winter's day, when Sarah called to tell me she was leaving David, all I could think of was Sarah's selfishness.

That and those deeply disturbing fears I had for Karly.

Chapter Four

Sarah was in town, hoping to bring Karly by for a visit, in February 2003 when she called. I didn't find that out until years later, during another heated exchange between the two of us. I don't know that it makes any difference now, but I like to tell myself that, had I known then, perhaps I would have responded differently, more thoughtfully, perhaps more carefully.

I'm ever mindful as I tell you this tale that I have my blind spots and my own difficult relationships with people I love, Sarah included.

Still, I do think each and every person connected to Karly and affected by her death ought to ask themselves the question Judge Holcomb raised: "Was there something (or something more) I could have done to prevent this?"

Several people in this case have been willing to answer that question honestly. Among them was former District Attorney Scott Heiser. It called for an exceptional degree of integrity for him to conclude: "This homicide was preventable and we in the system failed, and I'll carry that around for the rest of my life."

My own answer goes back to that angry phone exchange with Sarah.

I was driving my red Beemer north on Highway 395 between

Stanfield and Hermiston when my cell rang. I was on my way to the office, where I worked as the lone Oregon Bureau reporter for a Washington State newspaper. I was preoccupied, thinking about pressing deadlines and the mortal brawl I was having with an editor over a leave request.

I had asked for time off to make a trip to my father's battlefield in Vietnam with a group of other sons and daughters whose fathers had also died there. I offered to write an award-winning story documenting the trip. The editor informed me that he wasn't the least bit interested. "Choose the trip or choose the job," he said.

In response, I had turned in my resignation. In a week, I'd be boarding a plane bound for Ho Chi Minh City. I explained all that to Sarah early on in the conversation.

If I hadn't been so caught up in my own affairs, if I had been more attentive, Sarah probably would have let me know that she was in town and that she wanted to bring Karly by for a visit. But sensing that I was distracted by deadlines, or something else, Sarah never said anything about being in town or having Karly with her. For all I knew, she was calling me from the home she shared with David in Corvallis.

"How are you doing?" I asked.

There was a brief lull in the conversation, and then in one breath Sarah replied that she was taking one-year-old Karly, leaving David, and seeking a divorce.

I was driving past a grocery store at the time. I remember that because it has a big parking lot where I could easily have pulled off and parked. I could have put aside my own pressing agenda and taken the time to really listen to Sarah.

I felt panic rise up. My chest tightened. My stomach clenched up. I had this vision of a forlorn Karly sitting on the edge of her bed crying softly and missing her daddy, the way I had done countless times as a young girl. I was struck by an uncommon fear, of a kind I had not felt since leaving behind my own chaotic childhood.

My next visceral reaction was bombastic anger, all of which I'm sure was not fueled by Sarah's revelation as much as the discord of my own life; still, Sarah received the full brunt of my rage.

"What are you thinking?" I cried. "David adores you. He loves Karly. You can't do this!"

Sarah said nothing.

Taking a deep breath, I gripped the steering wheel with my left hand and the phone with my right one.

"Why?" I asked Sarah, in a tone more restrained. "Why are you doing this? Is David abusive? Is he cheating on you? What's happened?"

I thought back to that evening in 1998, when Sarah brought David to meet Tim and me and the kids. She and David were married by then. They married in a Reno rush. Sarah had always been a woman of passion and impulse. It was part of what I loved best about her, this reckless tendency to make every day seem like a fast ride in a Corvette, roof down, hair blowing, not a care in the world. It was also what worried me most about her.

I had been concerned that she'd made a mistake in choosing a husband so quickly, but my fears were unfounded. Tim and I appreciated David's quiet demeanor, his unassuming ways, and his adoration of Sarah. David and Tim bonded over all things soccer. We hoped that this marriage meant Sarah had finally managed to get her footing on something level, something solid and sure.

But headstrong as ever, Sarah grew increasingly defensive and argumentative as she outlined her reasons for leaving David: "I'm not happy anymore."

I was pissed. I could not believe that Sarah was going to walk out on her marriage. For what? The possibility of some future bliss in the wild blue beyond? Then, suddenly, it occurred to me that more likely Sarah wanted to continue courting the advances of the stable of lustful admirers she had always maintained. Swallowing my anger, I thought

I'd try a more gentle approach.

"Please, honey, don't do this. David loves you. He loves Karly. *Please*," I begged.

Sarah blew me off. "You don't understand," she said. "You don't get it. I'm not happy."

My fury flared again. I'd been through my own fair share of marital struggles. I wasn't about to let Sarah marginalize me in such a flippant fashion. I knew how to get down and scrappy.

"Listen, Sarah," I seethed, "you are not always going to be able to trade off your looks. One day you're going to wake up old and ugly, then what?"

I'd never spoken so harshly to her before, but somehow I knew that if Sarah left David, Karly would be neglected. I knew it as surely as I knew my mother's name.

"I don't care about your happiness!" I snapped. "You have a daughter to think about. You've got to think of what's best for Karly."

Sarah retreated. I waited for some reply, but none came and stone-cold silence pushed us to separate corners. After a brusque goodbye, we both clicked off our cell phones.

I left the next week for Vietnam, and the following year my husband and I moved from Pendleton to Hermiston, thirty miles west. That was the year I began to have a disturbing, reoccurring dream. This dream terrified me, because throughout life my dreams have served as a source of warning.

There was the dream I had the day we buried Daddy, where I saw my brother standing before me bloodied from head to foot. The phone call that startled Mama and me from our naps was a neighbor woman calling to tell Mama her boy was in a bad accident. Then came the knock at the door, and my brother was standing there awash in blood the way he had been in my dream.

There had been the dream I had of a girlfriend's husband searching room to room for his wife. I knew what he didn't know: she had been slaughtered. I woke with the urge to call and tell him to pray for his wife, whom I figured was in some sort of danger. He did as I urged, and three weeks later, she was diagnosed with the virulent breast cancer that would eventually take her life.

I seriously consider the dreams that haunt me. The one that came after my fight with Sarah was deeply disturbing. In that dream, I bury dead children. Not my children, but somebody's children. Upon waking, I have the awful sense these children are dead because I've murdered them and hidden their bodies. The dream is so vivid it is hard to know when I wake if I am really awake or still in the midst of a nightmare.

One morning upon waking from the dream again, I rolled over to face Tim. He was reading, one hand propped up behind his head, the pillow folded into the crook of his arm. With his other hand, Tim held an aging paperback copy of *The Problem of Pain*. Tim has read that book so many times over the course of our marriage I wonder sometimes if it is his form of therapy. The books pages are stiff and the color of smokers' teeth; a few have begun to loosen from the binding.

"I had a bad dream," I said, snuggling into him.

"You did." It wasn't intended to be a question, only a half-hearted acknowledgement that Tim had heard me.

"How many children have we killed?" I asked.

"What?" Tim dropped the book to his chest. "What are you talking about?"

"How many children have we killed?" I replied. "I dreamed we were burying dead babies. It seems so real, not like a dream, but like we really did kill them."

My dreams creep Tim out. Throwing back the covers, he hopped out of bed, his book in hand. "You have the strangest dreams," he said as he walked out of the room. It was Tim's way of letting me know he wanted no part in the conversation. I rolled back over and watched him leave. An outstretched hand of morning sun reached through the window and across the duvet in an attempt to soothe me with warmth, but I could not shrug off the chill that had woken me.

Four years would pass before Sarah and I spoke to one another again. By then, Karly would be dead.

CHAPTER FIVE

S ARAH ASKED US TO ADOPT her baby. Not Karly, but Hillary, who as I write this is a teenage girl herself, driving, dating, and dreaming of college.

Hillary is the baby Sarah had the year she came to live with us, and in a very conflicted way, Hillary feels like a baby I gave up.

It's hard to talk about it. There are probably hundreds of families out there with a similar tale: a daughter, a sister, an aunt, a friend, women who've suffered miscarriages or adoptions that failed. I imagine they all struggle with the same question. How do I tell others about the child I almost had? The only answer to that question is that you don't. Best to keep it to yourself, except for a rare few.

I'm pragmatic about the pitfalls of adolescence, having had an abortion my senior year of high school. Sarah was one of the half-dozen friends who knew the story of the baby I had aborted, and of my regrets. I am sure that is why she felt comfortable confiding in me. She knew I wasn't going to lecture her.

We talked, heart to heart, then Sarah left town. She relocated to a home for unwed mothers several hours away in Tacoma, Washington.

Sarah claimed the decision was her parents' idea. At the time, I accepted Sarah's explanation, but I never discussed the matter with Gene and Carol, even though I had strong opinions about Sarah moving away.

There was a time when being pregnant out of wedlock was socially unacceptable, a shameful thing. And while it's true Sarah's unplanned pregnancy would have been the scuttlebutt around Pendleton for a while, it would hardly have been headline news.

She was a college student, after all, plenty old enough to be considered capable, whether she planned to keep the baby or adopt it out. While having a baby was sure to interrupt her life, what was the point in hiding away until then?

Despite the distance separating us, Sarah and I grew much closer during her pregnancy. We talked weekly by phone, and when I could, I made trips up to see her. As I expected, she was miserable, living in a home where she had no emotional attachments to anyone. My sister and mother were within a short driving distance of the home, so I would make the six-hour drive, take Sarah out for a while and then head on over to visit with the rest of my family.

The home had rules dictating whom Sarah could see and when she was expected back if she went out. Like many nonprofit agencies, they'd bought the best house in the safest neighborhood they could afford, but it was a dingy place, full of cobbled-together donations: beds, couches, chairs, plates. While the people who ran the house were nice enough, I hated leaving Sarah there. I wanted to put her in the car, sneak her back into Pendleton under the dark of night, and hide her away myself.

Sarah was set on giving the baby up for adoption. The father of the child was reportedly a fellow from the nearby farming community of Heppner. Marrying somebody from a rural place like Heppner was not Sarah's vision for herself. She had a hunger for a more glamorous life.

It was during her sixth or seventh month of pregnancy that Sarah asked, "Would you and Tim adopt my baby?"

Stunned by the unexpected request, I tried to listen as Sarah thoughtfully explained why she wanted us to adopt her baby, but my mind was racing. Our children had been born in rapid succession. Our youngest daughter was nine, the twins were eleven, and our son was fourteen. Long gone were the playpens, diapers, cribs, strollers and Johnny Jump-Ups. We'd be starting from scratch with a newborn. Could we—more, *would* we do that?

I knew before I asked what Tim's response would be. He has always been the most devoted of fathers, so it was more a question of whether I would start over.

Tim responded exactly as I expected he would. He did a little hot-diggity-dog jig in the dining room and said, "I hope you told her yes!"

"Not exactly," I replied.

Tim removed his tie and walked into the bedroom. When he came back out, he asked, "Why not?"

I didn't know where to begin. Now that the kids were old enough, I had actually begun to figure out who I was, in addition to being their mother. I wasn't sure I was ready to let go of my newfound independence.

There was one other looming matter discouraging any elation I felt: What would Gene and Carol think? This would be their grandchild. How would they feel about Tim and me raising up this child across town from them? If they had, as Sarah maintained, sent her away to have this baby, then surely they wouldn't like the idea of the child virtually coming home.

I suggested to Tim that, if we were going to adopt Sarah's baby, we should only do it if Gene and Carol extended their blessings. Tim was in full agreement.

Sarah balked. She didn't see any need to ask her parents' blessing. "It's my baby," she said. "If I choose you and Tim, why should it matter whether my parents agree with my decision?"

The discussion over getting the Brills' blessing went on for about six weeks. I told Sarah I wanted her involved in the baby's life. The adoption would need to be an open one. This child would always know Sarah in some intimate way. On that matter, we agreed.

Sometime early into her third trimester, Sarah told us her father was okay with us adopting, but her mother was not. Carol did not want Tim and me raising her grandchild. I never asked Carol why. I'm not sure I wanted to know. I think it was because the hidden part of me was relieved.

Sarah was miffed when she told me her mother wouldn't give her consent. She was upset at me and at her mom. She didn't understand why it mattered what her mother thought. But now I wonder if Sarah really ever discussed the matter with her parents. Over the years, I've come to second-guess everything Sarah said.

I had one confidant in town whom I shared all this with, Janice Wells, who suggested an alternative couple for Sarah. Janice had friends in Portland who were possible candidates. Chuck and Missy McDonald already had a big family, like ours, but they wanted to add to it. Sarah was initially reluctant but eventually agreed to at least meet with Missy.

I didn't know much about the couple, only what Janice told me. But after several phone calls back and forth between all parties involved, and with Sarah's permission, I arranged for us all to meet. Missy drove up from Portland and I drove over from Pendleton, picking up Sarah along the way. We gathered in Westport, Washington, where my sister lives.

Out over the Pacific, and there in that harbor community, agitated clouds hung heavy and low. Looking back now, I might regard the darkening sky as an omen of the trouble sure to follow. But at that time, it made sense to trust fate to deal with whatever capricious winds were brewing.

CHAPTER SIX

SARAH WAS RAPED, OR SO she says now.

The first time I came across the rape claim I was leafing through a pile of documents Shawn's defense attorney gave me. Right there on Sarah's medical records was a request that she have an all-female delivery staff because Sarah said her first pregnancy had been traumatic: the result of rape.

The next time I read that statement was in a report filed by the detective who interviewed her parents in the wake of Karly's death.

"Sarah was a handful, a major challenge," Gene Brill told the officer. "One year we had to send her off to a Christian boarding school in San Diego because we were afraid she was going to run off somewhere."

"Was that the year she got pregnant?" asked Detective Mike Wells.

"No," Carol Brill said. "Sarah mimicked her birth mother. She waited to get pregnant until she was the same age her mother had been when she was born. Her mother was twenty. Sarah was twenty. She was trying to make some sort of connection."

"And that was a boyfriend? Or a rape she got pregnant from?" Detective Wells asked.

"A boyfriend," Gene replied.

Detective Wells was confused. Sarah claimed she'd been raped and that was why she'd been pregnant.

"It was a casual relationship," Gene said. "It wasn't anything long term."

That's exactly how I remember it. The baby's father was a cowboy from Heppner. Sarah told me they'd been drinking and got carried away. We even discussed whether she should get his consent for an adoption. I urged her to tell the young man she was pregnant with his child and to seek his consent. I would never have suggested it if I'd thought for one minute that Sarah had been raped. Sarah assured me they had talked and that he agreed with her decision.

Once she moved off to Corvallis, however, it appears Sarah's life took on the fictional characteristics of a James Frey memoir. She claimed she got pregnant from a date rape. According to several of her friends, who heard Sarah repeat different versions over the years, Sarah said a fellow she knew had climbed in her bedroom window and raped her.

Detective Mike Wells had his work cut out for him, trying to sort out fact from fiction. He interviewed Shelley, Sarah's best friend and sometime roommate, before speaking to the Brills.

Wells said, "The way Shelley understood it, when Sarah was fifteen or seventeen, she was raped, got pregnant, and was sent away to some type of boarding facility, and the baby was adopted out."

"That's not how it happened," Carol said. "Sarah had willingly gone to the home for unwed mothers." But Carol added, "It had probably been another mistake, sending her there."

"Yeah, it'd been a hard time for her," Gene said.

"Sarah didn't fit in well there," Carol explained. "All the other girls there were on welfare."

"Yeah," Gene said. "Sarah hated that place. I mean, they were really good Christian people and all involved there, but Sarah decided on her own to give that baby up, and in the end it devastated her. But Sarah was wise enough to know she wasn't ready to care for a baby. So she lost that one. And now look—this one is gone, too."

Gene and Carol never told Detective Wells that Sarah wanted to give her first child to Tim and me. They didn't mention how upset they'd been with her for getting pregnant. They didn't say that Sarah had returned to Pendleton after giving Hillary away and lived with our family, not theirs.

Chapter Seven

WE MET FOR LUNCH AT a touristy restaurant down on the docks, Sarah, Missy, my sister Linda, and me. Sarah barely looked pregnant. She wore a blue-jean skort, with thick white stockings and a denim blouse. Her baby bump was hidden under an oversized white knit sweater. Her hair, usually cut short, was longer now and softly curled.

Dancer thin, Missy looked more like a college coed than the mother of five in her jeans and leather bomber jacket. Her blonde hair was shoulder-length and curly, most likely the result of the spiral perms so popular then. Sarah was pleased that Missy was so pretty and I was happy that Missy was so genuine. She greeted us all with lingering hugs and an infectious smile.

Everybody had a case of the jitters. Meeting potential parents as a birth mom is a lot like going on a blind date; it's a search for the right mix of character and chemistry. The conversation started slowly but my sister Linda, who isn't really the sort to insert herself, filled in the holes with tidbits of information about Westport and its tourist trade.

Sarah has always been soft-spoken. She never had to demand center stage; when the spotlight was turned her way, no one shone brighter.

Hollywood might say she has that "IT" factor, a beguiling charisma that attracts people to her.

Carol Brill said Sarah is the sort of person who has many casual friends but few people really know her in an intimate way. I saw that in her, too. Sarah played everything close to the vest. No matter how well a person thought they knew Sarah, it was always difficult to know what she was thinking.

Yet, by midafternoon, it was obvious Missy had enchanted Sarah. The laughter came easy and the conversation soon turned to chatter, as though the two were old friends. Missy appeared to be all that Sarah was seeking in an adoptive mother. She was gregarious, warm, funny, and a good listener.

By early evening, I felt like the dying woman who had just introduced her husband to his next wife. I was elated for everyone else but grieving the loss up ahead. Sarah was so comfortable with Missy, I felt replaced. It's one of my least favorite emotions: an ugly mix of jealousy and insecurity, undergirded by the fear that I no longer matter. I couldn't tell Missy or Sarah what I was feeling, so I confided in my sister, who assured me it was normal, and part of the process of letting go.

I knew before we left the beach the next morning that Sarah would adopt her baby out to Chuck and Missy. She never said so but I knew it deep in my bones. I uttered a prayer of gratitude; Missy was going to be the perfect mother for Sarah's child. However, I cried as I drove, knowing full well I had given up something very precious.

Sarah called me from the hospital on a sunny spring day when the cherry tree was in bloom.

"I'm in labor," she said. "Can you get here as soon as possible?"

"That's terrific, honey," I said. "Is your mother there?"

"Yes."

"And Missy and Chuck? Are they there, too?"

"Yes," Sarah said.

"Great. That's just great," I said. "How are you doing?"

"Okay," she said. "But when are you getting here? You need to hurry."

I was pacing the floor between the living room and the dining room. I did a quick mental check. Everybody was pretty self-sufficient, and Tim would understand if I packed up at a moment's notice. He always understood when it came to Sarah. Nevertheless, I was torn between a desire to be there for the birth of this child and the realization that my presence, while a comfort to Sarah, would be uncomfortable for everyone else.

"Sarah, honey, I'm not coming," I said.

Silence sliced the air. Sarah had not imagined I wouldn't come when called, that I would ever in a million years miss this event.

"Why?" she cried.

"I don't belong there, Sarah. You have your mother. You have Missy. This is a time for you all."

"But I want you here," Sarah said, pleading. "Come on. *Please.* I need you."

Sarah's entreaties almost swayed me but the mother in me held me back. I didn't want to stomp over holy ground. This was a time, I hoped, for healing between Sarah and Carol. I did not want them to risk missing this chance.

I told Sarah she could call me anytime, day or night, no matter what. But I was not going to make the trip because I would be in the way.

"You need this time alone with your baby, with your mama, and with Chuck and Missy."

Someone called me later to tell me that Sarah had given birth to a healthy baby girl. Hillary Jane, called Hillary, was born the day before her mother's twentieth birthday.

The next call I got came from a very distraught Missy, who told me

Sarah was reluctant to relinquish the infant. I had expected as much. Missy was hoping I could talk some sense into Sarah, get her to realize she couldn't possibly handle motherhood. There was desperation in Missy's voice. She was afraid Sarah was going to change her mind.

I assured Missy I would talk to Sarah, try to figure out where her heart was in all of this. A flurry of phone calls took place over the next forty-eight hours. Janice Wells called. I called Sarah. Sarah called me. Missy called me.

If Carol was part of this decision-making, I didn't know it. Carol and I never spoke about Sarah's pregnancy, or Hillary's adoption. If Missy called Carol and spoke with her, she never mentioned it to me. It seems wrong now that I would not have welcomed Carol's input, but I'm sure at the time I was simply trying to honor Sarah's wishes.

I wanted to extract myself from the situation and to let things progress naturally, but here I was in the thick of it. If I felt that much pressure, I couldn't imagine how Sarah must have felt. I had wanted more than anything to protect her from that.

Chuck and Missy decided if Sarah wasn't ready to relinquish the infant child, well, by golly, they would take the whole kit and caboodle home with them. They invited Sarah to bring Hillary and come live with them for a while.

I have often thought that, had I gone up to Tacoma the day Hillary was born, all of this might have been avoided. Not the pain part— giving up Hillary was hard on Sarah. Anyone who knew her knew that. She really had mixed feelings about her decision, in part because Sarah needed to belong to somebody. She needed to be a mother.

Three weeks later, with Sarah still in their home, Chuck and Missy grew more worried. Would they get so attached to Hillary, only to have Sarah yank her out of their arms? Had they set themselves up for heartbreak? The few times I spoke with Missy she was every bit as emotional as Sarah. Everyone's nerves were on edge.

In the balance hung the welfare of an infant unaware, and a birth mother who was all too keenly aware of her separation from the baby she'd carried for nine months. Her child was in the arms of another woman. Sarah was not nursing or tending Hillary. Close as she was, Sarah was a visitor to Hillary, not a mother. If she left Hillary with Chuck and Missy, that's all she would ever be to Hillary: the visitor who had birthed her.

Sarah was struggling to figure out who she was and what she was going to do with the rest of her life now. She might as well have been trying to figure out how to maneuver around New York City on a zip line. Loneliness loomed before her like a dark street. Without a baby to care for, what was her purpose? She had no idea what she was going to do, or where she was going to go.

Tim and I suggested she should come live with us. It would allow her time to regroup and develop a plan for her own life. It didn't take her long to decide our offer was her best option.

Sarah came to our home and Hillary remained with her adoptive parents. When friends hosted a baby shower for Missy and Hillary, I drove to Portland, and took along a pair of tiny Nikes, a stuffed bunny and a poem Tim had written. It was the first and only time I would meet Hillary, though I've seen photos of her over the years. The week before I learned of Karly's death, I serendipitously came across a yellowed copy of the poem Tim had penned:

Ode to Hillary Jane
Welcome to the world, Hillary Jane!
Not as gentle an abode as that
from which you've come.

Yet, God, The Creator, carves out human souls,
and yours, Hillary Jane, He designed especially so.

Wear these shoes of Nike, classic messenger of God,
as honor to the mother who bore you,
and the family God appointed you.

Go boldly into this world, Hillary Jane.
step lively, step swiftly, along the path,
watch out for side roads,
stay within His lane, listen to the pace.

God, The Creator, designed you for a purpose,
Our Little Hillary Jane.

Sarah saw very little of Hillary during that first year of her life. The phone calls between Missy and Sarah that had taken place almost daily during the pregnancy became less frequent, once a month, then every other month, and then months would pass without any at all.

That disturbed me. I knew that if Hillary had been in our home, Sarah would have had regular contact with her. I thought Sarah needed and wanted that. Whenever I asked if she had heard from Missy recently, Sarah would shake her head no.

It was such a hard place to be in. In some ways it still is. When I look at photos of Hillary now, all grown up and dressed in blue satin, and I consider all those homecoming dances, the proms, the school musicals, the youth fellowships and all the late-night talks I missed out on, and of the story not written, it grieves me deeply.

Missy recognized that grief in me long before I ever did. Sometime shortly before Hillary's first birthday I wrote Missy a letter expressing my dismay at the breakdown in her relationship with Sarah. I blamed Missy for it, never allowing for the possibility that it was Sarah who was being unreliable or manipulative.

A month passed before Missy replied. The letter she sent me in May 1995 reads now more like a prophetic word than the defensive rebuttal I mistook it for then:

Dear Karen,

When I received your letter in February I wanted to respond right away, but I really wasn't quite sure how to. I went through a lot of emotions, first I bawled for hours. I felt very hurt by your disappointment in Chuck and me. For you to think we didn't care about Sarah and had closed the door on her was very hard to understand. But as I reread the letter and Chuck and I discussed it, I began to understand better where it was coming from. I think it comes from your heart and reveals your deepest emotion. I know that you care very deeply for Sarah, as though she was your own child. You have seen her hurting so much and you would like to stop it for her. I believe that you hear from Sarah, perhaps, a slanted view of the actual truth or fact. We both know Sarah has a way of making people feel sorry for her. I'm not saying she isn't experiencing some major emotions but there is also tremendous confusion in her life and she doesn't want to acknowledge where it's coming from.

Karen, not only were you expressing Sarah's pain, but also your own. I realize you must be going through a tremendous amount of your own grief. I know Hillary could as easily have been living in your home as ours. I'm sure you think about how you would have dealt with things if that had been the case. It's very easy to imagine what we would do if we were in a situation, but we can't always know until we are actually in it. The choices Chuck and I make are made with a lot of discussion and prayer. We do feel our first consideration has to be for Hillary. Sarah has to be second to that. If that means there will be times when we distance ourselves, it is because we feel it's the best for our whole family, not because we don't care about Sarah. We have tried to explain this to Sarah. We have also tried to get her to respond and tell us how she feels about everything. She said very little, but what she has said is that many people are trying to make her feel bad about not grieving over Hillary. She feels she has done that (not that I agree). She also expressed that she missed the relationship with Chuck and me that she had in the past. We have discussed the fact that things can't be the same as they were but that we will always be open to a relationship with her. I don't doubt that Sarah and Hillary will have a relationship in the future. How and when I don't know but it doesn't scare or threaten me in the least because Hillary will always know who she is and where she came from and that we love her very much.

Love, Missy

We never did speak much after that. I've seen Missy and Chuck only one other time since then, and I've only known Hillary from afar, in photos others shared, in the stories others told.

Hillary has Sarah's dark eyes and the same caramel complexion, but she's more petite and fine-boned than Sarah. She sings, writes lyrics, and possesses the passionate heart of a poet who cares about issues of social justice, especially when it comes to children.

When she was younger, Hillary would spend time in Pendleton with Gene and Carol, but that all changed when Karly died. That year, Chuck and Missy packed up and moved to Mexico, where they worked in missions for a short time. They moved back to Oregon for Hillary's high school years. At the time of Karly's death, Hillary was told her sister was dead, but not that Karly was murdered. I don't know if she has ever been told the real story.

I'm not sure anyone but Shawn, Sarah and Karly know the real story.

Chapter Eight

EXPECT HELL TO FREEZE FIRST. That's the gist of the reply I received from Shawn Field after sending him a letter, week after week, for a year. Only the date has changed.

> Shawn Wesley Field
> Inmate ID: 16002306
> EOCI
> Mr. Field:
> I am at work on a book about the murder of Karly Sheehan. I am interested in hearing your side of the story. But in order to do that I will have to be added to your list of approved visitors. If you will add me to your list, I will make an appointment to visit with you.
> I look forward to hearing from you.
> Karen Spears Zacharias

Detective Wells also attempted to interview Shawn Field. Field turned down the detective, too. Wells is the father of three daughters. His oldest daughter was only four years old when he was working the

Karly case. Having a daughter so close to Karly's age made this case more personal than others. Wells could easily imagine David's grief, but the detective could not understand the systematic senselessness, or the vile sickness behind the murder. Like me, Wells remains haunted by unanswered questions. Who is Shawn Field? Why did he kill Karly? What role did Sarah play in all of this?

I've been warned more than once that I ought to give up trying to get an interview with Shawn. "Short of a Grade B miracle, you will not get the chance to sit down with Shawn. That door is closed and he has no intention of opening it."

That warning came to me via an e-mail from a man in my community—Jack, I'll call him. Jack's in-laws are close friends of Hugh and Ann Field, Shawn Field's parents. Jack meets with Shawn on a regular basis as part of a prison ministry and he sends me intermittent e-mails, informing me of all the ways in which God is working in Shawn's life.

"God never ceases to amaze me with how he works through the grimmest situations," Jack writes. "Only God can change lives and I remain confident that he is doing that in Shawn's life. I pray that Sarah might come face to face with God here on Earth while she has a chance to receive his gift."

It's hard for me, when I receive notes like this, not to be put off. I've read thousands of pages of documents, police interrogations, evidence, and autopsy reports. I've studied the reports filed with the Oregon Department of Human Services Child Welfare Division in the months leading up to Karly's death. I've seen the photographs Shawn took in the moments before Karly died and the glossy color autopsy photos that caused me to flee the office of the Oregon Court of Appeals building so that I could cry unnoticed within the confines of my car.

I want to sit Jack down and walk him through all the evidence I've plowed through. I want him to study the photos of Karly's battered body that caused doctors and nurses alike to break down in tears. Yes, I'm disturbed and defensive over Jack's suggestion that Shawn is on some holy path that Sarah seems to have missed.

I wrote back to Jack and told him it's a good thing I believe in the God of Grade A miracles because I have every intention of continuing to pursue an interview with Shawn. And oh, by the way, I added, "I think if you were to ask Sarah she would tell you she is washed in the blood of the Lamb…or was at one time."

A week later, I received another e-mail, this one a little sterner in tone than all the previous exchanges:

> Karen,
>
> Shawn said you contacted him again. He also tells me his stance hasn't changed. The door is closed and locked to you. No matter how many times you contact him he will not answer any of your letters or add you as a visitor. I assume he isn't kidding.
>
> Have a nice day.
>
> Jack

I'm sure Jack believes it was his Christian duty to write me that e-mail, to persuade me to back off my pursuit of an interview. I am confident Jack means well, but we are at crosshairs on this issue. I don't know if I will ever get an interview with Inmate 16002306 but I will continue trying no matter how many testy e-mails I receive.

CHAPTER NINE

I DIDN'T KNOW ABOUT KARLY's murder or the three-year-old's desperate prayers for deliverance when Tim and I made the trek upriver to Bend, Oregon, in March 2007 to visit two of our four kids. Stephan, our eldest, worked at the High Desert Museum, one of the region's most popular tourist attractions. Our youngest daughter, Konnie, had just moved to town.

We'd spent the night at Konnie's new digs. I slipped out of bed at 7:45 a.m. Tim, who was wedged between the edge of the twin mattress and the wall, didn't flinch. Prying a peephole in the aged blinds, I glanced across the parking lot of the Boys & Girls Club. Half a dozen pines stood motionless, like trees in a picture book. Blue sky. No wind.

We didn't have big plans. After Tim got out of bed and got dressed, he and I grabbed a cup of coffee at the joint down the street, read the paper, poked around town a bit. Later that afternoon, Stephan gave us the town tour.

"What's *The Source*?" I asked, as he turned left past a brick building with a sign bearing that title.

"A newspaper," he replied. Parking the car in front of the saltbox house Konnie was renting, Stephan walked to the end of the block and grabbed a paper. He flipped through the weekly arts and entertainment guide while we huddled around a space heater in the living room.

Stephan opened the paper and leaned over to show something of interest to his father.

"What?" I asked.

Stephan turned to me and leaned in. "Isn't that Sarah?" he asked.

"It sure is," I said.

There she was holding up a dollar bill, wearing what was obviously her St. Paddy's Day t-shirt, the one with the four-leaf clovers that read, Feeling lucky.

"Does it say anything about her?"

"Nope," Stephan replied. "It doesn't even give her name."

It was a blip about some women who'd gone to a restaurant with an open fire pit. Their money had gone up in smoke after being blown into the pit by an unexpected wind. Sarah was holding up a dollar with burnt edges. She had that same engaging smile, the one that had slain dozens of men, and charmed nearly as many women.

"You think she lives here?" I asked.

"Maybe," Stephan said with a shrug.

The day after Stephan discovered Sarah's photo, I cranked the shower to a hot-as-I-can-stand-it setting and let it rain down over me.

"Please, God," I prayed, "if Sarah lives here, let me run into her today." Sometimes I have my best talks with God in the shower.

It was the morning of March 28, 2007.

At 5:30 p.m., Konnie burst through the door, ran to her bedroom, and changed into running clothes.

"Meet me at the bridge down by REI at the Old Mill," she instructed, as she grabbed her iPod and jogged off.

Tim and I walked down to the Old Mill shops and stood at the end of the bridge, watching for our daughter as brightly colored flags snapped overhead. I saw Konnie waving to us from across the Deschutes River.

We walked back, past the Old Mill and through the parking lot at Strictly Organic Coffee. At the top of the incline, we approached a man and a woman talking outside a small bungalow, their backs to us. The woman wore red shoes with three-inch heels, unusual in a town where flat, rubber-soled shoes are the most common footwear. Konnie strode a few steps ahead of us. When she got to the other side of the couple, she turned, cupped one hand over her face, pointed at the girl, and mouthed "Sarah!" to me.

I turned toward the couple.

"Sarah?"

It was the first time I had spoken to her since that nasty phone call in February 2003 when she told me she was divorcing David.

Sarah's jaw went slack. "Excuse me," she said to the man next to her. "These people are like my family and I haven't seen them in a very long time."

We embraced warmly.

"Do you live here?" she asked. Her dark-roasted eyes scanned the three of us, searching for some sign we were part of the Bend community.

"Konnie does," I answered. "She just moved here."

"Yeah, I live up the street," Konnie added. "Why don't you come up?"

The man shifted his feet anxiously. We had interrupted.

"Let me finish up here," Sarah said. "Then I'll come up."

Konnie gave her the address.

"How bizarre is that?" our daughter asked as we turned to leave.

"Pretty bizarre," her father said.

"Not bizarre at all," I said. They didn't know about the power of a shower prayer.

We'd barely walked in the front door before Sarah drove up. I met her on the stoop.

"I knew you were in town," I said, hugging her again.

"How?" she asked, laughing. I'd missed Sarah's easy laughter.

"I saw your picture in *The Source*. I wasn't sure if you lived here or were visiting but I had a strong feeling we'd run into each other."

"Yeah, that's pretty random," Sarah said.

"Not random at all," I said.

Then Sarah laughed again, but in a tense way people do when they are trying to appear confident but are anything but. I chalked it up to the normal anxiety that can exist between two people whose last conversation was an exchange of harsh words. I couldn't have been more wrong about the nature of Sarah's unease.

"How long have you lived here?" Tim asked from the corner of the sofa where he was sitting. A heater was pulled up next to him. Tim is a lean athlete who doesn't tolerate chill very well.

"Two years."

"Do you work?" I asked as I took a seat on the U-shaped footstool nearest the chair where Sarah sat.

"I manage the restaurant for one of the hotels in town," she said.

Sarah pulled a strand of her dark hair through her fingers. I recognized the nervous gesture. I'd witnessed it a thousand times back when she lived with us. Our daughter Shelby has the same habit.

"Do you keep in touch with anyone from Pendleton?" I asked.

"Not really."

"Are your parents still there?"

"Yes."

"How's Hillary? What is she, like, ten now?"

"Thirteen," Sarah replied.

I looked at Tim. "Has it been that long? God, I feel old."

"You are old," Tim said. Everyone laughed.

"Chuck and Missy moved to Mexico," Sarah added.

"Really? When?"

"Three years ago."

"So you haven't seen Hillary in all that time?"

"No."

"Do they write? Send photos?"

"Oh, yes."

"And what about Karly? Is she with David?"

Sarah had been in the house for nearly half an hour and hadn't mentioned Karly once. I wasn't sure how the custody issues had been ironed out. When we'd last spoken, Sarah said she and David would share custody of Karly. But with her living in Bend, and him in Corvallis, I didn't see how that would work. Karly would've turned five in January. She'd be old enough to attend preschool, at least. I assumed Karly was with her daddy.

A bad pause followed. That's how Tim described it later.

"If it had been good news, it would've come rushing out. But there was that bad pause," he said.

Tim swears he knew then, in that moment of silence, that Karly was dead. But I had no clue anything could be so wrong.

I watched as Sarah fumbled around with different phrasings before answering. I figured she was trying to find the best possible way to tell us she didn't have custody of her daughter.

"She has—" Sarah started, stopped, then started again, blurting it out in one breath. "Karly passed away. That's why I'm in Bend. But I'm having a very bad day so I don't want to talk about it. We'll have that conversation on another day." Sarah's eyes begged for grace.

My mind scattered like birds, startled. I'd spent the better part of the past two years on the road advocating for war widows and the children of those killed in Iraq and Afghanistan. If a war widow said to me that she didn't want to talk about something, I backed off. I knew she'd talk, eventually, when she was ready. I did as Sarah asked—I dropped it. Let it go.

Over dinner we talked about Sarah's current boyfriend—how she loved the boyfriend's family, but him, not so much. We talked about the job market in Bend, skiing, snowboarding, and the upcoming play at Second Street Theatre, where Stephan had the lead role.

"We'll be back next week to see Stephan in the play," I said, as we hugged goodbye.

"You can stay at my place, if you like," Sarah said. "I've got an extra bedroom."

"I'll call you before I leave in the morning," I said.

"Okay," Sarah said. Then she made sure I had her new phone number.

I called her first thing the next morning, as promised.

"Hey, Sarah. I'm sorry to wake you."

"You heading out?" she asked in her sleepy voice.

"In a bit. Listen, I'm sorry about that last phone call. I never meant for us to lose touch with each other that way."

"Yeah, me, too."

"I quit my job, went to Vietnam, moved away from Pendleton. Life got crazy." Then I said, "I'm sorry I wasn't there for you when you lost Karly."

Silence. There was no explanation from Sarah.

"Well, don't be a stranger, okay?"

"Okay," Sarah said.

Tim spent the night at Stephan's place, while I stayed with Konnie. He came by early the next morning and we loaded up the car.

"Can we go by Starbucks on the way out?" I asked, yanking on my seatbelt. I hardly looked at Tim as I began to chatter. "Konnie thinks maybe Karly died from a car wreck. Maybe Sarah was driving and that's why she can't talk about it, 'cause did you see how nervous she was? It's obvious she feels guilty. I don't think it was cancer."

There was that bad pause again.

"It wasn't a car wreck," Tim said.

"How do you know?" I asked.

"Stephan looked it up online when we got home last night."

"Looked up what? Karly's obit? What did it say?"

"I don't want to tell you," he said, clenching his square jaw. "You don't want to know."

"Well you might as well tell me because you know I'm going to look it up myself as soon as I get home."

"I wouldn't if I were you."

"Why? What happened?"

"Sarah's boyfriend tortured and murdered Karly."

My stomach fell to the floorboard. I wanted to vomit. I felt faint. My hands were sweaty, my heart racing. I couldn't breathe. I could only mumble: Oh, dear God. Dearest. God.

CHAPTER TEN

S ARAH SENT ME A MOTHER'S Day card the year Karly was born. In those early days, after I bumped into Sarah in Bend, that card fell out of a notebook I kept stashed in my office. The card is inscribed: *Our friendship is such a special part of my life. I'll always be thankful for that—and for you. Happy Mother's Day.*

In her own flourishing script, Sarah wrote me the following message:

> Karen –
>
> Here's hoping you have a wonderful Mother's Day. Although you're not old enough to be my mother, you were always the kind of mother I wished that I had, and now the kind of mother I hope to be to Karly. Thank you for always being there to talk, to listen, or just to hang out with. I love you & I love your family. Thank you for being wonderful you! Love ya! S-

I sat on the floor of my office and bawled as I read Sarah's words and recalled the laughter that had filled our home during the year Sarah lived with us. She was such an easy girl to love.

Sarah would get so unnerved when I cooked supper for seven. I'd invariably pull all the kitchen cupboard doors open during the course of the preparations and Sarah, who couldn't stand to leave a cupboard door open, would follow behind me, slamming them all.

In the mornings, after I'd gotten the kids off to school, I'd make my way through the maze of the unfinished basement we called the Dungeon and curl up under a white down comforter beside Sarah.

"Good morning, Sunshine. What are you reading now?"

Sarah loved to linger in bed and read. She liked to write, too. She kept a journal and talked of writing a book herself one day.

After moving in with us, Sarah signed up for classes at the local community college, and went in search of a part-time job. She was called back for an interview at a local bank, and afterwards, we sat in the kitchen rehashing the questions they'd posed.

"How'd it go?" I asked.

"Good, I think."

"What did they ask you?"

"They wanted to know if I had any experience with money."

"Did you tell them you have a lot of experience with other people's money?" I teased. Sarah laughed. Fiscal responsibility was not her strong suit. "Anything else they want to know?"

"Yeah," Sarah said. "They wanted to know what I'd bring to work with me every day if I got hired."

"What'd you tell them?"

"I said I'd bring my purse."

I waited for Sarah to crack a grin, when she didn't, I asked, "Really? Did you really tell them you'd bring your purse to work?"

"Yes," Sarah said, clueless. "Why? Something wrong with that?"

I was doubled over, laughing hysterically.

"What is so funny?" Sarah's dark eyes were filled with confusion.

"Oh my gosh, girl, they wanted to know what assets you would bring, your personal strengths. They didn't mean what would you literally bring!"

The memory of that conversation makes me laugh still, but it also reveals something of Sarah's character. She can come off guileless and very naïve. Sometimes she does it purposefully, other times it's just Sarah.

Wiping away hot tears, I removed the photos I kept inside that long-forgotten Mother's Day card. One was a snapshot of Sarah sitting on David's lap, cradling their newborn daughter. Karly wore a pink stocking cap and a bright-eyed expression. David was beaming; Sarah, smiling.

In the hours after learning of Karly's death, I could not get David out of my head. I knew without asking that Sarah had never told him about our ugly phone exchange in 2003.

Since then, I'd had no contact with Sarah or David. While Karly's death had been headline news in Corvallis, her connection to Eastern Oregon had gone underreported. Few people in Pendleton who'd been friends with Sarah knew her daughter had been murdered.

David must have wondered why I didn't show up when Karly died. Why I hadn't been present for her funeral or for the trial. I had been totally absent, and David had no idea why.

I did not Google Karly's death as I had threatened to do in those moments before Tim told me she had been murdered. Not that night and not for several months to follow. I didn't think I could handle what the news reports said.

But I called David that very night. I wanted to hear everything from him, all of it. I told David I had just learned of Karly's death. I told him about running into Sarah in Bend. I told him about the phone call in 2003, the one in which I pleaded with Sarah not to leave him. I told David that I had believed her doing so would put Karly at risk, and that I was afraid for Karly. Even so, I never imagined the terror Karly endured before dying.

I asked David to meet me for coffee. He agreed. It's a five-hour drive between my home in Hermiston and David's in Corvallis. I got up before dawn and headed out.

Driving west along the Columbia River Gorge, I thought how much more than distance in miles had separated me from David. I berated myself for not having kept in contact with him. I should have called. I should have told him sooner about that fight with Sarah. I should have assured him he could call, anytime, if he needed anything.

Why didn't I? It was very unlike me. I have friends from junior high school I keep in touch with: Jan Chaney Rabe in South Carolina, Sherri Davis Callaway in Georgia, Jerry Burke in Tennessee. I've cultivated friendships from Atlanta to Albuquerque, and maintained them over the years. I sent letters to Granny Leona in the hills of Tennessee as soon as I could pick up a fat pencil and write between the lines. The first thing I did as soon as I learned my daddy had died in Vietnam was to write a letter to Mrs. Eye, my third grade teacher. Mama helped me address it and send it to Oahu's Helemano Elementary School.

It was not like me to lose all contact with someone I cherished. What had happened?

My trip to Vietnam, mostly. I flew out of LAX to Ho Chi Minh the week after the blow-up with Sarah. I'd spent eight years researching and writing about my father's death in an unpopular war, how it had devastated our family. I sold that book, *After the Flag has been Folded,* to HarperCollins within a few months of my return from Vietnam. That propelled me into a role I'd never envisioned, as an advocate for a whole new generation of war widows and their children.

But David didn't know any of that. All he knew was that during a time when he could have used support the most, I wasn't there.

CHAPTER ELEVEN

THE MOUNTAINS THAT MAKE UP Oregon's coastal range were on my right as I drove into Corvallis. I can't look at those hills without thinking of Agnes Ferngren, the woman who was the mentor to me that I tried to be to Sarah. As a college coed, I'd lived with Agnes. Her husband, Gary, an Oregon State University history professor, was on an educational cruise ship, touring and teaching. I needed a place to live and Agnes needed help with the couple's three daughters, all preschoolers.

It was Agnes who taught me the mothering skills I would later employ with my own four children. Agnes taught me how to bake bread, how to French braid a little girl's hair—a skill I would later pass on to Sarah—and how to instill faith in a child.

Agnes and I were standing in the kitchen, washing up the dinner dishes one evening, when she brushed back her red bangs and looked out the window over the sink.

"Whenever I see those mountains I think of the Psalmist," Agnes said. "'I will lift up my eyes unto the hills. Where does my help come from? My help comes from the Lord, the maker of heaven and earth.'"

Agnes died in the spring of 2006 after a battle with a virulent lung cancer. I hadn't been back to Corvallis since her memorial service. I missed her terribly. I still do. Passing those mountains as I drove south into town, I asked God to help me, to give me the strength to write this story.

I knew if David gave his blessing for such a project I would tell Karly's story. I also knew doing so would enrage Sarah, and that troubled me deeply. I didn't know how I would handle that. I still don't.

David and I met downtown at Corvallis's New Morning Bakery. We sat at a back table. Slim as a seventh grader, David wore jeans and a navy Patagonia Henley. His fair hair was cut short. His brogue thick as the day he first came stateside.

David retained his proud Irish citizenship up until 2008, when he finally took the oath and became an American citizen. Honestly, given all I learned of what the Oregon legal system put him through, I was moved by his desire to become an American citizen. It speaks volumes about the kind of man David is.

David's sky-blue eyes grew misty several times during our visit as he spoke of Karly. He recalled that he took his daughter to Ireland twice during her brief life. The first time was in November 2002, when Karly was ten months old. David and his baby girl made the trip without the benefit of a mother's help.

Sarah had moved out when Karly was six months old. She would move back in once more, taking yet another stab at marriage and motherhood, but David was perfectly competent as a single parent. So traveling across the oceans alone with an infant or a toddler did not terrify him the way it might some fathers.

Father and daughter made their second trip to Ireland in July 2004. By then, Karly was on her way from potty-training toddler to full-fledged girlhood and she could talk the hind legs off a donkey. Karly displayed a verbal acuity that would make any Irish grandmother proud and any Irish grandfather exhausted.

The toddler's excitement about the trip could not be contained. She insisted on picking out her own carry-on luggage, test-driving a Dora the Explorer wheeled backpack in the aisles of a department store. She settled on that particular bag because it had a detachable pouch that Karly declared would be handy for the candy treats she'd need to sustain her on the long flights.

David had finished his master's classes at George Fox University on July 27, and the two of them flew out of Portland the next day. Any form of travel enchanted Karly, be it a boat, a horse, a bus, or a plane. David had taught his daughter the chorus to "Leaving on a Jet Plane," and the two of them sang it loudly like bar drunks as they packed bags and headed for the airport.

Their first long layover was in Chicago, a place that would one day play significantly into David's future—though, tragically, not Karly's. They walked all over O'Hare, grabbed some grub, and lollygagged around the towering Brachiosaurus dinosaur in the B concourse. The four-story-high, seventy-two-foot-long skeleton was on loan from the Chicago Field Museum. Karly called it a "disonaur," her own particular pronunciation for dinosaurs. Her quirky way with language tickled David. No matter how many times he corrected her, Karly liked her enunciation best, and truth be told, so did David.

It was nighttime when they finally left O'Hare, bound for Heathrow, but Karly retained her good-natured disposition. Traveling might make others cranky, but not Karly. She loved the way her tummy flipped on takeoffs. She played quietly with her toys, and was thoroughly delighted by the plastic cow that pooped out jellybeans with a lift of its tail, a trick that elicited endless giggles. She finally fell asleep in David's arms and they both woke bleary-eyed the next morning upon landing in London. After a short layover, they boarded the familiar green Aer Lingus for the short fifty-minute flight to Cork, where Grandpa and Grandma

Sheehan were eagerly awaiting the arrival of the granddaughter they hadn't seen since she was a baby, except in photos and in videos. It was good to see David, too.

Having made the trip enough times himself, David knew that the best way to deal with the jet lag was to stay awake until the local bedtime. So he made the rounds, taking Karly to his grandmother, then to visit his siblings and the many cousins. Later that night, as David tried to put Karly to bed, he started to sing her a lullaby but was stopped abruptly.

"Karly covered my mouth with her hand and said, 'Hush! Daddy! That's enough. You can never, never sing, and if you do, you must ask me first,'" David said. "I was astonished that my two-and-a-half-year-old daughter would say that, but then again Karly was very talkative. I laughed and laughed but Karly remained steadfast that I not sing, even after we returned home; she was adamant that I was not allowed to sing, although she did make exceptions if I sang 'Ring of Fire' or if I made up songs about her wearing striped shirts."

While in Ireland, David turned thirty. Doing her part to help with the celebration, Karly helped herself to the strawberries that adorned her father's cake, while her cousins ate the chocolate chips sprinkled on it.

Karly bonded easily with her cousins and the local kids, charming everyone with her laughter, her joy, and tales of her own imagination. She would boldly knock on neighbors' doors to see if the kids inside wanted to come out and play. During the day, she would happily spend time with her grandmother or cousins, but when evening rolled around it was David she wanted. She would get clingy if David wanted to go for a beer with his father.

"One evening I was able to reason with her to let me go out with Dad for a while, but Karly made it conditional, telling me that I had to run home, i.e. 'Don't be gone too long, Mister,'" David said.

Karly and her daddy crammed in a lot of life during the few weeks they were in Kenmare. They made a trip to the countryside, where Karly borrowed David's grandmother's cane and turned it into a rifle, the better with which to shoot pesky goats. They took a trip to the beach, where Karly romped around with her cousins in the shimmering waters.

As Karly and David held hands and walked through the town of Kenmare, where the streets are lined with buildings bright as Crayolas, the two chattered away, blissfully unaware of the dark clouds gathering back in Oregon.

And later, when Karly discovered their flight home to America was aboard an Aer Lingus plane called the "St. David," she was delighted. This thing Karly had suspected for a long time was true: her father really was a special man—he even had a big jet airliner named after him!

Over our coffee that day at New Morning Bakery, I asked for and received David's blessings to write this story. As far as I was concerned, he was the only person who had the right to ask me not to write about Karly. I didn't want to see him victimized any further, so I told him if he didn't want me to write this book, I wouldn't. But David gave me his blessings and his full cooperation.

There are many reasons why David wanted Karly's story told, but one of the foremost is because David wanted people to know that his daughter wasn't a tragic kid that nobody cared about.

"Karly is more than a statistic, a subject, a patient, a case number," David said. "She had many people that cared about her and loved her. She lived as full a life as a three-year-old can. She traveled to Ireland twice, charmed everybody she met, and made plans to buy a cell phone when she went to college."

Like most everyone connected to her death, David has his own regrets. "I did not do enough to protect Karly. I regret not standing up to the Children's Services investigation by pointing out the obvious things that were blatantly missed. I placed too much faith in the system."

David's naïve trust in Oregon Department of Human Services to help him protect his daughter did him far more harm than good. David was the primary suspect in the prolonged abuse case of Karly Sheehan.

CHAPTER TWELVE

S ARAH WAS NOT THE FIRST, nor the last, adolescent we welcomed into our home, but all came with the understanding that we had young children who would look to them as role models. Any potentially harmful behavior—smoking, drinking, or drugs—were taboo. Those who violated our rules were graciously asked to leave.

If Sarah abused our rules while living with us, I never knew of it. Sarah adored our children. If not out of respect for us, then out of love for them, she tried to set a good example. I appreciated that about her. Sarah's circle of associations was quite small, so I'm not sure where she had met her latest beau, Steve, but they quickly became a steady item.

Steve was a plain fellow, orange-headed and bony thin, but he had a good job and money to burn. He came to Pendleton to help establish Wildhorse Resort and Casino. Steve was one of a slew of financial people who swooped into town to help the Confederated Tribes of the Umatilla Indian Reservation (CTUIR) put their gaming business together. He pampered her with lavish gifts and elegant dinners out, spending as much time with her as his hectic schedule would allow. They would pop in and out of the house, coming from somewhere or going someplace else.

He was a nice enough fellow and always at Sarah's side, but, nonetheless, I was certain Sarah didn't consider him a keeper. The pickings of singles were slim in Pendleton if a girl ruled out cowboys and ranchers. Steve was simply someone to keep her entertained until she moved off to greener pastures.

At some point, perhaps while she was living with us, Sarah took up gambling in a bad way. Video gaming became her drug of choice, an addiction that would eventually lead to the break-up of her marriage to David. By the time the two divorced, Sarah had put the Sheehan household into tens of thousands of dollars in debt, most of it from gambling.

An estimated 2.3 million Americans are pathological gamblers, and experts say another 5 million adults have serious gambling problems. Research suggests those who suffer from attention deficit or hyperactive disorders, as Sarah does, are more prone to become compulsive gamblers.

Gambling is a socially acceptable behavior. For most, it starts out as harmless recreation. A compulsive gambler is expected to self-diagnosis and self-report. But the addict will resort to extreme measures of manipulations and deceitfulness, hocking possessions, lying, and outright stealing or engaging in other criminal pursuits to feed the frenzy created by their addiction.

If a person is a meth addict, physical symptoms will make it difficult to deny there's a problem. Their complexion gets bad. Teeth rot out. Muscle starts wasting away. It's easier to mask a gambling addiction than it is to mask a meth addiction. While many of Sarah's friends recognized she had an addiction to gambling, Sarah blamed her financial woes on poor fiscal skills.

"I'm shitty with money," she told Detective Wells.

That may have been the most truthful statement Sarah made in her numerous interviews with the police.

•

Money was one of the issues Tim and I addressed with Sarah during the time she lived with us. Sarah loved nice things. No sin in that, but there were times when the manner in which she obtained the things she wanted gave us pause. Sarah preferred easy cash to the hard-earned kind.

I didn't blame Sarah for trading off her looks and using them to her good pleasure. But over time, I came to question the extent to which Sarah capitalized on her physical attributes.

My unease switched to alarm after Sarah made a trip to Corvallis for a weekend and returned to Pendleton on a Sunday night driving a spiffy new pickup truck, glossy white with lots of shiny chrome.

Tim was driving around in a beater at the time, and he had a full-time job. Sarah was working at the bank part time. We were more than curious about how she could afford such a nice rig. But Sarah was twenty years old, and we respected her privacy.

Not long after she arrived back home with that new pickup, I started receiving phone calls from a young man asking for Sarah. I took his name and number and passed his messages on to her. For some inexplicable reason, Sarah refused to return his calls. The calls continued, almost nightly.

At first, I assumed it was some other poor schmuck who was smitten with Sarah, but there was something about the young man's tone that nagged at me. I kept telling Sarah to call him back. She never did. Finally, one night, I up and said, "Son, it's obvious to me Sarah isn't going to return your calls. Is there something I could help you with?"

"Yeah, maybe," he said, sighing. "I loaned Sarah $5,000 of my school loan money to buy a truck. Now spring term is here and I need to pay tuition, but I haven't heard from Sarah since she was down here."

Holy crap.

"I wish you hadn't done that," I said. "I'm afraid you'll never see that money again."

I doubt Sarah ever repaid him, but he didn't call our house anymore after that.

One dark night while a heavy rain fell, making the streets slick, the repo man came and towed Sarah's new toy away. That is what happens when you fail to make the monthly payments.

A year after Shawn Field was shackled and shuffled off to a prison cell for the murder of Karly, *Glamour Magazine* named Sarah their 2007 "What Are You Made Of? Reader of the Year." They flew her to New York, where they wined and dined her, and presented her with diamonds and a big fat check.

Sarah got the award for her work with the nonprofit, now-defunct Karly's Angels, a charity Sarah reportedly established to assist "single mothers" like her. David found out about Karly's Angels and the *Glamour* award via an e-mail announcement that Sarah apparently sent to her entire mail group:

> -----Original Message-----
> From: Sarah Sheehan [mailto:karlys.angels@gmail.com]
> Sent: Thursday, November 08, 2007 2:07 PM
> Subject: karlys angels gets props
> hiya - for those of you who aren't in the know, KA (Karly's Angels) was recognized nationally n NYC recently. I still have a lot of updating to do to the website, but now at least, i have some help! jilann's work donated a computer (awesome)! and my friend jaelyn, who is also a single mother, will begin doing research next week. karly's angels is pulling it together, with the second annual golf tournament to be held the first weekend in june. tbd. jilann, jaelyn and i travelled to new york city last saturday for a few days of sight seeing, sleeping and

attending some really fantastic events. i was chosen as one of three glamour magazine readers as woman of the year and was allowed to bring two guests. i chose jilann for all of the amazing support she has given me throughout the trial, and for being such an amazing friend to me since i moved here to bend and things weren't what i had expected. endless nights of vino and venting has fasted our friendship! i asked jaelyn to join because she is affiliated with karly's angels. we stayed at the fantastic hotel mela, which is right in the heart of times square. on monday we walked around the block to the conde naste building that houses not only glamour mag, but the likes of GQ and a zillion others. security was pretty decent. i am enclosing the link to the awards ceremony so that you may see pictures of it all. i would like to thank each and every one of you who has supported KA. i am excited to begin promoting for our next event, and with the generous donations from many of you, and a seriously generous donation from tag heuer and glamour mag, KA will be able to begin fulfilling our goals of helping children of single parent families! and that makes me happier than any of you can imagine ;) god bless, S.

There's more talk about the wine and the parties than there is mention of the murder that gained her the attention.

David had asked Sarah to stop copying him in on her e-mails. He'd even asked her to stop using Sheehan as her last name. That took me by surprise because Sarah told me David had urged her to keep her last name. She'd tagged that onto the conversation in which she'd told Tim and me Karly had passed. At the time, I'd thought it odd that it even came up in the conversation.

David called me shortly after he received Sarah's e-mail. Usually,

David is polite, congenial, always the essence of calm, cool, and collected. Not on this night. He was clearly and profoundly disturbed.

"What's next?" he asked angrily. "*Time's* Woman of the Year? The Nobel Prize? It's amazing a person with her background and trail of destruction is being feted like a hero of society. I found it interesting that nowhere in her e-mail did Sarah mention Karly except for Karly's Angels.

"And how ironic that she would play golf on the first weekend of June. Shawn commenced the final three-day beating ordeal while Mom of the Year was at golf—although she indicated to me that week that she would skip golf because she didn't have a sitter. "

I promised David that I would contact *Glamour* immediately. I sent an e-mail that evening to Nikki Ettore, at *Glamour*; to Ulrich Wohn, CEO at TAG Heuer, the diamond watch company that helped sponsor the award; and to Kris Kaczor, video editor at 750 Productions. All were people Sarah had copied on the same e-mail she sent to David.

It has come to my attention that Sarah Sheehan was recently named a *Glamour* magazine reader of the year. Sarah's daughter, Karly, was tortured to death by Sarah's boyfriend. Court documents are clear that Sarah was, if not complicit in this crime, at least very neglectful of her daughter. Before you highlight this woman as a *Glamour* girl, you should take a moment to read through the court documents. I think you might discover that there is much more to the story than just a woman and daughter being victimized. It could lead to some very embarrassing press for *Glamour* in the long run.

Karen Spears Zacharias, author/journalist

A representative for *Glamour* magazine sent the following response:

Thank you for your e-mail. To clarify, Sarah was honored in a WHAT ARE YOU MADE OF? contest, not a reader of the year. *Glamour* cannot comment on any allegations that may be made against the winner. It simply picked the winner based on her charitable efforts with Karly's Angels.

DANA ARISTONE | FASHION MERCHANDISING DIRECTOR | GLAMOUR MAGAZINE | P: 212-286-5392 | F: 212-286-4174

I passed *Glamour's* response to David, who sent me the following e-mail:

Karly's Angels was founded on 8/16/07 (according to the web site). Three months ago. Two weeks ago, she received donations from *Glamour* & TAG that would enable her to "begin fulfilling" their mission, emphasis on "begin." So what happened between 8/16 and 11/1 that would warrant receiving an award? Where's the track record? Did she receive an award because she got a tax ID, and has a web site under construction?

Ulrich Wohn did not respond to me. He did, however, send David a letter after David penned his own letter explaining how he had long nurtured an appreciation for TAG Heuer and their watches, ever since he was little boy growing up in Ireland. In fact, when David finally earned that master's degree he'd been pursuing the year Karly died, he'd rewarded himself with a TAG watch. The *Glamour* award to Sarah dulled the sheen on David's long-held infatuation with TAG. He urged Wohn to take action. To his credit, Wohn responded with compassion:

Dear Mr. Sheehan,

Thank you for your e-mail and bringing this to my attention. First and foremost, I am writing to express to you on behalf of the entire TAG Heuer organization my sincerest condolences on the tragic death of your daughter Karly and deep sadness for the anguish you and your family have had to endure.

With our recent awards, please know that TAG Heuer's intention was to honor women who have positively impacted their communities and to promote charitable action and giving. The winners of the contest were chosen by *Glamour Magazine* solely on the basis of the essays they wrote as contest entries, as specified in the contest rules.

While we realize that no amount of money can compensate for the pain of your loss, we have made a donation in Karly's honor to The Retreat, a wonderful charity for children who are the victims of domestic violence.

Again, I appreciate that you brought this very serious matter to my attention.

Sincerely,

Ulrich Wohn

Photos of Sarah collecting her award were circulated via the celebrity wire:

Early as it may have been, a perfectly coiffed Uma Thurman seemed pleased to emcee TAG Heuer and *Glamour Magazine*'s first What Are You Made Of? Awards breakfast last week. Thurman, who is a brand ambassador for Heuer and appears in the company's ads, joined Heuer North America president Ulrich Wohn, *Glamour* editor in chief Cindi Leive and *Glamour* vice president and publisher Bill Wackerman and others at Condé Nast Publications Inc.'s New York headquarters at 4 Times Square to laud three women who have positively impacted their communities.

Sarah Sheehan received an honor for starting Karly's Angels, a not-for-profit network of resources for single parents…Thurman presented each winner with an engraved diamond-studded Tag Heuer Carrera Chronograph watch.

— Sophia Chabbott

David was angry and unnerved by the manner in which Sarah exploited their dead child for financial gain. "If Sarah had undertaken five percent of her maternal responsibility, then Karly would still be alive," David said. "She has gotten away with so much. I can't let her rewrite history and make this artificial life for herself."

Sarah was not a single mother, abandoned, left to raise a child without support from Karly's father. Nothing could be further from the truth. Sarah was never a single mother. From the outset, David was Karly's primary caregiver. Even the chart notes made by nurses following Karly's birth document that fact:

"Husband is supportive. Father of baby very concerned and primary caregiver. Baby has been rooming in and father doing most of baby care while mom rests. Offered newborn class. Mom feeling too sore and wants father to go. Father took baby to class. Husband helps with baby. Patient anxious, needs lots of support and detailed explanation of procedures."

Within a couple of months of Karly's birth, Sarah returned to her freewheeling ways and resumed her social nightlife as a regular fixture at various clubs around town.

CHAPTER THIRTEEN

THE CITY'S NINE-HOLE COURSE AND club, called Par 3, located north of town on Highway 20, is a favorite among locals. Parents bring their children out to play the putt-putt course. Couples sit in the booths, sharing fries off each other's plates and ordering another local brew. Women and men weathered by too much golf and too many cigarettes totter on bar stools in a trance, pushing the chiming buttons of the video poker machines.

Eric DeWeese was manager at Par 3 the afternoon I stopped by following that phone call from a very distraught David. David said he'd heard Sarah had posted a flyer at Par 3 announcing a benefit golf tournament in Karly's honor, but it was all part of Sarah's newest moneymaking venture.

It was one of those rare dry winter days in the valley with a hand-drawn sun stuck to a felt-board sky, looking all make-believe. I sat in the parking lot at Par 3, gathering notebook and pen, and praying to learn what became of the Sarah I once knew.

A cursory scan as I passed through the door didn't reveal the flyer mentioning Karly's Angels. Overstuffed booths on my right, bar on my left. One man sat hunched over his bourbon, another over his second beer, the first bottle still on the bar.

A television blared from behind the bar. Leaning between the two men, I asked the girl wiping a glass if the manager was around, and if I could please speak to him. I could smell a burger sizzling on the grill, and beer sloshed on the floor for the last how many years.

Eric slid into the booth across from me. He was darkly handsome, all khaki and yellow polo, clean-shaven as a deacon. He sat sideways, back to the window, face to the bar, ready to hop up at a moment's notice. The barmaid turned the TV down a notch.

"What can you tell me about Sarah?" I asked.

"She's very attractive, very pretty, very flirty," Eric said. "A fairly big gambler, though. If she had $500, she'd spend it. If she had $1,000, she'd spend it. She was a party girl, always liked to have a good time."

He paused, and in his best manger voice asked, "Can I get you something to drink?"

"I'm good," I said. "Did you know Karly?"

"I knew Sarah for four years before I even knew she had a daughter. Crazy, huh? I assumed Sarah didn't have custody. She wasn't much of one to talk about personal things. She was the kind who'd ask you to watch Karly for ten minutes and come back eight hours later. Sarah was kind of a lost soul.

"I feel sorry for what happened and all, but anybody who thinks Sarah is a victim is a fool. Sarah put Sarah first, not Karly. Good mothers don't go out gambling. That gambling thing is a big turn-off."

"Is that why you never took up with her?" I asked.

"Yeah," Eric said. "I hired her as a cook but after a couple of months I moved her to the bar. But then $300 to $400 came up missing. I never came right out and accused her of stealing but I had to let her go. She quit coming out for a while after that but then she showed up again. She'd have a mimosa, gamble, golf, have lunch, drink, smoke and gamble some more."

"You ever see her use hard drugs?" I asked.

"I've seen her smoke some pot. She was taking pain pills left and right. She'd had some kind of surgery—I don't remember what. But she was popping those babies left and right. You damn sure shouldn't be taking those if you're drinking."

"Do you think Sarah is an alcoholic?" I asked.

"I don't know. Maybe," Eric said. He shifted around in the booth, so he could see the ESPN scores better. "But she didn't have the same kind of addiction to alcohol as she did to gambling."

"You think Sarah was involved in her daughter's death in any way?"

He pondered that question for a minute before answering.

"It's not too farfetched to think she could do this. Why would you go off and leave your child the way she did all the time? I never saw any signs of abuse but she sure had a lot of free time to spend here."

"How'd you learn of Karly's death?"

"A customer from HP told me. It was shocking, that's for sure. I don't view Sarah as a victim. I think she ought to be accountable for some of it. You should talk to those people over there." Eric nodded toward a round table back past the bar.

"Friends of Sarah's?" I asked.

"Used to be," he said.

I looked out the window, too dark to see anything but the out-buildings. The sun had long slipped beyond the green velvet coastal range hemming west Corvallis. I wasn't in any hurry. There was a warm bed waiting for me at Carlene Moorefield's house. Come anytime, Carlene said, and meant it.

"No telling when I will be coming and going," I had warned her.

"No worries," Carlene said. "Here's a key. Come and stay anytime." This was the third or fourth of many such visits.

"You think those people back there will want to talk to me?" I asked Eric.

"Sure, why not?"

"Oh, I don't know. If they are good friends of Sarah's they might find me intrusive."

"Not a chance," Eric said. "People around here aren't sorry to see Sarah go. She can stay on the east side. Good riddance."

I was surprised by the curt tone in his voice. "When's the last time you saw Sarah?"

"She was by here not long ago," Eric said. "I gave her permission to hang up the flyer."

"The flyer still there? I looked for one but didn't see it."

"Nah. I heard that her ex was a pretty stand-up guy and I got to wondering if he knew about this nonprofit of Sarah's. I wanted to know if he was involved in the charity. I had some reservations and my immediate thought was, is this legit or is Sarah in Bend gambling all this away? So I asked somebody who knows David."

That's when Eric found out David didn't know a thing about Karly's Angels. Just another get-rich-quick venture of Sarah's, Eric figured. So he ripped the flyer out of the window. He hasn't seen hide nor hair of Sarah since.

Friendships formed over barstools can wear thin during the drought times in a person's life. After Sarah e-mailed God and everybody and told them about being honored by *Glamour* magazine, her former pals at Par 3 sucked on filtered cigarettes and discussed the matter over glasses of chilled Chardonnay and foamy beer.

"Have a seat," Lee said, scooting to the right and offering me the chair next to Gina. Pam sat at the far end, opposite Lee now. I don't think anyone ever introduced me to the squatty fellow sitting directly across from me. The regulars had seen me earlier, talking with Eric. Who's the new chick? What's she want?

I put down the notebook and told them about how I knew Sarah.

Invited them to ask any questions they wanted. They didn't have any.

Lee, a Desert Storm veteran, looked more poet than soldier in his long black wool overcoat and rocker hair the color of barbwire. Lee ran around with Shawn's brother Kevin back in the day, before that nearly forgotten war, and before Kevin overdosed.

"We'd raise hell together," Lee said. "Shawn's parents were the nicest people. If we were at their house, his mom would bring us sandwiches and Shawn would yell at her to take them away. I asked him once, why do you treat your parents so badly? His parents were so nice, but Shawn was a fat, spoiled, rotten kid. A really horrible guy. He was nuts."

Lee knew Sarah, too, from her bartending days. "She wasn't a bad person," he said. "Just somebody who made bad choices. She was always the same weak girl, a heavy gambler."

How had Sarah's gambling problem escaped me all these years?

"So you ladies belong to the Sand Tramps?" I asked. Sarah had pulled together the all-girls league. Gina nodded. Even in the dead of winter, Gina has the honey glow of someone who spends a lot of time in the sun, planting flowers, pulling weeds. "Matt, that's my husband, would take care of Karly a lot," Gina said. "Our daughter Mia and Karly were playmates."

"What kind of mom was Sarah?" I asked.

"I love Sarah to death but she was not cut out to be a mom," Gina said. "Sarah treated Karly more like a possession than a daughter. She wanted Karly to have the best clothes; she was all about that trendy stuff. She liked to show Karly off but she wasn't about spending time with Karly. Moms put their kids first. Sarah never did that."

"Shawn, now he was trouble," Pam interrupted.

"What do you mean?"

"He was controlling. Sarah took up running because Shawn told her she was getting too fat. I was scared of him from the start."

"Really? Why?"

"It was gut instinct," Pam said. "When Sarah introduced me to him, I just thought, he's not a good person. Sarah and I quit hanging out after she took up with Shawn. She was always in a hurry to get home to him."

"Well, not always," Gina said. "Matt would watch Karly a lot. He is pissed at Sarah. He doesn't think she should have gotten off scot-free. Sarah's a good manipulator, good at getting her own way. Karly was at our house the week she died, running around crying, puking and shaking, 'I want my daddy! I want my daddy!'"

Hearing Gina quote the dead Karly punctured something in Pam. Holding back her corn-silk hair, she hunkered over the rim of her wine glass. A fierce thunderstorm gave way to tears. A fellow sitting nearby moved his beer and handed her a napkin.

We all grew silent. There was no talk of Beaver basketball or what a beautiful day it was in the Valley. Gina placed a hand on Pam's shoulder. There's a time when tears are the only appropriate response. Pam's shoulder-heaving sobs are what I would have expected from Sarah the day she told me Karly had died. How had she remained so calm about that?

"That e-mail Sarah sent out after her trip to New York, that upset a lot of us," Pam said.

"Yeah," Lee said, taking a draw from his beer.

"Sarah is all about the money," Pam added. "Anybody who knows Sarah knows she's all about the money."

"You think she had anything to do with Karly's death?" I asked.

"We never saw any abuse," Gina replied. "I mean it bugged the hell outta me when Karly showed up with all her hair missing. You don't lose that much hair. It's not normal. I told Sarah to take her to the doctor. You can't tell me as a mother she didn't know Karly was being abused. Toward the end, Sarah was spending much more time with Shawn's daughter than she was with Karly. I didn't know what to think."

CHAPTER FOURTEEN

Betrayal can only occur in relationships built on love and trust. The kind of relationship I had with Sarah at one time. The sort she had with David, briefly. The devoted kind of relationship that any child ought to be able to expect from her mother.

I worry about how betrayed Sarah is going to feel reading these words. Several people have asked whether I fear Sarah. I don't know the answer to that question because I no longer know Sarah. There are times when I wonder if I ever really knew her, if any of us ever did. Or was she betraying our affections the entire time we were loving on her?

It's the betrayal that Karly experienced that propels me onward. She comes to me in my dreams, not as the dead Karly, per se, but as a little girl distraught.

The young girl cries in my dream, begs to be held, and to be comforted. She pleads with me not to leave her alone. She is eight or nine, close to the age Shawn's daughter Kate was when Karly was killed, but it's not Kate. When Sarah and Shawn first began dating, Kate was eight and Karly was two, almost three. I hold the girl in my dreams and comfort her. I hold her close and tell her I will never, ever leave her alone, not for one second. When I wake, I'm the one crying.

When I began writing this book, I asked Jack if Shawn's parents, Hugh and Ann Field, would be willing to be interviewed by me.

> Karen:
>
> Just wanted to let you know I talked with S's parents about the issues you mentioned and they chose to stay with their original stance. They do not want to talk. I tried to explain the advantages but they politely declined.
>
> They want truth and at the same time are leery of the price they might have to pay in addition to what they have had to pay already. Good luck on the investigation and writing.
>
> Jack

I'm not sure what Shawn's parents want revealed, and as long as they refuse to speak with me I'm not likely to learn. But the one thing I do know from my years as an investigative reporter is that only those who have something to hide do the hiding. Everybody else talks.

Hugh and Ann have been covering for Shawn for a very long time. As an adolescent, Shawn was a bad attitude sprouting. He was arrested at sixteen with a couple of buddies full of bravado gone sour. The three of them broke into several homes and took hostage one of the boys' own mothers. They intended to steal Shawn's brother's truck and joyride to Colorado—to do some skiing—but local lawmen caught them before the trio could finish the chorus of "Ride Like the Wind" and then hauled their butts to juvie.

Ann and Hugh can protest all they want that their son is too good of a boy to have killed a child. Oh, bless him, he wouldn't pour salt on a slug, wouldn't flick a fly from a watermelon. Shawn couldn't possibly have hurt a child. But the evidence doesn't support their view.

Well, yes, Hugh told the courts, the boy-turned-man had stolen his credit cards, had forged his name, and run up a bill in the thousands of dollars without any way to pay for it. Shawn found working such a distasteful bore. Points of contention with his son are seen best in the clenching of Hugh's jaw. Getting along with a son intent on not getting along with anyone can sap a good man, but that's no call for airing dirty boxers on the public square. Nope. In front of God and everybody listening, Hugh and Ann declare their son has been wrongly accused.

But I suspect that when they sit silently across the dinner table, they avoid looking into each other's eyes and seeing the truth of their son. I bet Hugh and Ann have stood shoulder to shoulder in the kitchen pouring black coffee, peeling a banana and asking, "Do you think he could have done this thing?" And I'd bet they've howled against the bitter winds that delivered to them one son dead from an overdose and one imprisoned.

Not long after Jack sent me his note that Shawn's parents didn't want to talk to me, I received another one from him saying Ann Field was worried that digging all this up would harm her granddaughter.

Jack said he talked to Shawn's mother and that she was suffering, thinking about the book. "Her fear is that Kate will be the one most likely to suffer when your book comes out," Jack said. "She can't understand how you can push ahead on this book when you know you are going to hurt people."

I hope to never know the kind of grief Ann Field endures. It is not my intention to add to Hugh or Ann's heartache. Nor do I want to harm Kate in any way. David is concerned about her, too. He considers Kate, not Sarah, to be Shawn's other victim. Kate is not her real name. I told Jack to tell Ann I wouldn't use her real name.

Not that it really matters. It's not as if Kate doesn't wake up every morning knowing that her daddy puts on his prison jumpsuit one leg at a time. It's not as if she hasn't sucked back salty sobs, thinking of how hateful her father had been that last morning of Karly's life.

I didn't tell Jack but I came across some postings on an online forum discussing Karly's death. I can't be sure the remarks are Kate's but that's the claim made:

> "Im shawn fields daughter. He never abused me so i dont understand why he would abuse karly. She was like my sister and sarah was like a secind mom. PLEASE DONT ACUSE SARAH OF THIS CRIME. she had nothing do with her daughters death. She loved her more than anything. I was there so i know the BIG details. I was at school when karly died though."

If she had lived, Karly would have turned nine in January 2011, the date of the above post. Loving daughters are a delight at almost any age. Nine-year-old girls are all ankles and elbows, throwing back the covers on the day and running barefoot over our hearts. If Kate really did author that post, she might have been thinking about her own ninth birthday in 2005 and the trip she took to Disneyland without her father. He couldn't go because he was in jail, awaiting the outcome of an ongoing murder investigation.

I replied to Jack and told him I think Ann's fear is misplaced. Kate's suffering is going to be far more reaching than any book I write. The deceit we buy into is the belief that as long as we aren't talking about our hurts, they have no power over us.

Ann Field and I disagree over how one softens the blow for Kate growing up with her father imprisoned for murder. I don't think such a thing can be "softened." I think it ought to be dealt with, openly and honestly.

Even during midday, when I'm wide awake, I hear the words of Judge Holcomb echoing: "Might there have been an intervention that could have saved this child's life?"

Of course, an intervention could have saved her. Absolutely. Sarah, alone, could have offered her daughter salvation. Instead, she betrayed her.

Karly's death is not simply a tragedy—it's an unforgivable shame.

It takes the complicity of a community, and a nation, to stand by in silence as a child is tortured to death. That ought to give us all nightmares of children weeping.

CHAPTER FIFTEEN

ALARMED BY TROUBLING CHANGES SHE observed in Karly, Delynn Zoller was the first person to file an official complaint of possible abuse. Delynn, owner of Rugrats Traditional Home Child Care, was required by law to call Oregon Department of Human Services Child Welfare if she suspected abuse. That first call was made nine months before Karly's death and a few short weeks after Sarah started dating a man named Shawn Wesley Field. He was a nice-looking guy. Clean-shaven, lean, with expressive eyes. Dark mirrors that reflected shadows of things yet unseen.

Sarah met Shawn in late September at Suds and Suds, a beer-only bar located inside Woodstock's Pizza Parlor. Woodstock's is a multipurpose facility that caters to families and the college crowd. Sports jerseys and posters line the parlor's high walls. On the building's east side is a coin-operated laundry facility.

Suds is a typical neighborhood bar, not unlike the one seen on the popular television series *Cheers*, only smaller, about a quarter of the size.

"I thought he came from a good family," Sarah said. By "good", Sarah meant he came from a family with money. "He was driving a Volvo. His parents had homes in Corvallis and in Arizona. Shawn had a daughter. He presented this package that said, 'Hey, you're lucky you have me.'"

Shawn's neighbors would later describe him as athletic, like a runner or something, but Shawn's classmates at Crescent Valley High knew him as a pudgy, awkward kid. Crescent Valley, the school on the north side of Corvallis, is generally regarded as the rich kids' school. The Fields' home bordered a golf course.

On their first meeting, Shawn smiled disarmingly and introduced himself to Sarah. A flirt by nature, Sarah responded without reservation. They hooked up that very night. "We hung out at my place, playing cards," Sarah told the court. "I consider that as when we began dating."

The M-word came up within a couple weeks of their first date. Shawn was the first to raise it. It wasn't exactly a proposal but, as Sarah explained, it was close enough. "We were at Suds. I wasn't working. I was there socially. We were sitting outside on the patio with some of my friends. Shawn picked up my left hand and said, 'A ring would look really good there.' Shortly after that we talked of moving in together."

Shawn was living in a duplex off Aspen Street, in a quiet, residential part of town, close to Hoover Elementary School, the kind of neighborhood college professors and Hewlett-Packard employees call home. An area where barking dogs are the most common complaint.

Sarah, who had been sharing an apartment with a girlfriend, decided to move in with Shawn, though she barely knew him. She insisted they had this rare thing: chemistry, a connection, the kind that doesn't come along every day.

"I really liked Shawn at that point and was very interested in being in a committed relationship. Besides, I didn't have Karly most nights; David did. It was Shawn's idea, not mine, that I bring Karly for an overnight visit. He thought it was time that Karly and Kate meet."

Shawn's first marriage, to a girl named Molly Church, was annulled in 1994. Molly's father, Jim Church, a Portland attorney, told investigators it was out of concern for his daughter's well-being that he sought an annulment on her behalf.

If the annulment bothered him, Shawn didn't mope around much. He met his next wife, Eileen, on a blind date shortly thereafter. Two weeks later, just like in Sarah's case, Shawn raised the idea of marriage. When Shawn and Eileen married in 1995, Eileen was twenty-two years old and two months pregnant with the couple's only child, the daughter I call Kate. According to Eileen, the marriage was fraught with violent outbursts. The couple divorced in July 2002 and shared custody of Kate.

David forewarned me that Delynn probably wouldn't want to talk to me. "I think she wants to put all this behind her," he said. David was right; Delynn was reluctant. It was nearly a year after I first contacted her before Delynn e-mailed me.

"I got your message but have had to pray about this a little so forgive me for not getting back to you sooner," Delynn said. "Yes, this is a painful subject for me, but a happy one as well and I sometimes forget that."

In early 2008, I made a trip to Salem to the Court of Appeals office to look at the evidence that had been presented to the jury. At the time, I was teaching at Central Washington University in Ellensburg, Washington, and preparing to head off to Fairhope, Alabama. The Fairhope Center for the Writing Arts had invited me to be their writer-in-residence, and I needed to gather as much information as possible before I headed south. I wanted to wrap up interviews and compile the information I'd spent the better part of the past year collecting. Delynn's e-mail gave me some hope I could also meet with her face to face. But I was running out of time, and if Delynn didn't meet with me now, I wasn't sure when, or if, that meeting would take place.

It was late afternoon on an unusually warm day in Oregon's Willamette Valley. I'd left the Court of Appeals after spending the better part of the day holed up in a corner under the watchful eye of the court administrator, rifling through boxes of evidentiary materials. Bracing myself for a look at the post-mortem photos of Karly, I'd inadvertently pulled out a photo from a stack of 8x10s, and nearly collapsed in a heap when I discovered I'd grabbed hold of an autopsy photo.

I was prepared, but barely, to see Karly as the police had found her that afternoon in June, 2005. I knew I would have to look at those photos in order to understand the documents I'd spent the past eight months studying. But I didn't yet know about the autopsy photos.

Tough as I can be, I don't watch *CSI*, or any of those other forensic shows. I've been on the scene of all sorts of crimes, but I don't want to see people carved up, even on television. I'd kept my act together while I was in the Appeals office, but as soon as I got to the car, I broke down sobbing. I called Connie, a dear friend in nearby Albany. "This is one of those moments when I think I might actually have reached my breaking point," I said. "I'm not sure I can go on with this." Connie calmed me with words of thoughtful encouragement. As soon as we hung up, my cell rang. It was a number I didn't recognize.

"Hello," I said.

"Hi. Is this Karen? This is Delynn Zoller."

No matter how many times it occurs, I continue to be amazed by such strong coincidence.

Delynn agreed to meet me for dinner at New Morning Bakery, the same place where I'd met with David. We picked a table near the front window where we could talk freely, out of the eavesdropping range of others. The evening rush was in full swing. A steady line of people shuffled past the glass and chrome cases filled with spinach and mushroom quiche, fruit salads, hazelnut tortes, and lemon bars. Steaming soups, thick with tomatoes or white sauce, were ladled into heavy ceramic bowls. People called out to one another from behind the self-service coffee pots.

A pretty woman, Delynn is bright-eyed. Her back is strong and straight. She sits erect on the edge of her chair, ready to move at a moment's notice to put out whatever fire might need it. She'd be a ringer for the actor Julianne Moore if she dyed her brown hair red and put on a smack of red lipstick. Delynn is a reserved woman who lacks the self-confidence and the assertive attitude common among women who know they are pretty.

Delynn began caring for Karly in June 2004. Providing childcare for over two decades has made Delynn a keen observer of children's behavior. She knows when something is not right. Her intuition is sharp. Yet the daycare provider's voice, as that of a high school dropout, may have been easily dismissed in a community where over half the population has at least one college degree. Some may have tuned Delynn out simply because she was a born-again evangelical and openly expressed her faith in God.

At her home, Delynn kept a framed photo of her deceased mother on a coffee table. Karly would point to it and ask Delynn about her mom, about heaven, about Jesus. "Karly talked more about God than any of my other daycare children," Delynn said. "We talked a lot about Heaven, about what would happen there. I told her Heaven is the most wonderful thing. I told her how much God loves us, how much I love God. Karly said, 'I love God, too, Delynn.'"

When tussles broke out among the other children, Karly would often intervene. "She would referee," Delynn recalled. "She understood what was right and wrong." Karly was a peacemaker. She wanted everybody to play nicely, to get along, and to be happy. Much more verbal than other children her age, Delynn said, "Karly could carry on a conversation like an adult."

But Karly refused to tell others about the ongoing horrors she endured. Whether she did that because of threats from her abuser or because of her own tender heart is something we will never know.

Picking through the grapes and melon of her fruit salad, Delynn paused her fork midair and said she regarded Sarah as a distant mother. "Sarah really had this unnatural way about her."

"What do you mean?" I asked.

"Karly would cry and this blankness would wash over Sarah," Delynn said.

"Like she was ignoring Karly or didn't know how to handle her?" I asked.

"Maybe a bit of both," Delynn said.

In October 2004, Karly arrived at Rugrats Daycare with her blonde, wispy hair tightly wound into an elegant French braid.

I'd taught Sarah how to French braid. I'd spent untold hours on school mornings fixing my daughters' hair. They'd come to me, hair ribbon or bow in hand, and ask me to put their hair in a ponytail, to crimp it, curl it, or to French braid it. Sarah would sit on the stool at the kitchen island and watch as I divided a head of hair into three strands, wrapping one end over the other. What I did for one daughter, I did for three daughters.

"Will you teach me to do that?" she asked.

"Sure," I replied, and I did.

Despite the bakery's suppertime crowd, Delynn wept unabashedly as she recalled how lovely Karly had been on that particular day.

"I told Karly how pretty her hair looked but I could tell she had been crying. Her eyes were all red and watery. 'Karly,' I said, 'you have princess hair,' which is what I call a braid."

Instead of being delighted by Delynn's comments, Karly was agitated. "My mom said I don't have princess hair," Karly said. "She said I have ogre hair."

Karly's comment startled Delynn. She thought the young girl must have misheard her mother.

"I told her, 'No, your hair is beautiful, just like Princess Fiona's hair.'"

Delynn recalled that Karly behaved oddly all day long. She slept a lot. When Sarah came to pick her up that evening, Delynn remarked to Sarah that Karly had been worn out. She asked if Sarah had put any gels or anything else like that on Karly's hair, some kind of allergen, because Karly's eyes were so irritated. Sarah said no, nothing came to mind.

The next day's events startled Delynn and haunt her to this day.

"Sarah called and said Karly would be late to daycare because she had to take Karly in to get her hair cut. I said, 'Gosh! That's so sad. Her princess hair?' And Sarah said, 'Yes. It got in a big mat and there was no way I could comb it out.'"

When Karly showed up later that day, her soft blonde locks had been hacked off. Her eyes were swollen and red. She had been crying. "I think Karly was very embarrassed by her short hair."

Sarah told Delynn she'd left the braid in overnight and she'd woken to find the braid matted. "Here, I'll get it," Sarah said, rushing out to her car. It was a disquieting moment when Sarah displayed the braid.

"I am sure my face registered shock because I was thinking about what Karly said the day before about having 'ogre hair.' I was so upset for Karly," Delynn said. "Sarah kind of laughed and said, 'Can you believe this?' She said she wanted me to see it because she couldn't believe it and wondered what I thought about it."

What Delynn thought was that Sarah was strange as all get out. She didn't believe one word Sarah was saying. "I couldn't figure out what may have happened, but I was thinking it was weird that any little kid's hair could do that over one night and that it was even weirder that her mother would show it to me."

"What did it look like?" I asked.

"It looked like the mat on a dog," Delynn said.

Why are you showing me this? Delynn wondered. "I'd never had a parent do something like that before. It made me wonder if she was hiding something. To be honest, I didn't believe her. In my gut I thought, 'This mom has done something to her daughter's hair.' I didn't trust Sarah was telling me the truth."

Her suspicion of Sarah left Delynn feeling guilty. "I didn't have a good relationship with Sarah. I felt bad that I didn't believe what she said, but I didn't."

Despite her issues with Sarah, Delynn put on a front for Karly. "I told her that I loved her haircut." But the haircut shamed the little girl.

"My mommy said that I don't have princess hair now and that I'm not going to be Princess Fiona," Karly said.

It infuriated Delynn that the haircut humiliated Karly.

"I told Karly how pretty she was, that she looked like a little pixie."

Karly snapped at Delynn: "I'm not a princess anymore!"

"Well, you can be a fairy princess because fairy princesses have short pixie hair like you," Delynn reassured Karly.

But Karly never again referred to herself as Princess Fiona. From that moment on, Karly referred to herself as Prince Charming.

Chapter Sixteen

When Sarah had Karly's hair chopped off, it was the first sign of trouble. Police investigators, Delynn, David and Karly's doctor all agree that something bad happened to Karly that night. Did Shawn jerk Karly upside the head? Did Sarah?

That's sheer speculation, of course. A badly matted braid is not proof of abuse, but that hair incident was the first hint of the violence that would follow. It would be the event that a host of people would puzzle over as the investigation, which had started as potential child abuse, turned into an investigation for murder.

David had a couple of extended business trips in October and November, 2004. Prior to leaving, he'd made daycare arrangements with Delynn. It gave David peace of mind to know Delynn was watching after Karly.

He was out of town, but Sarah warned David before he returned home that she had taken Karly in for a haircut. She also casually mentioned she and Karly had spent three nights at her new boyfriend's place. David didn't like it one bit, but divorced parents all over this country understand you cannot dictate the ex-spouse's dating behavior, even if children are involved. Shawn wasn't the first man Sarah had introduced into Karly's life since her breakup with David. In fact, there had been several. David worried that Sarah's lack of discernment would negatively affect their daughter.

On Monday, November 15, 2004, David wrote a letter to Sarah. He was trying to find a civil way to let her know he was worried about her lifestyle choices:

> Hi Sarah:
>
> I have something I need to talk to you about, and figured that this was the best way to initiate it—and remove the tone of my voice from the picture. I definitely don't want to appear unreasonable or confrontational, so bear with me.
>
> I am really dismayed that Karly has effectively moved in with Sean (not sure if name is spelled that way or 'Shawn'). While maybe you haven't officially moved in, it looks like Karly spends her nights with you at his house. I think it is very irresponsible of you to do this again. You only started dating in September, and by the end of October you have our daughter living at his house. How can this possibly strike you or him as a good idea? I think you have a long track record of making bad decisions in relationships by rushing into things, and now you are with a guy who is also content to rush in, and both of you are bringing two young girls along for the ride.
>
> I firmly believe that Karly does not like the situation at all. Of course, it is hard to believe everything she said, so I won't go by what she tells me about not liking it over there. What I will go by is what Karly doesn't say to me—she never asks for you anymore. I don't hear her say, "I want my mama" the way she used to say a month ago.
>
> Hopefully you can at least have a think about things, and reflect a little on what's best for Karly. On Saturday night after

you dropped her off, she slept from 7 p.m. until 9 a.m. on Sunday morning (when I decided to wake her). Any thoughts on why she is so tired over the last few weeks? Similarly, why she has experienced such dramatic hair loss over the last few weeks? I think we should take her to Dr. deSoyza and have her take a look at Karly's scalp.

    David

He never got around to mailing that letter to Sarah. He decided against it because he feared Sarah would dismiss the letter as a rant from a jealous ex, and David didn't want to be mistaken for that by her or anyone else.

Sarah said she and Shawn discussed whether Karly should go to Delynn's daycare. "It was a fairly reoccurring conversation between us," she said. "Shawn's opinion was Karly shouldn't be in daycare. He said if I was a good mother, she would be with me all the time."

And once Sarah took up with Shawn, Karly's attendance at daycare became sporadic. It was one of the things Delynn kept track of in a journal, following more obvious signs that Karly was in distress. Delynn's relationship with Sarah grew increasingly strained.

"If it hadn't been for David," Delynn said, "I would not have taken care of Karly because I don't work for people I can't get along with and I couldn't get along with Sarah. She always acted like she was irritated or annoyed with me. I guess we just didn't click."

David was traveling a lot that fall and Delynn noticed Karly's eating and sleeping patterns were changing.

"That's when I began to keep a journal, writing down all the things that worried me. Karly always seemed hungry. She was asking for food all the time. She hadn't done that before. And she was complaining about being tired all the time. Karly would tell me that she wanted to take a nap. When a kid wants to take a nap, you know something is up. Three days in a row, Karly fell asleep while watching *Barney*. Something just wasn't right."

Delynn wasn't the only one who started keeping a journal. Sarah kept notes, too. She later told a jury Shawn had forced her to keep a diary. Her so-called diary consisted of a few notes scribbled on notebook paper. Sarah's "diary" seemed to have a clear agenda: to frame David for the abuse of Karly Sheehan.

> Thursday, Oct. 10, 2004
> Karly woke up this morning very upset again. She repeated the phrase "I'm scared of my daddy" several times. Could not get her to say why though. I asked her what's scary about Daddy, and she cried more. Very upsetting.

> Saturday, Oct. 30
> Karly woke up stressed out again this morning. After a long night of being awake, whimpering over breakfast and needing to be held. When I told her everything would be okay, that nobody was going to hurt her, she said, "My daddy hurts me" and began crying hysterically. After calming her down a bit I just held her some more.

> Saturday, Nov. 13
> Went shopping with Karly, she seemed fine until the AT&T store. After playing for a little while, she came up to me crying & saying she was scared of her daddy. Over & over & over again. It was quite disturbing.

Not only was Sarah not married to Shawn, she wasn't financially dependent on Shawn, either. She had a job, made her own income. Throughout the time she was with him, Sarah maintained a separate apartment with her friend Shelley. Sarah was free to come and go as she liked. She spent a great deal of time at Par 3. She had only met Shawn two months prior to writing these notes.

By mid-November, Karly's hair was pixie short, and appeared to be thinning. Delynn noted that Karly "cries uncontrollably for her daddy several times during the day," a direct contradiction to the notes Sarah kept.

Delynn further expressed her concerns about Karly. "I talked to Sarah about Karly being so tired. Sarah said she sees the same thing at home. Karly cries constantly for her daddy."

For several weeks, between the braid mess and the crying jags of November, Delynn debated notifying authorities. Weighing heavily on her mind was another child, Jasara, a young girl she had cared for some years prior.

Delynn kept Jasara from the time she was born until she was two, when the family moved to California. It was shortly after the move that the little girl was brutally beaten by her mother's boyfriend. The last time Delynn saw Jasara, she was being carried to the car by her mom's new boyfriend.

"When the sleeping Jasara opened her eyes and realized that she was being held by Jacques, she turned to me and reached out her arms," Delynn recalled. "I felt that the look in her eyes was pure fear. At the time, I could not shake that away. I thought logically that it was probably because she did not know him very well, but I will never forget the way she looked at me and reached for me, and now I know why. It was to save her from him."

It's a haunting memory.

•

Karly was an articulate, sunny-natured, inquisitive child, until Sarah hooked up with Shawn. Then Karly became withdrawn and moody. In mid-November, Karly made a startling proclamation to Delynn.

"My daddy hits me," she said.

All the daycare kids were sitting around the table, munching on crackers and turkey slices, apples and grapes, or sucking on their sippy cups when Karly put down her juice and began slapping her head to show them how she was being hit. "I'm scared of my daddy," she added.

Stunned, Delynn asked, "You mean your daddy David?" And Delynn could have sworn, and indeed did swear later, that Karly answered "Yes." But it was noisy and kids were chattering about one thing or another, all vying for attention. Surely Delynn must have heard her wrong. David would never hit Karly. Delynn was sure of that. She told investigators and the jury that.

"Delynn, you need to talk to my daddy," Karly said.

"What do I need to say to your dad?" Delynn asked.

"You need to tell him no! Don't hit me!"

On Tuesday, November 16, 2004, Delynn waited until the lunch table was cleared and all the kids were down for a nap before she called the state's child abuse hotline. She kept a detailed log of the conversation.

Delynn talked first to an intake officer who took the information and told her someone would call her back. Meanwhile, David called to check on Karly, something he did as a matter of routine to see how his daughter's day was going. Delynn didn't mention what Karly had shared with her but she did suggest that David needed to take Karly to see a doctor. David agreed and said he would see to it.

Later that afternoon, when Sarah arrived to pick up Karly, Delynn told her the same thing: Sarah needed to get Karly to a doctor to evaluate her. "She's tired all the time and, look, see how her hair is coming out in patches?" Delynn said, pointing to the bald spots.

But Sarah, defensive, acted as if Delynn was making a mountain out of a molehill. She told Delynn she had spoken with her mother about the hair loss. According to Sarah, her own sister had suffered extensive hair loss when she was the same age as Karly. Sarah said the sort of hair loss that Karly was experiencing "was normal in our family."

Such a statement made absolutely no sense. Any genetic propensity toward hair thinning or balding was not passed along to Karly from her Aunt Kim or her Grandma Carol or Grandpa Gene. There was no genetic legacy passed along to Karly via the Brill family at all. Sarah was adopted.

Unfortunately, Delynn was unaware of the embedded deceit.

Leaning over the table at the bakery where Delynn and I sat long after our meals had grown cold, Delynn took a sip of Pepsi, pushed her brunette hair back off her high forehead, and exhaled a deep sigh. Her regret over Karly's death was palpable.

I waited. Silence no longer makes me uncomfortable. Grief will not be bossed, coerced, or cajoled. It comes and goes as it pleases, and if you try to hurry it along, it will refuse to leave.

A few minutes passed where the only noise was the clanging of dishes and the chatter of people trying to decide what to order, whether to have that slice of apple pie. After a few minutes, Delynn jumped back into her story.

"It was almost like God was talking to me. Karly said, 'Delynn, my daddy hits me. My daddy bites me.'"

Delynn said now she was sure Karly had to be talking about Sarah's new boyfriend. "I knew she couldn't mean David. I had never seen him act in any way wrong." But when she first called authorities, Delynn had to tell them exactly, verbatim, what Karly said. "I was just sick," she said. "I knew it meant I would get David into trouble, and I knew Karly loved her daddy."

Delynn said she never believed David was the one harming Karly.

"I did not trust what Karly was saying when she said, 'My daddy bites me, hits me,'" Delynn said. "I just had this gut feeling she could not tell who it was for some reason and maybe she was saying 'Daddy' in order to tell somebody, but not to tell on the somebody she was very scared of."

Or could it be that Karly's abuser coerced her into hiding the truth?

CHAPTER SEVENTEEN

D R. SHANILKA DESOYZA AGREED TO meet me at a coffee shop near the campus of Oregon State University. The doctor, a native of Sri Lanka, was Karly's doctor from birth.

An afternoon rush crowded the shop. I chose a seat near the storefront window, put down my bag, and placed my order. I was halfway through my latte when a small-boned woman in dark slacks, a periwinkle-blue sweater and black flats approached me and introduced herself.

Dr. deSoyza's hair is black, cropped short, stylish but functional, perfect for a mother on the run. She has two children. Her oldest child, a girl, is a high-functioning autistic. She told me that and much more as students, fueled by caffeine, hovered over newspapers, laptops, and textbooks.

The doctor maintained a professional demeanor but she also had a vulnerable quality to her. It rose to the surface the minute she began to talk about her own children.

She was in her fourth year of medical school in Cincinnati, Ohio, when her first child was born.

"I had no idea she wouldn't be a typical child," deSoyza said. Her daughter would not sleep or take a bottle. Residency turned into a nightmare; overwhelmed, deSoyza left medical school. She and her husband relocated thousands of miles away to Hermiston, Oregon, a town where they had friends.

Five years passed before deSoyza felt comfortable enough to leave the pastoral life of Hermiston to return to the tyranny of residency. The couple returned to Ohio, but planned to raise their family in Oregon as soon as deSoyza finished her program.

They needed to relocate to an area where their daughter could get the best medical and educational care possible. So the couple settled in Corvallis in 2001 and deSoyza went to work for Samaritan Health Services.

Dr. deSoyza was Sarah and David's general physician. When David mentioned that they needed to find a pediatrician for the baby they were expecting, Dr. deSoyza told David that she was capable of treating children. Dr. deSoyza had seen her share of children in her practice. For a time, she treated the children at Corvallis' Children's Farm Home, a residential treatment facility for children with behavioral problems.

The family doctor was very familiar with Karly, and her parents. "Karly was a little girl with a big personality," Dr. deSoyza said. "A little bit mischievous."

She knew David and Sarah were divorced. Dr. deSoyza considered David a very good father. Sarah, however, often seemed overwhelmed. "She was flaky," deSoyza said. "But I've dealt with moms a lot flakier than Sarah."

After the couple split, it was usually David who brought Karly in for medical care. Karly saw the doctor in June 2004 because David wanted to discuss some digestive issues Karly had been experiencing. Dr. deSoyza didn't see Karly again until November 17, 2004. This time it was at the request of an official with Department of Human Services Child Welfare, who wanted Dr. deSoyza to evaluate the child for signs of possible child abuse.

Before making that first call to the state's abuse hotline, Delynn had attempted to collect more information from Karly.

"Does your momma work at night?" she asked Karly.

Karly nodded yes.

"Who takes care of you when your momma is gone?"

"Shawn does," Karly said.

"Do you like it when Shawn takes care of you?" Delynn asked.

"No, Shawn spanks me," Karly whimpered.

That was exactly the answer Delynn expected. Suspicious of Sarah and her lifestyle, Delynn needed to get as many details as she could. She repeated what Karly had said back to the child in hopes that Karly would elaborate.

"Shawn spanks you?"

"No," Karly said, shaking her head. She was clearly agitated now, panicky even. "My daddy spanks me," she said, and began to cry. "I'm tired, Delynn."

Troubled that she had upset the fragile child, Delynn said, "You eat a little now and then you can lay down on the couch, okay?" Karly nodded.

When David called after lunch, Delynn told him Karly had been listless all morning long, preferring sleep rather than playing with the other children. She did not eat her lunch.

"You need to get her in to a see a doctor," Delynn said.

"Okay," David said. "I'll do that."

"You know as a daycare provider I'm required by law to report the changes I'm seeing in Karly," Delynn warned.

"You do what you need to do," David said. He was at his wits' end trying to figure out what was wrong with Karly. David had asked Delynn if she had ever seen hair loss like Karly's before. She had not. David welcomed the idea of the complaints about Karly coming from someone besides himself. Any time he questioned her, Sarah would accuse him of being jealous and controlling. David didn't know if Karly had some undetermined illness or if she was miserable about her mother's new living arrangement. He knew, however, that Sarah lived in a constant state of flux, changing jobs, changing boyfriends, and changing living arrangements every few months.

On Tuesday, November 16, 2004, Matt Stark was working at the Oregon Department of Human Services (DHS), the state agency responsible for protecting children from neglect and abuse, when he first received a referral for assessment alleging possible physical abuse regarding Karla Isabelle Ruth Sheehan.

That next day, in the early afternoon, Stark called Delynn, who carefully outlined her concerns: Karly's erratic sleeping pattern, her hair loss and an occasional odd bruising. Delynn told Stark she'd insisted the parents get Karly in to see a doctor immediately. David had called to say Karly had an appointment that very evening with Dr. deSoyza at Samaritan Health Services in Corvallis. Oh, yeah, and there was one more thing Stark should know: Sarah, Karly's mama, was upset and she was a force to be reckoned with.

"David told her I'd called the state and that it was her fault," Delynn said. "Sarah accused me of getting David mad at her. In the meantime, I'm looking at their daughter asleep on my couch, thinking, why is Karly sleeping for six hours here? Why is she behaving this way?"

Stark collected background information from Delynn. After discussing the case with one of his coworkers, he called Detective Karin Stauder of the Corvallis Police Department.

Stauder handled most of the child abuse cases for the police department and served on the Linn/Benton Counties Child Abuse Response Team (CART). The two discussed the case in detail. Then

Stark called Dr. Carol Chervenak, the medical director for the child victim assessment center, known as the ABC (All Because Of Children) House, in nearby Albany.

"I asked Dr. Chervenak for some guidance," Stark said. "And I reported the disturbed sleeping patterns and hair loss specifically."

Dr. Chervenak should have evaluated Karly. That was standard operating procedure for any suspected case of child abuse—but Stark made an exception, allowing David and Sarah Sheehan to take Karly to see her doctor instead.

Stark's decision proved to be a critical blunder, an error in judgment in a long line of such miscalculations. The moment former District Attorney Scott Heiser referred to as a "failure."

Another key piece of information overlooked was that Sarah's live-in situation had recently changed. There was a new man in her life, and in Karly's. Instead, Shawn Field was about the last person investigators suspected. He was a hometown boy. His daddy was a longtime employee of HP. He came from good stock. Shawn had yard signs and bumper stickers on his car urging people to vote conservatively—to protect family values.

Dr. deSoyza agreed to see Karly at 4:30 p.m. on Wednesday, November 17, 2004. Shortly before Sarah arrived to pick up Karly from Rugrats, Delynn attempted to pry information from the child. "I asked how she got the 'owies' on her head. I hadn't noticed them the day before, but they were little scabby areas. She told me, 'My dad did it. He bites me.'"

Delynn was more confused than ever. She drafted a letter for the doctor, insisted Sarah read and initial it.

> Nov. 17, 2004
>
> To whom it may concern:
>
> Today Karly slept over 5 hours at daycare. On Friday, Nov.

12, she slept 4 hours (2 naps). Tuesday Nov. 16, she slept 4 hours (2 naps) as well. Karly is requesting to take naps. She complains of being tired. She fell asleep 2 times before lunch 2 different days the week of Nov. 8 while she was sitting up watching "Barney."

These 2 days are NOT the same days I have allowed her to nap in the morning. Karly has been eating very well (not as much today) and requests "more" food often. Karly is listless and will not wake up from noise (other children) and seems uninterested in childcare routine and activities.

She fell asleep (after asking to go take a nap) on the couch at 9:20 a.m. and I could not wake her up until lunchtime. She ate sparingly and requested to go back to sleep. I laid her down again at 1:00 and she fell back to sleep at approx. 1:15 p.m. She will not wake up readily to prompting and at 3:30 I tried to wake her. She would not wake up. Her hair loss is noticeable and I am concerned about her health. Delynn Zoller.

Delynn was the first person to file a report of possible child abuse. Had she failed to do so, Delynn could have been in trouble with the law herself.

David and Sarah had no idea a caseworker would join them at the doctor's office. They were talking with Mona Schneider, Dr. deSoyza's nurse, when Matt Stark showed up. A bookish-looking fellow with straight brown hair, Stark looks like the sort of person who might pluck a guitar and write songs rather than a man who spends his afternoons jotting graphic notes about child abuse.

After introducing himself, Stark asked David and Sarah what changes they had observed in Karly. As her parents talked, Stark scribbled some details about the toddler's appearance that he would later translate for investigators:

"Karly had short, patchy hair and it appeared that she had lost some hair in areas concentrated to the left and right sides from the center of her head. I also noticed a yellowish spot at the top of Karly's head. It appeared at first glance to be bruising, an aging bruise or fading bruise."

Stark asked about Karly's recent sleeping patterns and, of course, the hair loss. To his credit, Stark also asked Sarah whether or not Karly was ever left alone with her new boyfriend.

Was Karly ever left alone with Shawn? That one question had been burning the edges of David's sanity for weeks now. David's heart quickened as he searched Sarah's eyes for any hint of deception. Surely, Sarah wouldn't lie to a state investigator when the welfare of her own daughter was at risk. Sarah stared directly into David's eyes as she answered Stark's question.

"I was looking right at her as she told Matt Stark that Shawn was never alone with Karly," David said. "Like an idiot I believed her. I didn't think Shawn was ever left alone with Karly, so how could he possibly be harming her?"

David would later learn of other lies Sarah told him about Shawn. "I can't believe all the lies she told to protect him from the start. She told me they met at a playground, but in fact it was at a bar."

Stark was pleased with how cooperative David and Sarah were, but as soon as Stark told Sarah and David that he wanted to speak to Karly without them present, the little girl got visibly upset. Worried about Karly's reaction, Stark asked Nurse Schneider to stick around and assist him with the interview. She did.

Karly never made eye contact with Stark, nor did she answer to any of his direct questions, even the simplest ones. The stuffed animals and the action figures the nurse had retrieved from a toy bin distracted her. Karly nodded her response to most of the questions. Whenever Stark attempted to ask more detailed questions, specifically, "Tell me about your father," Karly immediately began crying for her daddy.

Stark ended the interview.

Dr. deSoyza greeted Karly warmly and noticed right away that the toddler wasn't her typical self. During routine visits, well-baby checks and such, Karly was always talkative, vivacious, and full of mischief. Generally, she liked to pull out all the drawers and explore the exam room, but not on this night.

"Karly seemed a little clingy, a little subdued," Dr. deSoyza noted. The doctor spotted a small bruise on Karly's right cheek and hair loss at the crown of her head, toward the back. The spot wasn't tender to the touch but it did have some discoloration.

After speaking with David and Sarah, Dr. deSoyza ordered blood work to test for lead poisoning. She also ordered an iron and thyroid panel. All the tests came back within normal range. Karly's tiredness, bruising and hair loss were not the result of an underlying medical condition. At this visit and the ones that would follow, Dr. deSoyza was stumped by Karly's ongoing symptoms. It was difficult for the family doctor to contemplate child abuse, given her long-standing relationship with David and Sarah. She regarded them as caring parents. It was her reluctance to entertain child abuse that would help throw the investigation off-course.

But that night, before leaving the doctor's office, Matt Stark told David and Sarah that the state would continue its investigation, in cooperation with the Corvallis Police Department.

It was an ominous statement, and embedded within it was a warning for David.

CHAPTER EIGHTEEN

THE NEXT DAY, STARK ATTENDED a meeting with other members of the Child Abuse Response Team (CART). He briefed the team, which included Detective Stauder, about the previous night's visit with Karly and her parents. The team urged him to conduct another follow-up visit.

That afternoon Matt Stark paid a visit to Rugrats Daycare. Delynn had remembered one other thing she thought Stark might need to know: Karly's recent haircut. She told him all about the French braid incident.

The braid incident was something even Dr. deSoyza later described to me as disturbing. Sarah gave the doctor the same story she'd given Delynn: that Karly woke up with her hair so badly matted she'd had to cut it short.

"It was a pretty weird story," deSoyza said. "Why would you cut hair in that fashion? Instead of trying to untangle it, you cut it off? I thought it was a strange way of dealing with a problem like that. You don't cut off somebody's hair because it's too tangled to deal with. It was all too weird."

It seemed odd at the time, but it was just one more puzzling thing in a long list of puzzling things.

Matt Stark hoped that if he visited with Karly in the safe environment of her daycare provider, the toddler would be less suspicious of him.

The children were sitting around a table, having a snack when Stark joined them, making small talk. Again, Karly avoided eye contact and remained quiet.

Stark asked her about her haircut.

She didn't respond.

He asked her who took care of her hair.

"My daddy," she said.

He asked if her daddy washed her hair.

"Yes," she said.

He asked what else she could tell him about her hair.

Karly didn't respond.

He asked what she liked about her daddy.

Karly began to cry and ask for her father, in much the same manner as she had night before at Dr. deSoyza's office.

"As soon as I mentioned him, Karly was immediately distraught and wanting her dad," Stark said. "This was more than quiet sobbing and tears. It was to the point that I had to respect her emotional state and end the interview."

Again.

Stark's methodology frustrated Delynn. She felt he mishandled the interview. "I was very unimpressed by the way he just bluntly asked Karly questions," Delynn said. "She was very distrusting anyway. Karly cried and said her classic response to any question: 'I want my daddy!'"

Stark called David and Sarah and left them each a voice message letting them know he had talked to their daughter. He may have been baiting them, trying to figure out their level of concern, to see if he could get a clear read on them.

Sarah made it easy: she was mad and she let Stark know it.

"She sounded like she was pretty upset about this investigation,"

Stark said. "I didn't notice her crying or anything, but she was concerned."

Once the state launched its investigation, Sarah promised David she wouldn't take Karly around Shawn anymore. They agreed that from here on out Karly would stay with David.

CHAPTER NINETEEN

ONE HAPPY DAY DURING THE fall of 2004, David and Karly took a stroll, kicking golden leaves high off the tips of their boots. "Karly, why are you so good?" David asked.

"Because I am," Karly replied.

"Karly, why are you so lovely?"

"Because I am."

David paused as Karly jumped down hard on a pile of crunchy mulch.

"And precious too?" Karly asked, smirking slyly at her father.

"Karly, why are you so precious?" David asked, accepting the cue.

She gave a dismissive but confident shrug and replied, "Because I am."

The first week in December 2004, David took Karly to a rodeo at the Benton County fairgrounds. It was a first for the both of them. Karly whooped it up for the cowgirls on fast horses making sharp turns around big barrels and giggled through the antics of the big-footed clown. And every single time the big bulls came snorting out of the holding pens, Karly let loose with a loud guttural "ROAR!" sending others sitting nearby into fits of laughter. But halfway through the show, shortly after she'd finished her hot dog lunch, Karly grew restless.

David noticed her inching away, exploring the dusty bleachers. He told Karly to stop rolling around and to sit down beside him. His tone was firm. Frustrated, Karly responded by slapping at her head, open-handed. David took hold of Karly's hands and told her that if she didn't start behaving properly they were going to leave. Tired and crying, she continued slapping herself, so David picked her up and took her home.

The whole incident unnerved David enough that he mentioned it the next day during a phone call with Matt Stark, who made a note of it: "Karly got mad and started tugging at her own hair. Father is convinced she has been pulling her own hair." Those were Matt Stark's words and his assessment. David recalls telling Stark that Karly tugged on her hair, but David never saw, or said he saw, Karly pulling her hair.

Stark told David that Karly needed to see her doctor again. Then Stark called Delynn, who told him Karly was much better. She wasn't crying nearly as often, nor as clingy or tired. Delynn attributed the changes to Karly spending less time with Shawn and more time with David. Stark made a note of that, too.

During the previous week, Stark had stumbled across troubling information while running a routine background check on the adults in Karly's life: Shawn Field's history of domestic violence with his ex-wife, Eileen. The state investigator did not bother to mention it to Dr. deSoyza or Delynn Zoller or even to Dr. Carol Chervenak. Despite the documented history of domestic violence, Shawn wasn't even on the radar as a suspect for child abuse.

The same day that David spoke with Stark about Karly's behavior at the rodeo, Stark called Dr. Chervenak again, seeking her advice. Dr. Chervenak had personally examined more than 1,500 children on suspicion of abuse. But in Karly's case, Dr. Chervenak relied on two people to provide her with an on-site evaluation: Matt Stark and Corvallis Police Detective Karin Stauder. The fact that Dr. Chervenak did not examine Karly prior to her death indicates that someone suggested such an assessment wasn't warranted. That oversight would be identified later as one of the first major foul-ups in a case chock-full of them.

On Monday, December 6, 2004, per Matt Stark's suggestion, David and Sarah took Karly back to Dr. deSoyza's for a follow-up exam that afternoon. David told the doctor about Karly slapping herself during the rodeo.

Dr. deSoyza knew David Sheehan had recently changed jobs and was driving back and forth to Hillsboro, due west of Portland—a three-hour round trip from Corvallis, even longer in bad traffic. David was also working on his master's degree at George Fox University one night a week, a seventy-five-minute drive from home. But as David explained to Dr. deSoyza and Matt Stark, on the days Karly was with him David worked shorter days, so that the time he spent with her was the same as it had been before the job change and long commute.

In Karly's medical file, Dr. deSoyza made note that Sarah had recently moved in with a new boyfriend shortly before Karly started displaying bruises, thinning hair, and exhaustion. Dr. Chervenak, who had vast experience in identifying child abuse, would have automatically suspected Karly was being abused, given the physical symptoms and all the changes in Karly's life: her dad's prolonged absences, her mother's new boyfriend, and the new living situation.

Dr. deSoyza, however, wondered if Karly was under too much stress. Maybe all these changes had created anxiety for Karly, causing her to act out. Anxiety in children can sometimes result in hair loss. Maybe Karly was displaying symptoms of trichotillomania.

Trichotillomania is a hair-pulling disorder, a mental disorder that creates an irresistible urge to yank out hair from the scalp, eyebrows, eyelashes, or pubic area. Less than one percent of the nation's population suffers from it. Most often hair is pulled from the scalp, causing unsightly bald patches, the kind observed in Karly during that visit. Anxiety, tension, loneliness, fatigue, and frustration are all common triggers.

Lots of little girls and even some big ones will sometimes chew on long strands of hair, or twirl a strand round and round as a nervous gesture. Sarah did this. Like people who bite their nails, they'll unconsciously tug at their hair. Someone who suffers from trichotillomania will actually yank the hair out.

Dr. deSoyza told me she never intended trichotillomania to be a definitive diagnosis.

"There was never an official diagnosis," deSoyza said. "It was just one of several possible causes for Karly's hair loss that were discussed. I found it so bizarre that it was made into such a huge thing. Well, I didn't even know it was a huge thing until I was testifying in court. I wondered why everyone kept asking about it and talking about it. Like I said, it was very strange to me that they made it a central thing when it never was an official diagnosis."

Assumptions can be like poorly packed luggage, always in need of resorting. There was never any material evidence that Karly was yanking out her own hair. There were no reports of globs of hair found on pillows where Karly slept, or hairballs on any of the bathroom counters, or even in front of the television set. There was not indisputable physical proof that Karly was in any form or fashion harming herself. That opinion was all based upon false assumptions and a handful of lies.

Sarah was adamant that she wasn't taking Karly around Shawn, wasn't leaving her alone with him. Everyone assumed she was telling the truth. *Why would a mother lie about such a thing?* Dr. deSoyza asked.

Dr. deSoyza has a difficult time reconciling her image of Sarah with the woman who repeatedly put Karly in danger. "One of the reasons the state investigators didn't pursue things further is because Sarah told us she observed Karly hurting herself. Sarah said she saw Karly hitting herself, pulling her own hair. You just don't think a mother would lie about something like that," deSoyza mused. "It was obvious that when Sarah was with her boyfriend Karly wasn't tolerating the situation very well. When Sarah said she was moving out, we were all very pleased. It didn't occur to me that she would go back to him. I don't know who is responsible to check up, to make sure Sarah kept her word. I'm a doctor, not a policeman."

And policemen aren't doctors, either. If a child's own doctor doesn't suspect child abuse as the primary cause of deteriorating health, why should anyone else?

"When Sarah said she had moved out of her boyfriend's place, I thought, 'Finally a good decision. Shoosh! We dodged a bullet there!'" Dr. deSoyza said.

The relief Dr. deSoyza felt was short-lived.

Chapter Twenty

KARLY LOVED THE CHRISTMAS DRESS her daddy bought her. With its red-velvet bodice, white satin sash, and white organza skirt, this was a dress befitting a true princess. Karly got all dolled up and twirled around the room, repeatedly calling, "Look, Daddy, look!"

Then she perched on the couch, ankles crossed daintily, so David could take her picture to send to the family back in Ireland. Her blonde hair, cut in a long pixie style, framed her sweet face. She playfully put a shiny silver tiara, replete with fake jewels, atop her head. All the while Karly smiled coyly, like a girl who knows she's pretty and oh so loved. Like a little girl who knows that as long as she's with her daddy, she's safe.

David noticed the gun as soon as he walked into Matt Stark's office.

It was Monday, December 6, 2004, the same day that David and Sarah took Karly for a follow-up visit with Dr. deSoyza. Matt Stark asked David to come by his office for a little chat. David was unaware that Detective Karin Stauder was going to be there as well.

It was her gun David noticed right off the bat. The cop kept it holstered at her hip. The room was business bleak. Cheap chairs, a sturdy table, and a whiteboard.

From a purely physical standpoint, Detective Stauder wasn't imposing—not particularly tall or broad of shoulder or hip, but with the tomboy look of a girl who played softball. Her dark brown hair was thick and cut efficiently short. Around kids, Stauder has an engaging and kind smile. Around adults, however, she could appear stone-faced. But it was the gun that put David on alert, gave him a chill.

David naïvely thought Stark wanted to meet with him privately to discuss the problems created by Sarah's ongoing relationship with Shawn. Given the chance to tell investigators, David would say that though he had nothing specific to blame on Shawn, he had his suspicions. He would say it was evident to him that Karly's emotional and physical deterioration could be traced back to the appearance of Shawn in Sarah's life.

He would let detectives know that when he attempted to ask Karly anything about Shawn, the child would get visibly upset. David was sure something bad was going on. He hoped Stark and Stauder would be able to get to the bottom of it—they were the experts after all, right?

Stark offered David a chair and made it clear his position was to act as an advocate for Karly. He told David the reason he and Detective Stauder had called him in was that he was under investigation for child abuse.

Allegations of child abuse?

David wasn't sure he'd heard them correctly. How could he be under investigation? Nobody loved or cared for Karly better than David. Everyone knew that, didn't they?

David outwardly kept his cool but inside he was angry with both Stark and Stauder.

"I spent the next thirty or forty-five minutes defending myself, drawing diagrams on the whiteboard recounting recent travel dates, answering their every question," David recalled. "I mentioned Sarah's moving in with Shawn but Stauder quickly responded that she had talked with Shawn and he had insisted Sarah had not moved in. Later that afternoon, when I was driving back up to Portland, I remembered Sarah had told me herself she was paying Shawn's rent. I called Stark and pointed out that discrepancy."

But Stark remained wishy-washy. He told David that he and Detective Stauder were "on the fence" about him.

David didn't have to ask a second time what that meant. He understood that as far as Stark and Stauder were concerned David was guilty of something; they simply lacked proof to charge him.

Following their visit with David, Detective Stauder wrote up the following report:

> I asked David if he has any ideas to the reason why Karly suffered from hair loss. David told me he first thought it was from stress due to the change in her visitations with him and Sarah. David said Karly is very regimented with regards to her schedule and when things change, she has a difficult time. David gave me an example of when he was scheduled to pick up Karly up from daycare. David was unable to pick her up, so Sarah picked her up instead. Karly yelled and screamed, throwing a temper tantrum and wanted him instead of her mom. David told me since about mid to end of October 2004, Sarah has moved in with Shawn and that Karly has sporadically stayed the night. David believes this change in Karly's routine has caused her stress. I asked David if he suspects Sarah is abusing Karly and he said absolutely not. I asked David about Shawn and he said he did not have any reason to believe Shawn was hurting Karly.

David takes issue with Detective Stauder's report. "I would never have described Karly as being regimented. If anything she was quite the opposite, and was very easygoing."

Detective Stauder's report also bothered me. Why would David tell the investigating officers he didn't suspect Shawn? David may not have known all the ways in which Shawn was terrorizing his daughter, but David was sure Shawn was the source of Karly's distress. I asked David why he told Detective Stauder otherwise.

"I clearly remember answering the question," David said. "And diplomacy definitely played a part. I'd spoken with a good friend the weekend prior to the interview and he told me I was coming across as very angry about the whole thing. He suggested I should tone down my rhetoric, because 'they' would pick up on it."

Once Matt Stark told David at the beginning of the interview that he was under suspicion of child abuse, David immediately went on the defense. "I felt the interview changed from how to protect Karly to how to get me."

David worried Detective Stauder and Matt Stark were setting a trap for him. He was not being paranoid. Detective Stauder did, indeed, ask Sarah the next day if she believed David was abusing Karly. But state's investigators never singled Sarah out as a suspect for child abuse and neglect the way they did David.

If anything, the system granted more protection to Sarah than it did to Karly. Too many officials who implement family law in our states cling to an archaic belief that mothers are good, and any mother's failure is more likely the result of ignorance than intent. Even when, as was the case with Karly, there is reason to warrant charges of willful negligence, if not downright abuse, many people in the system are loathe to recognize some women are unfit mothers.

David was guarded in speaking about his dealings with Sarah. It seemed to David that those charged with protecting Karly viewed Sarah more as a victim than as a perpetrator.

David entertained thoughts of taking Karly and running with her, perhaps back to Ireland. But he worried running would make it look like he had something to hide. And suppose law enforcement officials caught him? He risked being deported and losing Karly forever.

Believing he was trapped, David could only trust the system. It failed him—miserably. The state's investigation did little to resolve the issues confronting Karly. On the other hand, it fueled David's fear of deportation. He thought about it constantly. "Blithely saying 'deportation crossed my mind' downplays the reality of it for me. I was acutely aware of it," he said. In truth, David was terrified of being sent away from Karly.

We usually associate the term "deportation" with illegal immigrants, dark-skinned people with dark eyes, not the blue-eyed blonds among us.

Yet, despite his whiteness and the fact that he was in this country legally, David was keenly aware that when it came to matters of the state, he was an immigrant, an outsider, a person of suspect.

"The authorities have significant leverage over immigrants," David said. "I think being an immigrant diminished the fact that I was a law-abiding, taxpaying, economically active responsible parent. I was unlike Shawn in every way. I was the stability in Karly's life. I was very concerned about never seeing Karly again. I could not bear to think of her growing up thousands of miles and a border away from me."

Sarah had nothing to fear the following day, December 7, 2004, when she met with Matt Stark and Detective Stauder at the state offices in Albany. Stauder kept notes about that meeting as well:

I asked Sarah if she has any ideas to the reason why Karly suffered from hair loss. Sarah believed it was due to stress. Sarah told me that after she moved in full time with Shawn, Karly would ask her where "daddy" was and why he didn't live with her. Sarah mentioned Karly was fine as long as they were just visiting at Shawn's, but once she moved in full time it really seemed to bother Karly.

Sarah mentioned that Karly gets used to a set schedule and when it changes she has a difficult time coping. I asked Sarah if she thought David was abusing Karly and she told me no. Sarah told me David is a "terrific dad." When I asked Sarah about Karly saying David hits her in the head she told me she did not know why Karly said that. She does not believe he does.

I told Sarah sometimes an abuser will pick the pulling of hair to abuse their victim because there are no visible signs of injury, just the complaint of the victim. Sarah told me she spoke with Karly's doctor at length and she said the doctor told her about a disorder called "Trichotillomania"—the pulling of hair and that Karly may suffer from the disorder.

Sarah clearly said that the problems with Karly didn't arise until after she moved in with Shawn. That should have been a red flag for investigators. Following the interview, Matt Stark filed the following report:

12.07.2004

Sarah indicated that Karly's hair loss was due to stress around changes to her schedule and spending more time at Shawn's house. Ms. Sheehan said Karly can't accept that her mom and dad are not together and she is not happy sharing her mother with Shawn and Kate.

Karly was only three months old when her parents first separated. How could she not be adjusted to her parents living apart?

Stark made a similar record of the interview.

Ms. Sheehan does not suspect abuse by Shawn or David. She indicated that David is a good dad. She could not explain why Karly said her dad hits her head and does not believe it is true. Ms. Sheehan indicated that she talked with Karly's doctor regarding a condition called Trichotillomania and that Karly may have suffered from the disorder. Ms. Sheehan agreed to contact the Old Mill Center to get Karly into counseling.

If Sarah believed David was a good dad, and not abusing Karly, why was she keeping a detailed journal to the contrary?

11.19.04. Friday

Karly woke up in a good mood, having had a good night sleep. She had a bath and breakfast. While helping me put laundry away, Karly began to cry & told me she did not like it when her daddy pulled her hair. I said, "Who pulls your hair Karly?" & she said, "Daddy David pulls my hair like this." She then grabbed a small strand of hair & lifted up, but did not pull it out. I asked her to stop crying & told her it was okay. She stopped crying, but said she was scared of her daddy several times. Later this morning, again Karly saying she is scared of her daddy, that he pulls her hair. I ask why & she said, "It's not fair, Mommy."

This whole entry is a total fabrication that Sarah later admitted to in court. Karly wasn't with Sarah that night or the next morning; she was with her father the entire time. Sarah said Shawn forced her to make these journal entries targeting David as Karly's abuser.

Most every failure in this case is tethered to some lie, some deception, and some denial. The question must be asked: why would a woman who has only been in a relationship with a man for less than three months go to such great lengths to construct elaborate lies? What would compel Sarah to frame her ex while allowing her child to be abused by a man she barely knew?

Addressing Shawn before a crowded courtroom, Sarah identified who she considered responsible for Karly's death: "I'm angry at God for allowing you into our lives, only so you could take hers."

We blame God when children die as a way of deflecting the truth, a way to shift responsibility away from the real source: ourselves.

Chapter Twenty-One

UNFOUNDED FOR ABUSE! On December 7, 2004, upon the recommendation of Detective Karin Stauder and Matt Stark, the Oregon Department of Human Services ruled the case for abuse of Karly Sheehan closed. Detective Stauder's report stated:

> Case Unfounded. Based on the information I learned in my investigation, I do not believe Sarah or David are physically abusing Karly; nor anyone else I identified. I believe the cause and start of Karly's hair pulling is the result of her new living arrangement with her mother moving in with her boyfriend. According to Sarah, Karly was fine when she visited her at her boyfriend's house, but when she actually moved in with her boyfriend it caused a great deal of stress for Karly.

Stauder did not reach this ruling in isolation. She depended upon the insights and input of Matt Stark. Tasked by the Oregon Department of Human Services with providing for the protection of minor children, it was Stark who decided "there was no reasonable cause to believe

Karly was the victim of physical abuse. She did not provide a statement herself to indicate she had been."

Ninety percent of the 1,500 children who die in this country every year as a result of child abuse are age three and under. Experts believe abusers choose their prey based upon a child's very inability to tattle.

Experts in the field say fear is the most common reason children don't report their abusers. Many victims recount stories of telling their mothers of abuse, only to be confronted with doubt and disbelief, or worse yet, to be accused of lying outright. Karly may have tried to tell her mother that Shawn was hurting her, only to be dismissed or reprimanded for it.

It is oddly coincidental that I sit typing this six years to the day since Detective Stauder and Matt Stark concluded three-year-old Karly was not the victim of child abuse. It's a cold, rainy, dark day in Oregon. Over the random airwaves of Pandora, Celtic Woman, a female ensemble, is singing "Away in the Manger": "Be near me, Lord Jesus, I ask you to stay close by me forever and love me I pray. Bless all the dear children in thy tender care and take us to heaven to live with you there."

I am overcome with a sorrow darker than a starless midnight. As a woman of faith, I look for comfort in my beliefs, but if faith becomes our balm for such heinously wrong acts, doesn't that serve to make us bystanders, if not participants, in such evils?

Up on the mountain where Karly's maternal grandparents reside, the driving conditions are often dangerous during the winter. Years ago, the new head football coach from Pendleton, his wife and two daughters were killed there. The family had gone in search of a Christmas tree. They were headed back to town with it loaded onto their truck when angry winds bit off a chunk of an evergreen near the road and spit it out. The tree struck the truck's windshield and killed them on impact.

Theirs was the only group funeral I've ever attended. I remember the younger girl's casket best. It was shiny pink, and oh, so tiny. A bassinette crafted from cold metal, designed to deliver a child straight to God's front door. The Bentley of coffins. A coffin not unlike the one that delivered Karly from evil. The "system" was supposed to do that, and keep her alive, but we all failed her. We are all guilty.

On what should have been Karly's sixth birthday, I sent David a note telling him I didn't have any idea what it must be like to have a daughter's birthday without the daughter around. In postscript, I added my wish that he didn't know either.

David wrote back: "Thanks for acknowledging Karly's birthday. She was so big, bright, loving, and such good company at three that I wonder what she would have been like now. I imagine I will wonder that for the rest of my life, with every passing age."

Everything outside on this cold day is as still as a child in death. Silent tears will fall into soft pillows this Christmas season and seasons to come as those who loved Karly best, and even those who only know her from the stories retold, continue to remember the cries of a child distressed.

Others have spoken to me about the tears that Detective Stauder has shed. It's difficult to read the words of her report, knowing what we all know now, and not see the warning "Danger Ahead" embedded in Stauder's own words: *"I believe the cause and start of Karly's hair-pulling is the result of her new living arrangement with her mother moving in with her boyfriend."*

CHAPTER TWENTY-TWO

As David drove by a gleaming glass office building shortly before their last Christmas together, Karly pointed at the mirrored building and said, "When I'm big and I'm a dada, I'm going to work there."

David corrected her and said, "But Karly, when you're big you won't be a dada. You'll be a mommy."

"I don't want to be a mommy!" Karly cried. "I want to be a dada! I want to be a dada!"

David would recall that incident later in court as the moment when he knew something was terribly amiss between daughter and mother. "I told Sarah, 'Your relationship with Karly is beginning to crumble here and you'd better take some steps to address it.'"

Delynn was expecting Karly at daycare on Tuesday, December 7, 2004, the same day the state ruled the abuse case unfounded, but Sarah called and said she wouldn't be bringing Karly that day because she was taking her Christmas shopping instead. Delynn was flustered by the call. By this time neither David nor Delynn trusted Sarah, yet Delynn felt she didn't have the authority to intervene. "I was in a weird position between

David and Sarah. I didn't trust Sarah, but I thought, what could I do? The state's been notified and nobody's done anything."

There were times when Delynn considered she could be wrong. "I was hoping things would get better," Delynn said. But Sarah called on Wednesday, too, and said Karly was sick and she wouldn't be bringing her that day either. And then, on Thursday and Friday, Sarah didn't call or bring Karly to daycare.

Delynn was worried. "She was gone for the whole week she was with her mom," Delynn said. With David in Portland for work that week, Delynn didn't know what to do about Karly's absence, if anything. If she called David and complained, Sarah would get angry with her. It was clear David and Sarah weren't on good terms with one another. Delynn didn't want to contribute to the aggravation between the two of them. Besides, really, what business of it was hers if Sarah wanted to keep her daughter during the week her daddy was out of town?

On the weekends, David and Sarah had a routine for swapping Karly. They would meet at the Starbucks at Timberhill Mall on Saturday mornings. But on that Saturday, December 11, 2004, Sarah called David to make different arrangements for the swap. Sarah wanted to know if it would be okay if they could meet at his place instead of at Starbucks. Sure, he agreed, suspecting nothing out of the ordinary.

"She said Karly didn't look all that good," David recalled. "I thought she meant Karly had the flu or something like that."

Sarah showed up with Karly in tow at about ten o'clock that morning. David was completely unprepared for what he saw: Karly was completely bald, save only for a few wisps of flyaway hair. Her face was bruised. There was some yellowing—evidence the bruising was a day or two old. One eye was slightly swollen. There was a teardrop-shaped scratch under her left eye. Her lips were badly chapped, like those of a person severely dehydrated. A silent, shell-shocked Karly reached for her daddy. David wrapped his frail daughter in a protective embrace and stared, open-mouthed, at Sarah, waiting for her to say something, anything, to explain what had happened to their daughter.

"I was in shock," David recalled. He questioned Sarah, demanded to know what had happened to Karly. What had she done to their daughter now? The only thing Sarah said as she handed Karly over to David was, "This happened on my watch."

David didn't know what the hell Sarah meant. Was that some sort of admission of abuse on her behalf? Sarah turned to leave before he could spit out another word but not before David realized making the switch at his house had been a very bad idea. Nobody had seen Sarah with the battered Karly.

Bloody hell.

It was a trap designed to fix suspicion on David. Under any other circumstances David would have done what any reasonable person would do, the thing her mother should have done, and taken Karly straight to the hospital. His mind was racing, his blood pumping as David sought to soothe his distraught daughter.

"It was very out of the ordinary for Sarah to drop Karly at the house, instead of at Starbucks," David said. "I thought she was reckless and irresponsible. She gave me no prior warning that anything was wrong with Karly. She simply dropped her off and washed her hands of it."

A trip to the hospital would ensure the abuse case would be reopened, but it would be his word against Sarah's, and the state agency had already made it abundantly clear he was the primary suspect in the investigation they'd just closed. Besides, David worried that if he took Karly to the hospital the staff would insist on separating him from Karly, and there was no way he was letting her out of his sight now.

Terror seized his stomach. Clenching his jaw, he carried Karly into the house and sat on the couch. Karly clung to him like a baby chimp, frightened. Nuzzled in her father's neck, she didn't cry, didn't move, and didn't speak. She wanted nothing more from her father but that he never let her go.

David was furious. He no longer questioned whether Shawn was abusing Karly—he was sure of it. The problem was figuring out a way to convince the investigators they had the wrong person. "I was very concerned about getting blamed," he said. "I was frustrated with their decision-making process. I thought it was ridiculous they were accusing me."

David was convinced the state agency was looking for any excuse to take Karly away from him. "They were so busy trying to compile a case against me, they never bothered to find out what was happening to Karly," David said. "They continued to assume I was abusing Karly, despite overwhelming evidence to the contrary."

David put balm on Karly's lips. He tried to get her to drink as much as possible. He knew he had to document the condition she was in, so he held out a digital camera and snapped pictures of an emaciated-looking Karly, battered and bruised, clinging to her daddy. Then, around two o'clock that afternoon, he took Karly next door to the home of his good friends, Dave and Jennifer Woolley.

Jennifer and Sarah had been friends since 1994, but their friendship had worn thin in 2000. Jennifer told police investigators Sarah often failed to pay her share of the rent when they were roommates, and Sarah still owed her quite a bit of money. Moreover, Jennifer said she wanted to distance herself from Sarah's irresponsible reputation. Sarah simply could not be trusted. Despite the breakdown in the relationship between Jennifer and Sarah, David had continued his friendship with the Woolleys after the divorce.

David knocked on their front door.

"David was holding Karly," Jennifer said, later recalling that disturbing day. "She was very pale. Her hair sparse. She looked like a cancer patient. She was bruised and scratched from head to toe."

David haltingly explained that Sarah had brought Karly to him in that condition and he wanted Jennifer to be an eyewitness.

"He was very somber," Jennifer said. "He seemed to be at a loss for words."

Jennifer Woolley was not alone. She had a friend visiting who did not know David, who did not know what kind of father or man he was. She only knew she saw a man holding a battered child.

Karly clung to her father so much that every time he'd attempted to put her down, Karly woke up whimpering and terrified. His daughter refused to be left alone. But finally, and probably out of sheer exhaustion, David was able to get Karly to sleep.

As soon as he was sure she was asleep, David put her to bed and attempted to file a report with DHS. He called Matt Stark at about 7:30 that evening but Stark's phone went to voice mail. David left him a message, asking him to return the call.

Exhausted emotionally and physically, David crawled into bed around nine o'clock. Earlier that evening Corvallis Police Department received a phone call from a woman who identified herself as a teacher, and thus a mandatory reporter. She wanted to talk to a police officer about a possible abuse case. The child, bruised and bald, was at her father's home on Walnut Street. Her name was Karly Sheehan.

Hours after David had fallen asleep in his own bed, someone banged on his front door. Roused by the pounding and still a bit dazed, David opened the door.

"Officer Cox with the Corvallis Police Department," said the young police officer.

Cox was a general patrol officer. He'd been with the department for three years, but he'd already distinguished himself, earning an Officer of the Year award for his extraordinarily high number of arrests for

DUIs, drivers impaired by drug or alcohol abuse. (Cox would later resign from his post at Corvallis following an internal investigation into the aggressive and questionable tactics he employed to earn that award.)

Officer Cox told David he wanted to see his daughter. David told the policeman Karly was sleeping but the officer insisted he needed to see her. So David escorted Cox upstairs to Karly's room. The officer shined his bright flashlight on the sleeping toddler. Alarmed, Karly bolted upright and commenced crying.

"I took a look at her body," Officer Cox recalled later in court. "Much of her hair was missing. It looked like her hair had been pulled out of her head."

Cox studied the bruises splotched across Karly's face and head and made note of the numerous scratches on her face and the side of her head. He did not take any pictures of Karly, but he looked at the ones David had captured earlier on his digital camera.

David explained how Sarah Sheehan had dropped the bald-headed and badly bruised Karly off that morning. The lawman told David he was headed over to visit Sarah, but before leaving he issued an ominous warning: "If your story doesn't check out, I will be back for you."

After the officer left, David checked on Karly. She was in his bed, snuggled under the covers and so physically exhausted she couldn't keep her sleepy eyes open. David knew his own fate and Karly's would be determined in part by Sarah. Would she lie and say Karly had been perfectly fine when she'd dropped her off earlier? If she did, David figured the policeman would be back to arrest him. Such an arrest would undoubtedly mean he would lose his job, and it would likely mean deportation. At the time, running seemed like the worst of his options, but David didn't yet know the full extent of the evil Karly encountered, or he might have snatched up his daughter's hand and caught the next plane.

Every loving parent understands that while their best dreams revolve around their children, so do their worst nightmares. David had woken up in the middle of Karly's nightmare and he was at a complete loss as to how he should rescue them both.

Even though it was well past midnight when Officer Cox left David Sheehan's home, the policeman drove straight to Shawn Field's duplex at 2652 NW Aspen Street. He knocked on the door and both Sarah and Shawn answered.

It is standard procedure for a lawman to separate people he thinks may have conflicting stories, such as suspects or victims, but Cox didn't separate Sarah and Shawn. Shawn made it clear he didn't want Sarah talking to the police alone. That should have set off all sorts of alarms in Officer Cox's head.

Shawn and Sarah could have easily have said that the last time they saw Karly, she was perfectly okay, and no one would have been the wiser. But instead of denying Karly's condition, Shawn gave Officer Cox a ready explanation for Karly's injuries. He told Cox that earlier in the week he'd seen Karly balling up her fist, rubbing her eyes, and pressing her thumbs into her forehead. Those bruises on Karly's forehead? Those were the corresponding marks left by her thumbs.

And that hair loss?

Well, Sarah explained to a none-the-wiser officer that Karly had recently been diagnosed with trichotillomania, a weird hair-pulling disorder. It was a little psychotic, for sure, but they'd been getting treatment for her. Kids. They do the craziest things.

Cox glanced around the tidy duplex. He noticed the Beaver blanket thrown over the couch and the framed professional photographs of Shawn's daughter hanging in the hallway. He saw no sign of anything to give him cause for concern. No half-spilled prescription bottles. No worn roach clips. No empty Jack Daniel's bottles. Cox concluded there was no indication Sarah or Shawn were under the influence of drugs or alcohol. He'd know that. He was, after all, the leading cop in the state on such arrests.

Before leaving, Cox urged Sarah to get Karly to the doctor again, pronto.

No problem, she assured him, they were taking her to a specialist later that week. Then Sarah thanked the officer for his obvious concern.

Back at the police station, Officer Cox filed an incident report. It was posted at 4:46 a.m. and marked *No Press*.

> Welfare Check:
>
> On 12-11-04, I responded to 4111 N.W. Walnut Blvd. on a welfare check. Karla Sheehan's (age 2) parents (David and Sarah Sheehan) are divorced and she rotates who she stays with. Karla has recently started pulling her hair out and hitting herself in the face and scratching herself with her hands/fingernails while staying with Sarah at 2652 NW Aspen. Karla's hair was very thin and much of it had been pulled out. Karla had several small scratches and bruises on her face and head. David and Sarah believe that Karla may have psychological problems and are getting her an appointment with a specialist on 12-13-04. The scratches, bruises and the missing hair that I observed on Karla appeared consistent with self-inflicted injuries.

Cox sent his report to DHS, and to Detective Karin Stauder, as required, standard operating procedure for any potential child abuse case.

Nobody wants to be called out on a child abuse case, but patrol cops like Cox, in particular, don't like them. Child abuse cases are labor-intensive, requiring a lot of paperwork and follow-up. There's little glitz and glamour attached to the work, and very few awards, but a lot of heartache.

Cox was the state's eyes that night, and he did not take photos of Karly. He did not take the time to interview Sarah and Shawn separately, to look for any inconsistencies in their stories. Cox did not approach Sarah or Shawn with the same level of distrust that he did David. The officer had threatened David with arrest but took Sarah and Shawn at their word. Some of his peers at the Corvallis Police Department feel that Cox's investigation that night was shoddy, done haphazardly so that he could hurry back to the work that brought him the most notoriety: trolling for drunks.

Cox should have taken photos of Karly that night but he didn't. The only documentation was the report he made based upon his own observations. A photo would have told an entirely different story than the one Cox reported. There was no way anyone could look at photos of Karly from that night and think all was well. As the father of young kids himself, Cox should have approached the case with more due diligence. His conclusion that Karly's condition was self-inflicted threw the entire abuse investigation off the grid, and it was one of the primary reasons why Shawn Field was not considered a suspect until after Karly's death.

Back at the house on Walnut Street, David waited and waited, but Cox did not return to make an arrest. It was well past one o'clock when David crawled back into bed. His head sank into the pillow. It had been the most draining day of his entire life. There would be more days like this to come. But David didn't know that yet, so he fell into a still and silent sleep.

Chapter Twenty-Three

THE LAST LETTER I SENT to Shawn Field came back marked "Return to Sender, Refused." He has the right to do that, refuse to speak to me. I understand why he doesn't want to talk to me. He believes because Sarah was once part of our family that I'm biased. He and his parents, Hugh and Ann, fear anything I write will put Shawn in a bad light.

Shawn continues to deny that he had any part in Karly's death. Jack, the fellow who meets with Shawn weekly for Bible study, told me, "Shawn is very upset with God. He doesn't understand how a loving God could allow many of the things that have happened."

And that was before the cancer was discovered.

Three years following Karly's death, I received a note from Jack alerting me that Shawn was seriously sick and asking I pray. "Shawn has been ill for nearly three weeks and yesterday they discovered he has a good-sized tumor in his chest. At this time, I don't know if it's malignant. He is in tremendous pain. Ann and Hugh wonder how much they can take. I would appreciate your prayers."

The tumor proved to be a very aggressive cancer. Shawn was moved from the prison in Pendleton to one in the Willamette Valley, where he received the best medical care our state is able to provide.

I saw Shawn's cancer as one more sad twist in an already tragic tale. David summed up my feelings best: "I think the mom in you probably senses the anguish of Ann Field."

It's true. I feel a good deal of empathy for Shawn's parents. I wonder if they feel they failed at parenting. Much like Sarah's parents have done, Hugh and Ann have picked up the pieces of their son's messy life since he was a high school student at Santiam Christian High School in Corvallis, Oregon.

Hugh and Ann enrolled Shawn in the private school in hopes that, being surrounded by "good" kids, Shawn might be inspired to make better choices. Instead, he got kicked out. Superintendent Stan Baker didn't have any trouble recalling the troubled teen. Baker considered Shawn an ill fit for the Christian school. "He was known to participate in satanic practices and rituals," Superintendent Baker told investigators. "He dressed in black clothes and would go to cemeteries at night. He was not liked well by other students."

Baker kicked Shawn out of school in January 1988 after he and another Santiam Christian School student were arrested for a series of burglaries in the Vineyard Mountain area of Corvallis, the neighborhood where Hugh and Ann Field made their home.

I wanted to speak with Hugh and Ann about Shawn's tenure at Santiam, as well many other events that shaped young Shawn's life, like the death of his brother. So I called Hugh and Ann at their home in Redmond, Oregon.

Hugh answered the first call.

"Hi, this is Karen Zacharias," I said. "Is this Hugh Field?"

"I have nothing to say to you," Hugh replied, sharply, gruffly. I expected as much. People had warned me Hugh is a tough guy. "Control freak" is a term I often heard others, attorneys and law enforcement folks alike, use when describing Hugh.

"I don't really want you to…" I was going to say "…talk." I wanted to give Hugh a chance to ask me questions, but he hung up before I finished my sentence.

I called back straightaway. This time Ann answered the phone. She wasn't gruff, but she was curt. As soon as I identified myself, she hung up.

Not at all surprisingly, I received the following e-mail that same night:

> Karen,
>
> I received a disturbing phone call tonight. Hugh called to tell me that you had started calling Ann and Hugh. As a professional journalist, I know you are working every angle to find more information on the case, but Ann and Hugh would appreciate it if you would not call them again. They have no desire to talk to you about anything. Period. They consider your phone calls a severe invasion of privacy. Shawn also has no desire to talk to you in person, by letter or any other means.
>
> How you run your business is up to you, yet as a friend I ask that you would please consider my request.
>
> Thank you,
>
> Jack

Jack is willing to forgive my tenacity. While he insists neither Shawn nor his parents are ever going to grant me an interview, he understands I'm probably not going to quit asking for one.

To be honest, Jack's relationship with Shawn intrigues me, bugs me somewhat. I can't help but wonder, if he knew what I know about Shawn, if Jack would be so eager to defend him. I wrote and asked him about it:

> Jack,
>
> I don't have a clue what you know about this case, but based

upon what you know or have been told, whom do you think killed Karly? Care to share how you reached your conclusions?

Because it occurs to me that if you think Shawn killed Karly, how are you able to sit with him and guide him through the Scriptures? If you believe Shawn killed a three-year-old child, do you really truly believe that God offers grace to such an individual?

On the other hand, if you don't believe Shawn killed Karly, then you are sharing Scriptures with an innocent man, wrongly convicted. And in that situation, what hope does Jesus offer such a man?

ksz

Jack sent me a note back:

Karen,

Journalists never rest, do they?

I have heard many things and have many other questions I would like the answer to. Most of my opinions are best kept to myself but I can tell you this. I am a firm believer in redemption and the power of God's love. God called me to be a friend to Shawn. I am not his counselor, Father Confessor, judge, or conscience. Shawn is a friend who I care deeply about. I visit him not because I have to but because I want to. I listen to him, question him, tease him, debate with him, laugh with him and cry with him, and share the gospel with him.

The questions you ask are good ones and tough ones. God is obviously the only one who knows all the answers in this case and though I would like to know more and might have a chance to later, I will willingly spend time with Shawn as long as he and

I are on this Earth. When you visit a person in prison you don't ask other people what the person they are visiting is doing time for or how long their sentence is unless they volunteer it, but one day a woman, who I assume was a newbie, asked when my friend was getting out and I said, "Until they carry him out or I die." The look on the lady's face told me I might have gone too far, but she asked a tough question and she received a tough answer.

There are things that this case raises and throws in my face regularly about justice, forgiveness, redemption as well as the role of believers and what we are called to do. Mercy and love are hard to give. This whole ordeal has stretched me and made me reconsider my own beliefs.

I regularly pray for the players in this play and pray that they might come to know God as Lord and Savior and one day experience his love, mercy, forgiveness and peace.

Jack

During the time in which Shawn's cancer was discovered and treated, I lost two of my dearest friends to cancer. As I type this, Shawn's cancer is in remission and he enjoys good health.

CHAPTER TWENTY-FOUR

K ATE FIELD, AGE EIGHT, SCHOOL Journal.
Sept. 2004.
A bully is someone that make bad daseson and
sometimes they can hert you. I have never been bullied by a
bully and I have never seen a bully. A bully is big. They ruen
your life. They can be really dangerus. They never say sory. Their
not smart at all. They torger you. They can easly stell from you
when your not looken so thats why you have to be really carful
case you never no when there is a bully around. Bullys hert your
mom and dad.

Matt Stark was out of the office on Monday, December 13, 2004, the first
business day after Officer Cox's midnight visit to investigate a reported
possible child abuse. In Stark's absence, his coworker, Elizabeth Castillo,
received Cox's report regarding the child Karly Sheehan.

Castillo arranged to meet David late Monday afternoon at the DHS
offices. David, who'd had Karly with him all weekend, brought Karly
along. Castillo attempted to talk to Karly, but as usual, Karly wasn't
having any of it.

"She didn't want me being close to her," Castillo said.

Most of Karly's hair was missing. She had scratches on her face, a couple around her left eye, and yellowing bruises on her temple and forehead. Karly kept picking at the scratches around her eye.

David explained the whole situation to Castillo. He told her about Sarah dropping Karly off on Saturday in this horrific state with no more of an explanation than "this happened on my watch." He told her about Officer Cox's late-night visit on Saturday.

David held out hope that state investigators would finally see what had been clear to him: for Karly's sake, Sarah needed to put some distance between herself and Shawn. His hopes were completely obliterated by Castillo's response.

"Hispanic fathers are known to pull their kids' hair out as a form of discipline," she said pointedly.

David was stunned. What the hell was that supposed to mean? He wanted to blurt out, "As a Catholic I see lots of Hispanic kids in mass. They are not bald!" Besides, where in this situation was the Hispanic?

Castillo was insinuating David had snatched Karly bald.

"I couldn't believe what I was hearing!" David said. "This is the treatment I got from the people who were supposed to protect children? Any foreign father in my situation would have felt like he was under a microscope. I've had problems with that statement ever since Castillo made it."

David was pissed but he kept his emotions in check. He told Castillo he had taken photos of Karly on Saturday, and would be happy to provide those to DHS. Great, Castillo said, but said she needed to take pictures of Karly herself. No problem, David said. Castillo got out the digital camera and took some snapshots of Karly. She told David that Matt Stark would be in touch.

Earlier that day, David and Sarah had taken Karly in to see Dr. deSoyza.

"What happened over the past week?" deSoyza asked. The doctor was disturbed by Karly's condition.

Sarah explained that Karly had gotten upset when Sarah took her over to Shawn's house.

"She refused to sleep. She yanked out her hair, and clawed at her face," Sarah said.

The doctor urged Sarah and David to consider taking Karly to see a pediatric psychiatrist. Sarah said she'd already made an appointment for Karly to see a counselor at Old Mill Center for Children and Families. Sarah also assured David and Dr. deSoyza that she was moving out of Shawn's house *that very day*, admitting her new situation was too stressful for Karly.

"Hopefully a change in environment will have a positive impact on the patient's symptoms, but the underlying causes for this do need to be looked into," the doctor wrote in Karly's chart.

Dr. deSoyza knew something was terribly wrong with Sarah's new living arrangement, and she had her suspicions.

Matt Stark returned to his office the following day, Tuesday, December 14, 2004. He retrieved two voice messages left by David Sheehan. Delynn Zoller had also called and left a message. Stark returned her call first. Delynn asked if he had seen Karly. He had not.

"My god, she looks awful!" Delynn exclaimed. "You need to get a look for yourself."

Stark called David, who said Sarah had taken full responsibility for Karly's battered condition. She had assured David she was moving out of Shawn's place immediately. Sarah agreed for the time being that David would have full custody of Karly.

Stark put in a call to Dr. deSoyza and spoke with Mona Schneider, deSoyza's nurse. Yes, she said, the parents had indeed brought Karly in yesterday. She described the abrasions around Karly's eye and the wispy tuft of hair on the child's head.

Stark decided to make an unannounced call to 2652 N.W. Aspen Street. Despite telling Dr. deSoyza and David she was moving out of Shawn's place, Sarah was still at Shawn's the next afternoon when Stark showed up. Because it was winter break at school, Kate was there too.

Sarah stepped out on the porch to talk with Stark. She did not invite him in.

"Karly hasn't been sleeping well," Sarah said. She added that she didn't have much sleep herself on Friday or Saturday because she'd been up with Karly those nights. "I had to restrain Karly to keep her from clawing at herself."

Sarah said that whenever she tried to get Karly to quit playing around and go to sleep, Karly responded by digging at her eyes.

"On Friday night, I made a bed for Karly in the living room in front of the TV, and I lay down with her. I hoped she would sleep, but Karly kept digging at her eye," Sarah said.

It wasn't until morning's light that Sarah realized how badly Karly had hurt herself.

"It wasn't just the scratching at her eyes," Sarah added. "Karly was also smacking at her head and pulling out her hair. And she climbed up on the bunk bed and jumped off the top bunk. That's how she got the bruise on her forehead. She hit the Barbie house on the way down!"

"How long have you been at Shawn's?" Stark asked.

"Pretty much all week," Sarah said.

"And how was Karly earlier in the week?"

"She was fine on Tuesday and Wednesday, but she'd started acting out some on Thursday," Sarah said.

"Why do you think Karly's behavior has gotten worse over the past few days?" Stark asked.

"I think Karly really needs a schedule," Sarah said. "Whenever she gets off her schedule she gets out of control."

"How come you didn't take Karly to daycare this week?" Stark asked.

"Because Karly had the stomach flu," Sarah said. "You can't go to daycare if you are throwing up."

"How does Shawn deal with Karly?" Stark asked.

"Shawn tries to be helpful," Sarah said. "He understands and agrees that Karly needs to be out of his home for a while."

"Is Shawn here?" Stark asked. "Can I speak to him?"

"Just a minute," Sarah said. "I'll get him.'

Shawn stepped out onto the porch. Neither he nor Sarah invited the state investigator inside. Shawn told Stark, "I'll answer general questions but nothing else without my attorney."

Stark thought it odd that Shawn would immediately be on the defensive when he hadn't asked a single question yet. He reassured Shawn he was there to inquire specifically about Karly's recent visit to the doctor's office.

"You don't have to answer any questions you don't want to," Stark said.

"I have my own daughter to take care of, and I don't want you guys snooping around, threatening my daughter's safety."

"I just want to ask you a few questions about Karly," Stark said. "Have you noticed any changes in her behavior recently?"

"She hasn't been sleeping well," Shawn said. "And she throws these big fits for no reason. Karly's been unhappy ever since Sarah moved in."

"Do you think someone is abusing Karly?" Stark asked. He studied Shawn's face as he answered.

"No," Shawn said, shaking his head. "When she has these temper tantrums, she slaps her head and pulls out her hair, fistfuls of it."

"What do you do when she does that?"

"We—me and Sarah—will grab Karly's hands and tell her not to do that," Shawn said. "We've even threatened to send her to the corner if she doesn't stop, but that doesn't do any good. Karly will go to the corner on her own, punish herself. Karly does not want to be to here, and she does not want her mom here."

"Do you think Karly's afraid of you?" Stark asked.

"No," Shawn replied. "She'd be that way even if I weren't around. Karly acts out because of the change in routine, not because of anything I do."

"Was Karly sick this week?" Stark asked.

"Sick?" Shawn asked. "No, she hasn't been sick. She was really thirsty but otherwise she ate okay. She did throw up once, but I think that was more nerves than anything else."

"Would you mind if I spoke with Kate?" Stark asked.

"Sure," Shawn said. "But only with me here."

"Okay," Stark agreed.

Shawn called Kate to the door. He stood off to one side as Stark asked Kate some questions. "Do you remember me from our previous visit?"

"Yes," Kate said, nodding.

"How has Karly been?" Stark asked.

"She's been sick," Kate said. "She threw up."

"Did you see her throw up?" Stark asked.

"No," Kate said. "I think I just heard her."

"Do you know what happened to Karly's hair?" Stark asked.

"She's been pulling at her hair," Kate said. "And slapping her face."

"What did your daddy or Sarah do when Karly did that?"

"I dunno," Kate replied.

"You can't remember?" Stark asked.

"No. I think I was asleep then," Kate said.

"Thank you, Kate," he said. "Would you tell Sarah I want to speak to her again?"

"Sure," Kate said.

Stark asked Sarah about her plans to move out of Shawn's place.

Sarah said she'd decided to let Karly stay with David for now.

Back at the office, Stark went over the day's events with his supervisor. "We were both concerned over Mr. Field's apparent defensiveness," Stark said.

Two days later, on Thursday, December 16, as promised, Sarah took Karly for evaluation at the Old Mill Center for Children and Families. Sarah told the counselor, Caitlyn Chisholm, that Karly had been having extreme fits of anger, marked by Karly screaming until she turned purple and sometimes hitting herself. Sarah said it was heartbreaking to watch Karly behave in this fashion because she was usually such a vibrant, bouncy, and fun girl.

"Do you know when Karly started acting out?" Chisholm asked.

"Yes," Sarah said. "A couple of months ago. In October. It was right after I moved in with my new boyfriend, Shawn."

Sarah said DHS got involved after Karly made some startling statement about her daddy hitting her. Sarah was so concerned she'd had a long talk with Karly about whom she meant when she said "Daddy hits me." Sarah said Karly would only identify David as her daddy, not Shawn. DHS had been investigating the issue, and closed the case out a week ago.

"But then Karly went crazy last week at Shawn's house and pulled nearly all her hair out. So my ex called Children's Services again," Sarah said. "The real reason he made the call is because he's angry that I've moved on in my life. He got pissed and took Karly to the neighbor's house and told my girlfriend there what a terrible parent I am. He even sent a police over to my boyfriend's house at midnight. My ex is crazy jealous. Now Children's Services has reopened the case and that's why I'm here."

Chisholm noted that while Karly seemed calm and cooperative, because of the balding, Karly looked like a child undergoing chemotherapy.

"Have you or Karly seen other counselors?" Chisholm asked.

"I've pretty much been in therapy my whole life," Sarah said, chuckling. "I'm adopted and my parents made me go. I don't have the best relationship with them."

"And Karly? What about her?" Chisholm asked.

"No," Sarah said.

"Any other symptoms she's having that concern you?"

"She has nightmares," Sarah said. "And she talks a lot about monsters."

Chisholm turned to Karly who was playing nearby.

"Tell me about the monsters, Karly."

"Sometimes the monsters bother me," Karly said.

At the end of only one short session, Chisholm diagnosed Karly with acute anxiety and depression. Chisholm concluded that Karly was suffering adjustment disorder. When Sarah repeated this to David, she seemed elated. David thought the diagnosis was complete bullshit and he told Chisholm so in Karly's only follow-up visit.

At no time did Sarah mention to either Dr. deSoyza, David, or the counselor at the Old Mill Center that Sarah had been bedridden the week Karly reportedly "went crazy." Sarah was in bed that week, the result of a miscarriage or an abortion. Police were never able to determine if she really had either one. But Sarah said she was knocked out with sleeping pills, pills she later claimed Shawn Field had been plying her with while he looked after Karly. None of that came out, however, until five days after Karly's death, during an interview with Corvallis Police Detective Mike Wells.

Since their divorce, David and Sarah had a formal custody agreement, which included rotating holidays. It was Sarah's turn to have Karly for Christmas.

Shawn and Kate were headed to Arizona to visit his parents at their winter home. Shawn was angry with Sarah about the investigation. He blamed her for getting him and Kate involved. He wanted to end his relationship with her but the two were wildly attracted to each other, in all sorts of unhealthy ways. Shawn thought going to Arizona would give him breathing room, time to clear his head of her. Sarah was not invited along, and that pissed her off. They fought over it but Shawn didn't change his mind.

Before he and Kate left, Sarah gave him his Christmas gift: a BB gun. By Sarah's own admission, it was an odd gift for a thirty-three-year-old man.

On Christmas Eve morning, Shawn dropped Sarah off in Portland on his way to the airport. Sarah was going to visit her mom, Carol, who was in the hospital again, dealing with cancer and a multitude of serious ailments. Sarah was often dismissive of her mother's ongoing health problems, referring to her as a hypochondriac. David, who was working in Hillsboro, agreed to pick up Sarah after work and give her a ride back to Corvallis. They went together to get Karly at Delynn's that evening.

Afterward, Sarah asked David to drop her at Shawn's place. As David made the turn onto Aspen Street, to pull into the driveway at Shawn's duplex, Karly began to whimper from her car seat in the back. David looked in the rearview mirror and saw a look of sheer panic on his daughter's face. Rapidly maneuvering the steering wheel, David swerved away from the driveway and edged up to the curb instead. Karly calmed down after David reassured her that he was just dropping Sarah off.

The next morning, Christmas Day, he went back to the apartment that Sarah shared with her roommate Shelley, to be with Karly as she opened her gifts. Sarah cooked a holiday meal for the three of them.

Then David took Karly and went back to his place. Later, with Karly dressed in the beautiful lace and red velvet dress David had bought, the two of them headed out for a Christmas gathering at John Hogan's house. Hogan was one of David's best friends. David covered Karly's bald head with a Santa hat.

"I was feeling very hurt for her," David recalled. He knew Karly was very much aware of how startling she looked. Somebody asked Karly to go stand by the inflatable reindeer so they could take her picture. Karly complied but then pulled her father close and whispered, "That reindeer is not Rudolph because Rudolph has a red nose and that reindeer doesn't!"

Nothing escaped Karly's keen eye. She was intuitive and inquisitive, perceptive and observant. Girls born to neglectful mothers learn early that the world is fraught with dangers and they need to stay alert.

Karly didn't see her mother again until a week later, on New Year's Eve, when Sarah dropped by David's place for a brief visit, after David asked if Sarah intended to spend any time with her daughter during the holidays since it was "her turn" to have Karly. Sarah popped in but only for a few minutes. She had a full night of partying ahead.

On January 4, 2005, Karly's third birthday, David presented his daughter with a delicate necklace adorned with a crucifix. Some of Karly's friends at daycare had started to shun her, undoubtedly scared off by her rapidly deteriorating condition and her appearance. For that reason, David decided against having a birthday party for Karly. If David hoped the crucifix would ward off the monsters that threatened his daughter, it did not work. Karly did not see another birthday.

CHAPTER TWENTY-FIVE

SARAH'S PARENTS WERE UNAWARE OF the ongoing investigation. She'd never mentioned it to Gene or Carol.

In early November, Sarah and Karly met Gene at Timberhill's Starbucks in the neighborhood mall on Corvallis's north side. Carol was ill and unable to attend. Gene and two other grandkids were on their way down to Springfield to visit Sarah's sister, Kimberly, and her husband Tony. One of the grandkids was having a birthday party, and they were taking Karly along.

Gene saw that Karly had a bruise on her left cheek. It looked like Karly had been slapped. Gene asked Sarah about it and she dismissed it as nothing. Karly had run into something, Sarah said. Gene studied his granddaughter for a moment. She was running frantically around Starbucks.

"She didn't hardly stop," Gene said. "She ran almost constantly, in a nervous way." But by the time Karly arrived at her aunt and uncle's home, an hour away, she didn't want to play. Gene recalled she seemed unhappy over everything, which wasn't like Karly. Kim was so troubled by her niece's behavior and by the bruise on her face that she took Karly aside and asked her about it. All Karly would say is that she fell.

"It was very suspicious to Kim," Carol later told police investigators. "She was mad."

When David drove down to pick up Karly a day later, Gene asked David how it was that Karly came to have such a bruise. David said he thought she had fallen or run into something.

Karly saw her grandparents again over Thanksgiving. They noticed she had even less hair than before, but Karly's appearance in November left them ill-prepared for what they saw on February 8, 2005.

Carol had a doctor's appointment at Oregon Health Science University Hospital. David met Gene at Washington Square Mall, just outside Portland, to drop off Karly. She was going back to Pendleton with her grandparents for a brief stay. Karly was prepared for the trip, with her backpack in tow and wearing a jaunty traveling hat. Gene and Karly headed back up to the hospital on Portland's west side. Because it was early, Gene and Carol took Karly to get some breakfast in the cafeteria. Karly seemed famished. She ate all of her breakfast, and then helped her grandfather finish off his.

Carol's doctor, who had joined them for breakfast, asked Karly to take off her hat so he could see her princess blonde hair. But when Carol lifted it off, everyone gasped: Karly hardly had any hair at all.

"My doctor couldn't believe she wasn't a chemo patient," Carol said. "She looked just like one."

Neither Sarah nor David had warned Gene and Carol ahead of time about Karly's hair loss. Gene and Carol knew that Sarah was seeing a new boyfriend but they had never met Shawn, and knew nothing about him other than his name. Sarah did not like her parents asking questions, and she volunteered very little information. Gene and Carol had a better relationship with David than they did Sarah, but David hadn't wanted to worry to them, so he hadn't said anything either.

It is a four-hour drive east from Portland, where Gene picked up Karly, to where Gene and Carol live. After Sarah and her siblings grew up and moved away, Gene and Carol sold their home and built their dream home on on a hillside, east of Pendleton, designed for comfort and grandchildren, with breathtaking views that span the Blue Mountains.

During that particular February visit, as Carol was washing up the dinner dishes, Karly let out a bloodcurdling scream. Carol ran to her granddaughter and found Karly cowering next to an overturned plant.

"I'm sorry, Grandma," Karly cried. "I broke your plant!"

"Oh, honey," Carol said, wrapping the trembling child in her arms, "you never, ever have to be afraid in Grandma's house. There is nothing in my house more important than you."

Karly came back for one more visit that winter, in mid-March, to join her cousins for an early Easter celebration. She was thinner than ever and pale as death. Her eyes were red-rimmed and seemed full of an unspoken strain. Carol asked Karly what she thought of Shawn. Karly replied he "was poopy."

The usually gregarious Karly refused to participate in the Easter egg hunt with her cousins. She had to be taken by the hand and led through the motions.

"She looked so lost, so forlorn, so sad, scared," Carol said.

Sarah, who had agreed to pick up Karly, arranged to meet her parents halfway. Karly spoke to Sarah on the cell phone several times as her grandparents drove west through the Columbia River Gorge that afternoon. Each time, she asked for David, over and over again. Karly's begging for her father upset Gene Brill.

"I remember it so vividly because I was hurting for Sarah. I knew Sarah just wanted to talk to her daughter, but the whole time Karly kept saying, 'I want my daddy. I want my daddy,'" Gene said.

Gene and Carol discussed their concerns about Karly with other family members, but they stopped short of naming the thing they feared most: that their granddaughter was being abused.

Gene and Carol had a handful of uneasy observations, but nothing more came of it. Karly's grandparents didn't learn of the state's abuse investigation until after Karly's murder, when the Corvallis police called them in for interviews.

Chapter Twenty-Six

CAROL BRILL'S MOTHER DIED THE first week in May. Sarah called her brother, Doug, and asked if she could hitch a ride down to Redding, California, for their grandmother's funeral.

It was a grueling trip: eight people packed together in an SUV for the six-hour drive: Doug, his wife Gretchen, their four kids, plus Sarah and Karly. Sarah sat in the very back between Karly and her cousin Emily.

Somewhere north of Redding, Doug pulled the car into a rest area to give the kids a break. They ran. They hollered. They jumped in puddles. No one could remember what exactly set Sarah off, but something did. She grabbed Karly by the shoulders, shook her, and then threw her sobbing daughter into the car seat in the very back of the vehicle and began to scream at her.

"Be quiet!"

Karly continued to cry.

"Why don't you just shut your mouth? I don't want to hear any more of it!"

Doug and Gretchen were stunned.

"She's just being a kid," one of them muttered.

At the family dinner following the funeral, Sarah complained to those within earshot that David would hardly have anything to do with Karly, that she was a single mom having to manage all by her lonesome, putting herself through college. Sarah probably didn't notice the family members who knew better rolling their eyes.

Gretchen walked away. "None of it was true," she later told detectives. It was more fiction crafted to evoke sympathy for Sarah.

Meanwhile, as Sarah stood in the church fellowship hall, talking about herself, Karly was running around the church parking lot unsupervised.

"The thing that disturbed me the most was Sarah just seemed so disconnected from Karly," Gretchen recalled. "Karly would run inside and see her mom and she didn't get anything out of her mom, attention or anything.

"Sarah would keep talking to whoever she was talking to, and just totally ignore her, so Karly would run back to where the excitement was with the kids," Gretchen said. "There was no emotional attachment that I could see at all. Karly was just a little prize, kind of: this is my daughter."

The next day, Karly rode back with her aunt and uncle while Sarah rode in her parents' car, sleeping mostly. Nearly every five minutes, Karly asked the same questions, over and over again.

"Uncle Doug, do you know how to get to my daddy's house? Are you sure you know where my daddy lives?"

Karly's anxiety made the trip seem twice as long. Finally, she went absolutely wild with joy when Doug pulled over at a gas station along Interstate 5 and David was there to get her.

That Sunday, Mother's Day, Karly spent the day with her father. Sarah dropped by briefly. She spent less than an hour with her daughter.

The very next week, after Sarah had her for a couple of days, Karly came to David's with a knot in the middle of her forehead. It was a bruise about an inch long and very narrow. Angry and distraught, David sent Sarah a text message: "We have 2 talk in the morning re: Karly. She has new cuts & bruises, and I haven't seen her this upset since the hair loss. I'm worried about her."

The message was sent at 9:40 p.m. on Friday, May 13, 2005.

Sarah called him. There was an exchange of heated words.

"Karly's got a knot on her head," David began. "What happened?"

"She ran into a tree," Sarah said.

"Really?" David replied, disbelieving. "She just ran into a tree? She couldn't see the tree in front of her?"

"You know how clumsy she is."

"No. No, I don't, Sarah. I don't know anything about Karly's clumsiness. I think that maybe we ought to take her back to Dr. deSoyza. Have her take a look at Karly."

"That's ridiculous," Sarah said. "We can't be taking Karly to the doctor for every bump or bruise she gets. She's a kid. Kids run into things and get banged up all the time. I did it when I was a kid and my parents weren't carting me to the doctor every single time I skinned my knee."

"Yeah, well, when you were a kid, were state investigators involved in your life?" David prodded.

"Yes. Yes, they were," Sarah snapped back.

David noted a marked difference in Sarah's tone. In December, when she'd brought Karly to him so badly bruised and with her hair missing, Sarah had been conciliatory, apologetic. This time Sarah was defensive, accusatory.

"Karly is perfectly safe with me," Sarah continued. "Besides, how do I know she's not getting bruised with you? I'm going to start taking pictures when she arrives at my house."

Sarah later testified that the picture-taking scheme had been

Shawn's idea. He wanted to document the bruises on Karly and use those photos as evidence so Sarah would get full custody of Karly, and the check that would go along with it.

Sarah knew as she argued with David that the bump on Karly's forehead appeared after she left Karly alone with Shawn. The promise never to leave the two of them alone was one Sarah had broken early.

That next day, Saturday, May 14, David drove Karly to Pendleton for another short stay with her grandparents. By late Saturday, the bruising on Karly's forehead had begun to seep downward, turning the corner pockets of her eyes a shocking blue. At dinner, Karly ate like a field hand. Later, while bathing her granddaughter before bedtime, Grandma Carol noticed scratches in Karly's armpits, as if she had a rash of some sort. She dried Karly off and rubbed Neosporin under her arms.

After her bath, Karly began to cry. "I miss my daddy. I want my daddy. Can we call my daddy?"

Her grandparents were rattled by her cries. Every time they'd been around her since the previous fall, Karly had done the very same thing. And it didn't seem to matter if it was day or night. Karly cried for her father; she did not cry for her mother.

Karly refused to sleep in her own bed. Her grandparents usually made her a bed on a cot in their room, but on this trip, even that wasn't close enough to soothe Karly.

"She slept with me," Carol said. "She was too scared to go anywhere else. She slept in my bed, right up next to me. She refused to go to bed unless she could lay right next to me."

David called to check on Karly at least three times a day. Sarah rarely called. One afternoon, Carol and Karly were in the kitchen baking cookies. Karly told her grandma all about her daddy's new girlfriend, Kendall, about how they sometimes made cookies together, too.

"I really like her," Karly said. "She's nice."

"What about Shawn?" Carol asked. "Do you like him?"

"NO! Grandma!" Karly said.

Carol paused and studied her granddaughter for a minute, and then asked, "How come? Does he spank you?"

Karly looked down, averting her grandmother's curious gaze. "No," she muttered softly. Then, climbing down out of the chair, she went off to play by herself.

When Gene and Carol's Bible study group came over for their weekly meeting, Carol put on a video for Karly to watch downstairs in the family room, as was their routine whenever their grandchildren came to visit. Distraught over being left alone, Karly began to sob uncontrollably, "I want my daddy! I want my daddy!"

Carol held Karly and soothed her throughout the rest of the evening. When David picked up Karly on Thursday, May 19, 2005, he told Gene and Carol he was planning to move with Karly to Portland in August.

"We love our daughter," Carol said, "but Karly will be better off with you."

The pockets around Karly's eyes had really begun to turn a deep purple. David and Gene Brill talked about possible reasons why a child's eyes might do that. Gene had worked for a medical lab. He urged David to get Karly in to see her doctor, to get a blood test. David called when he got back and scheduled Karly for a visit with Dr. deSoyza for the following Wednesday, May 25. David told the doctor what Sarah had told him, that Karly had run headlong into a tree almost two week previously, sustaining a significant bump and bruise on her forehead. Now she had two black eyes.

During the exam, Dr. deSoyza noticed Karly had some bruises on her back as well. She asked David if he had any idea how Karly got those.

David said he'd been working in the yard over the weekend and Karly had tripped over some rhododendron roots and fallen on her backside. David also told the doctor that when he'd picked Karly up from daycare on Monday she'd had a bruise on her left arm.

Dr. deSoyza made a note of the bruise on Karly's left bicep and the bruises on her back. She told David she thought the black eyes were caused by the head bruise seeping downward. It would, she suggested, continue to dissipate and be absorbed by Karly's body.

It wasn't until after Karly died that Dr. deSoyza learned that the day Karly reportedly ran into the tree, she was not with Sarah—she was alone with Shawn.

"If I had known Karly was back in that same environment, I would have looked at the last visit in a totally different context," Dr. deSoyza said. "But I didn't know."

Nine days later, Dr. deSoyza received another call regarding Karly. This one came from a colleague who worked the emergency room at Good Samaritan Hospital.

"Karly Sheehan is dead," he said. "I thought you'd want to know right away."

The doctor who had attended to Karly from the moment of her birth hung up the phone, walked into the living room, sat in a chair, dropped her head into her hands, and wept.

CHAPTER TWENTY-SEVEN

ARAH IS ANGRY WITH ME.

I knew she would be. That's why I put off calling her and telling her about this book.

I intended to sit down and talk to Sarah about it, but I knew before I wrote one word that Sarah wouldn't like it. And I knew why. This book is nonfiction. Sarah prefers made-up stories, what David calls her alternate reality.

My cell phone rang the minute I walked out of the Benton County courthouse. It was the spring of 2007 and I'd come to town to pull some documents, and to visit with folks at the courthouse about the case. Sarah had been on my mind all morning long. A woman who knew the case intimately had pulled me aside earlier that day and warned me to be careful when going through the documents.

"Those of us who work around this stuff all the time were shocked by what we saw," she said. "Don't look at the photos. I'm warning you. They were the worst ever, even for those of us used to it."

I thanked her for her advice, but assured her that as a former cop reporter, I'd seen my fair share of nightmares.

"Not like this," she said. "And your relationship with the family and all will make it even harder."

Then she paused, placed her hand over mine, and added, "I understand her."

"Sarah?" I asked.

"Yes," she said. Then taking me by the elbow and leading me to a quiet corner, she added, "My ex-husband was abusive. I understand how a woman can get caught up in a relationship like she did."

She proceeded to tell me how she never knew when her ex would be in a foul mood, could not tell what little things would set him off. Finally, after one terribly explosive evening, she called it quits. She left him.

"So I know how these things can happen," she said.

"Did you have children?" I asked.

"Yes," she said.

"Did he ever threaten or hurt your children?"

"Yes, once," she said. "That's when I made up my mind to leave."

"Exactly," I said. "That's the difference between you and Sarah. You protected your children. She didn't."

The lady nodded her head in the knowing way of mothers and grandmothers and sisters the world over. We will take a heap of abuse ourselves, but God help the person who tries to harm one of our children. Scorn us thusly and most of us will storm the Gates of Hell and do hand-to-hand combat with legions of demons.

Sarah looked the other way in hopes of hanging onto Shawn.

It pleased Sarah that David didn't like Shawn. And while David clearly had no affection left for Sarah at this point, Sarah fancied him jealous. And, in fact, told investigators David's jealousy was the source of all of Karly's problems.

Of course, I didn't have a clear picture of what had happened the day Sarah called me, the way I do now after spending hundreds of hours studying court documents and after talking to the people involved, and reflecting on all of it as the years have passed. I'd put off telling her I was writing a book because I wanted to know more first.

But I wasn't surprised when I answered the cell phone on the steps of the Benton County Courthouse and got an earful of Sarah's ranting. She was pissed. Why hadn't I called her? Didn't I owe her that courtesy? It was the first of many such phone calls to follow. In each one, Sarah spoke harshly, yelling at times. Sarah is usually very soft-spoken. It's part of her charm. She is usually so controlled, so controlling; she rarely allows her emotions to lead the way.

"I am sorry," I said. "I should have called."

Sarah grew quiet. We both did. There wasn't much left to say.

Since that day on the courthouse steps, I have called Sarah periodically to keep her up-to-date. I have offered Sarah as much opportunity for input into this story as I've given David. I would have welcomed what Sarah had to say, but Sarah has resolutely refused to participate.

"I am barely over the trial and now this," Sarah said. I'd called her from my home in Hermiston. "You don't know me anymore."

"True enough," I said. I was standing at the kitchen counter, taking notes, and watching the dog run across the backyard. "But I did at one time."

"The last time we spoke you bitched me out. You cut me out of your life," Sarah said. "Why would I speak to you after that?"

She wasn't referring to the very last time we spoke. We'd spoken several times lately. She was dredging up that awful phone call of February 2003.

"Because, Sarah, that's what families do," I said. "They get angry and say things, sometimes hurtful things, but then they get over it."

"Not in our family!" Sarah snapped. "When I got angry, I got sent off to boarding school."

This was exactly the sort of response I expected from Sarah. When-

ever the conversation grows uncomfortable for her, Sarah brings up
how it is somebody else's fault her life got derailed. Her parents sent
her away. Her mother didn't like her. She was the outsider. No one ever
really loved her. Sarah is skilled at deflections

"It's your fault I got involved with Shawn to begin with," Sarah said,
in her most accusatory tone.

That was a gut-kick I didn't see coming. I moved from the kitchen
counter to the living room. I curled over myself into the armless red
chair. I felt queasy, clammy. No one can knock the breath out of me the
way Sarah does.

"How's that?" I asked. My voice was thin.

"Those things you said! Well, at least one of them hasn't come true."

She was referring, of course, to when I said to her: "Listen, Sarah,
you are not always going to be able to trade off your looks. One day
you're going to wake up old and ugly, then what?"

"I was very angry at you for a long time," Sarah continued. "I
thought, 'Screw Karen. I found a guy better than David.' Of course he
wasn't."

Once Sarah had her say, she grew silent. I was pretty quiet myself.
I was nauseated at the thought of my anger being a compelling reason
for Sarah to get involved with a man like Shawn. On some level, I knew
she was just making excuses. But on a deeper level, I also regretted,
continue to regret, that during that 2003 phone call I didn't offer to
pray with Sarah, instead of yelling at her about her decision to leave
David. I should have prayed for Sarah, for David, and most of all for
Karly.

That what I was thinking, but what I asked Sarah was, "Wouldn't
you rather have someone who loves and cares for you write this?" I
asked.

"No!" Sarah said. "I'd rather have someone who didn't know me at
all. How would you feel if someone decided to write about some of the

painful things of your past? Interviewing your friends from childhood? How would you feel?"

Sarah had told me about the breakdown in her relationship with her brother Doug.

Sarah and Doug had maintained a close relationship as they grew up, bonding in sibling solidarity. But that all changed once Karly died, and perhaps before.

During one of our last conversations, I asked Sarah about Doug, and she said, "I haven't spoken to my brother." I was surprised to hear that, knowing how much she had adored him. I told her so.

"Family members are fairly easy to replace," she said. "You get a couple of new friends and move on. I don't hate him. I'm at peace with my decision. You can't keep people in your life forever."

CHAPTER TWENTY-EIGHT

K ARLY FASHIONED A GAME FROM her favorite movie, *Shrek*. She and David played it a hundred times or more. The last time they played, it was on Monday, May 30, 2005, at the playground at Hoover Elementary School. The school is located a couple hundred yards from David's house and within blocks of Shawn's place.

It was Sarah's week to have Karly. David's coursework on his master's program at George Fox University was winding up. Even though it was a holiday, he had a study group meeting in Salem, papers he needed to write, exams to study for, and his job to attend to. It was going to be a crazy, hectic week.

Father and daughter spent Saturday at the Oregon Zoo in Portland. They drove up in the morning, met up with David's girlfriend, and rode MAX, the city's mass transit system, out to the zoo. Karly loved seeing the hairy orangutan, the painted zebra, and the gangly-necked giraffe. She ran from animal to animal, standing on her tiptoes, tugging on David to pick her up so she could better see the sleeping polar bear. After Saturday's outing, both father and daughter were so tired that on Sunday, after Mass, they puttered around the house all day. Monday morning, after breakfast and chores, Karly and David walked over to the playground at Hoover.

"Higher!" Karly cried, as David gave her a gentle push in the swing.

"Betcha can't catch me!" she said, running from him. "Catch me, Daddy!" she commanded as she barreled down the slide on her tummy.

Then she climbed up on one of the play structures and spread across the colored tubing. She lay perfectly still, eyes closed, a slight grin on her face.

It was David's cue.

She was a sleeping princess, like *Shrek's* Fiona, who could only be awakened with a kiss from her daddy. And it had to be the perfect kiss or she would forever remain suspended somewhere between life and death. It was up to the prince to save her, to awaken her, and to bring her back to life. And love, true love, was the key.

David leaned over the sleeping Karly and kissed her. Then he stood back to wait her reaction. Ah. Nothing. The princess remained asleep. No magic in that kiss. He leaned over and tried again.

Aha! That's the one. Her blue eyes popped open, reflective pools that mirrored her daddy's eyes. The magic worked. Karly clasped her little hands around her father's neck and whispered, "Thank you, Prince! You saved me!"

"Good thing," David said. "Otherwise you might have missed your lunch."

The two walked hand and hand back to David's place. After a lunch of pizza, Karly's favorite food, they gathered her things and stuffed them into her backpack.

"C'mon," David said, "time to go." He grabbed his books and opened the door.

Karly reluctantly pulled her backpack behind her. "I don't want to go."

"I know, honey, but we have to get going. Your mommy's waiting for you and I've got to be in Salem soon."

"But I don't want to go to Mommy's," she whined.

David said nothing. Karly climbed into her car seat. He buckled her in as a fat tear rolled down her cheeks.

"I don't want to go!" she cried.

David looked at his daughter in the rearview mirror. What could he do? It was Sarah's week. If he refused to bring Karly, Sarah would raise holy hell. Probably call the police on him.

"I want to stay with you!" Karly was sobbing buckets now. Salty tears mixed with snot streamed down her face. "I don't want to go!"

"I'm sorry, honey," he said. "But your mommy wants to see you."

"How many times will you pick me up?"

"What?"

"How many times are you going to pick me up, Daddy? How many times?" Karly demanded.

"I don't know, Karly."

"Are you going to pick me up? Are you, Daddy? Are you coming to get me?"

"Yes, honey. I'm going to come get you."

"When?" Karly said, sucking back another sob.

"I don't know," he said. "Maybe Friday."

Karly would not be quieted. Her cries continued even as David pulled the car up to Sarah's place, the apartment she kept with Shelley Freeland, Karly's godmother. Karly loved "Auntie" Shelley, loved hanging out with her, but she did not want her daddy to leave her today, not for any reason. She continued pleading, "When? When are you going to come get me? How many times?" Karly continued to cry even as Sarah took her from David's arms.

Bloody hell, he thought as he kissed Karly goodbye.

On Friday, June 3, 2005, David was at work when he got the call from Gene Brill. It was 2:45 p.m.

"Sarah just called," Gene said. "Karly's in the emergency room."

David went to his supervisor and told her he needed to leave immediately. He tried not to worry. Doesn't every kid wind up in the emergency room at one time or another? And besides, David told himself, he had just heard from her that very morning.

Sarah had called around ten o'clock. David's phone was on vibrate, as was his habit while working, so he'd missed the call, but Karly left a message.

"Hi Daddy," Karly said. "I miss you. I love you."

It was the last thing Karly would ever say to her father. He not only missed the call, he'd erased it after he heard it.

David put his car in reverse and nearly hit a Hillsboro Police Department squad car in his rush. Taking a deep breath, David paused to compose himself. *Karly is in good hands*, he reminded himself. *You still have at least an hour and a half of driving to do. Don't end up in the emergency room yourself, or you'll be no help to her.*

Once he was on the highway, David called Sarah's cell. He got her voice mail.

"Sarah, I am Karly's father. If there's something wrong with her, I have the right to know. Why didn't you call and tell me she's in the hospital? Call me ASAP!"

It was the last thing he would say to Sarah in the coming weeks.

As he headed south on Interstate 5, David called Gene back.

"Have you heard anything more?"

"I haven't," Gene said. "But Sarah did say Karly wasn't breathing when she was admitted to the ER."

"Okay," David said. He took a deep breath and gripped the steering wheel. "I'm going to call the hospital. See what I can find out."

At 3:30 p.m., just a tad north of the Wilsonville exit, still about sixty-five miles north of Corvallis, David received a phone call from a man who identified himself as an emergency room doctor. Dr. Hochfeld didn't waste any breath making small talk.

"Your daughter was admitted to the ER this afternoon. She was not breathing. I am sorry. We did everything we could. Karly is dead," he said.

"No! No! No!" David cried out.

Hours earlier on that Friday morning, Sarah had called Gene Brill and told him that Karly had woken up with a badly swollen eye. Gene and Carol were at Oregon Health Sciences University Hospital in Portland, where Carol was being treated for ongoing health problems. Gene recalled later that Sarah sounded very distressed.

"Dad, Karly's eye is swollen and all she wants to do is sleep. Can allergies do that? Make a person sleepy that way?" Sarah asked.

"Yes, Sarah," he said. "Eyes can be affected by allergies. They can turn red. Sometimes there's swelling. Sometimes they get runny." He reminded Sarah that sometimes her sister's son got allergies, especially during the spring growing season.

"Kim gives her boy Benadryl. You might try that. Why don't you call Kim?" Gene suggested. "Ask her about it."

Sarah asked Karly if she wanted to talk.

"Grandpa! Grandpa!" Karly cried. "My eye hurts. My eye hurts."

"I know, honey. Your momma told me. I'm so sorry."

"Is Grandma sick?" Karly asked. "Are the doctors fixing her?"

"Yes, honey. They are fixing her all up. I'll tell her you called, and we'll see you soon, okay?"

"Okay," Karly said, handing the phone back to her mother.

Gene was disconcerted by Karly's cries. His granddaughter seemed to be in a great deal of pain, but he couldn't see what Sarah saw, what the police, EMTs, nurses, and doctors would later see—what made them believe this little girl had been beaten to death. Karly's eye was swollen shut. The eyeball was ruptured. She looked like a boxer who'd lost the fight.

•

David kept driving through his tears and anguish. He did not try to call Sarah. He did not want to speak to her. Instead, he called his girlfriend Kendall and told her that Karly was dead.

He asked Kendall to call his sister Andrea in Ireland, but not to tell her anything.

"Just tell her to call me ASAP, please," David said.

It was late in Ireland. The family had gathered at Castletownbere to celebrate a wedding. David and Karly couldn't be there with the rest of the family, but they had a trip booked for later in August. Karly had started packing her suitcase already. A week or two before, in a phone call, Karly had serenaded her Auntie Andrea. She sang "Leaving on a Jet Plane," the song her daddy had taught her the previous summer when they were preparing for their last trip to Ireland.

Shortly after midnight, Jason, David's brother, asked Andrea to check for messages on her phone from a U.S. number. Kendall had left a message, instructing Andrea to call David as soon as possible.

Andrea and Jason left the reception, stood in the hallway, and called David.

"David," Andrea hesitated. "What's wrong?"

"Where are you?" David asked.

"I'm at the wedding," Andrea said, "with the rest of the family. Why? What's wrong?"

"Karly's dead," David cried.

Andrea dropped to her knees. Jason dropped down beside her. Everything went hazy for them both. She assured David that she would tell their mom and dad. But after she hung up, Andrea had a sense that none of it had really happened. Not the phone call. Not the death. Perhaps the universe was playing some horrific hoax. Surely, she had misheard David. Or he had misspoken. There was no way Karly could be dead.

So unsure was she that Andrea rang her brother back.

"David, how do you know Karly's dead? She can't be dead! Are you sure?"

"As sure as I can be," David replied. "That's what the doctor just told me."

David's parents, James and Noreen Sheehan, were on the dance floor swaying to a slow song. Noreen had been facing the door when Jason had first come to get Andrea. She'd watched the two of them leave together. There was something about the way they were walking, an urgency to it that bothered Noreen.

"James, there's something wrong," she said. "Maybe something's wrong with one of the grandkids." The couple held their spot on the dance floor facing the door, waiting, watching, expecting.

Andrea was soon back, making her way across the crowded dance floor. When she reached her parents, Andrea took them both by the hand and led them outside.

"What's wrong?" Noreen asked first, then James. "Andrea, what's wrong?"

They kept repeating their question, but Andrea would not answer them. She wanted to get them as far away from the wedding reception as possible. Once outside, Andrea spoke as plainly as she could.

"Karly is dead!" she cried.

"Andrea! Don't say things like that!" Noreen scolded. But then she saw the darkness in her daughter's eyes. "Oh my God!" she cried. "Why? How?"

But Andrea didn't know why or how. Jason was kneeling on the ground, weeping. They all were weeping.

"We've got to get home," Noreen said. She turned to her husband. "We all have to get home. Right now! I need to talk to David."

A friend took them to the hotel, where they picked up their bags, and then drove them the thirty miles home to County Kerry.

"We were very anxious to get home," Noreen said. "David was going to ring us when he had information for us. At that stage, we had no details as to what had happened. Unfortunately, we had a fair idea that Sarah was involved."

Nearly all of Andrea's childhood memories include David. The two, who were born only a year apart, were as close as any siblings could be. They spent nearly every weekend with their own grandparents. In the mornings, David would tag along with their grandfather and Andrea along with their grandmother. In the afternoons, the two siblings would go off frogging.

"We would spend hours playing in the field, climbing into drains with old tin cans and catching frogs and putting them into a barrel," Andrea recalled "Our record was about fifteen frogs. We were very proud!"

As they grew older, David took pride in looking after his younger sister. When she was in her final year of college and pregnant with her daughter, Chantelle, Andrea developed a kidney infection.

"I didn't want to ring Mom and Dad as I was afraid that they would worry, and also I didn't want to put them under pressure financially as there were three of us in college that year, which can't have been easy," Andrea said. "So I rang David, who told me to get myself to a doctor, and that he would send down money for me. A check arrived in the post the following day."

Now her big brother was across a wide ocean from her, desperately hurt, and there was nothing Andrea, or anyone else, could do to bring Karly back.

Still driving south on I-5, David called his friend John Hogan. There were a million scenarios running through his head, but David was trying his best to stay focused as he told John what little he knew.

"John, when I get there, I don't want to see that prick Field," David said.

John was waiting at Good Samaritan Hospital when David pulled into the parking lot. Before getting out of the car, David dropped his head to the steering wheel and prayed for strength.

David felt lead-footed entering the ER. John embraced him and handed him a bottle of water. His priest, Father John Mitchell from St. Mary's Catholic Church, was there as well. They spoke briefly before Detective Karin Stauder and Detective Shawn Houck showed up to interview David.

Three hours and a penile swab later, when David finally emerged, John Hogan was still there. Despite the warmth of that June day, David felt a chill deeper than any he'd ever known.

Chapter Twenty-Nine

KARLA ISABELLE RUTH SHEEHAN WAS declared dead by Dr. Paul Hochfeld, the attending emergency room physician, at 2:20 p.m. on Friday, June 3.

Detective Mike Wells was at his desk tending to paperwork that afternoon when his cell phone buzzed. He turned it over, looked at the incoming number. It was Jason Harvey. Wells flipped the phone open.

"Mike?"

"Yeah."

"Maclean needs some help on a death investigation out on Aspen. I'm going out there. You want me to swing by and get you?"

"What kind of death?" Wells asked.

"A kid."

Wells had been with Corvallis Police Department nearly ten years, but he'd only been a detective for the past few months. Wells is a handsome man, with a runner's frame. He keeps his brown hair clipped in military style. He is deliberate man—some would say calculating. He's a thinker, but he's no diplomat. Wells says what he thinks, plainly and frankly. He's a take-charge, help-or-get-out-of-my-way kind of guy.

Harvey, by contrast, is a broad-chested fellow with a slow smile and an intimidating presence to those on the wrong side of the law. Harvey prefers the company of dogs to people.

Wells was still gathering up equipment—baggies, tape, swab kits, gloves, video equipment—when Harvey showed up a few minutes later. The two men loaded all the stuff they'd need to collect evidence into the back of Harvey's patrol car.

Picking up the radio handset, Wells called dispatch.

"What's the address of the death investigation that Maclean is on?"

"2652 NW Aspen Street."

"What do you know about it?"

"A child stopped breathing. Fire crew is there now."

Medics were loading a gurney into the ambulance when the two officers arrived. The emergency crew sped away with lights and siren blaring before the two men got out of their car.

Sergeant Fieman walked over to greet the detectives.

"Poor girl's been beat, beat bad," Fieman said. The veteran cop was visibly shaken.

"How old is she?" Harvey asked.

"Three," Fieman replied. "She wasn't breathing. Didn't have a pulse. I don't think she's gonna make it." He shook his head the way disbelieving people do. "I know her momma. Sarah Sheehan. Fire crew took her to the hospital. Her boyfriend, Shawn Field, is inside the house. Officer Teeter's with him."

"Wells, why don't you head on over to the hospital? Monitor the mom and kid," Harvey said. "I've got a couple of questions I'd like to ask the mom's boyfriend."

Wells located Officer Maclean in the emergency room. He had a box camera and was taking photos of the little girl.

"We'll do an autopsy to confirm it, but it appears she died of blunt force trauma," Dr. Hochfeld advised Detective Wells. "Her mom's in the waiting room. You want to come with me while I tell her?"

The two men walked the hospital hallway, heads down and somber, to a private waiting room where Sarah Brill Sheehan waited with her roommate, "Auntie" Shelley Freeland.

Shelley was sitting on the couch. She saw the men enter before Sarah did. With her back to the door, Sarah was kneeling on the floor in front of Shelley. The two women had weathered ten years of friendship, often strained by the fraying of financial or moral cords. They grasped at each other. Their hands entwined, they prayed and wept like the sisters of Lazarus, wailing for God's intervention. The two of them had made untidy promises, the way they had a thousand times before. They promised to be good girls if only God would heal Karly, right now, right this very minute.

Shelley knew when she saw the doctor's fretted brow that all their ardent prayers and silver-tongued promises could cease.

Sarah turned toward the door. A familiar blankness shrouding her face.

"Dr. Hochfeld," the man in the white coat said, introducing himself. He did not offer a handshake. Neither woman rose. They continued to grasp each other.

"Karla is dead," he said. His tone was terse—an even-tempered man standing two steps beyond agitated.

The wailing resumed.

"But they told me they got a pulse!" Sarah screamed through tears. Fists balled up, she beat the couch. "They told me they got a pulse!"

Shelley lacked Sarah's fury, but her tears fell, too, hard and steady.

The doctor and detective stood by, silently, waiting for a break in the squall. One minute, then two, passed before Dr. Hochfeld spoke sternly, eyes blurred by despair.

"Karla had numerous bruises to her face. Do you have any idea where those came from?" he asked.

Sarah looked up. Dr. Hochfeld turned toward the officer at his side. As a warning to her, he said, "This is Detective Wells with the Corvallis Police Department."

There was another pause as choking sobs subsided. Sarah was struggling to find her breath to speak.

"She jumped off the bed last night," Sarah offered. "Those bruises, they came yesterday, to her eye and her arm."

When a child lies beaten to death, a reckoning is called for. Dr. Hochfeld's next question let Sarah know he didn't believe her.

"Karla's eye was very swollen."

"She has very bad allergies," Sarah said. "She'd been rubbing her eye."

Unconvinced, Hochfeld left the room without another word. Never in his twenty-seven years of medical practice had he ever seen a child so severely beaten. The little girl's head injuries alone couldn't have been worse if she'd fallen from a two-story window.

Shortly before Karly was declared dead, Lieutenant Tim Brewer notified Benton County District Attorney Scott Heiser. Brewer told him a three-year-old child had been transported to Good Samaritan Hospital and that investigators on the scene were saying she had been badly beaten.

Heiser was serving his second term as DA, a job he'd held since 1999. Heiser has a sharp chin, disarming smile, and clipped hair. He was a local boy who obtained his undergraduate in Economics from OSU and his law degree from Northwestern School of Law at Lewis and Clark, a private college in Portland.

Heiser prosecuted a number of child abusers, though most were sex offenders, but among his cases he couldn't recall any abused child who had died. As he headed across the street to the Corvallis Police Department, he hoped Brewer was wrong, and that the EMTs had been able to revive the little girl.

•

In a private room at the hospital, a police investigator pulled up a chair in front of Sarah and Shelley.

"I'm Detective Wells with the Corvallis Police Department," he said.

Both women nodded, still crying.

Wells placed a tape recorder between them.

"I'm not really good at writing things down so I'm going to go ahead and just record this so I can make sure I get everything when we talk, okay?"

The women bobbed their heads, unable to say anything coherent.

"What's your name again?"

"Sarah."

"And what's your relationship?" Wells asked, looking at Shelley.

"Um, she's my best friend and my roommate," Sarah replied.

"Okay, and your roommate?"

"But we're not lesbians," Sarah said.

The detective thought that was an unusual clarification to make at such a time. He asked Shelley to spell her name. Both women were crying so hard that even with the recorder it was difficult to decipher their answers.

"I'm Karly's godmother," Shelley Freeland said. She added that Karly and Sarah lived with her. They covered all the basics, including that Shawn Field lived at the duplex on Aspen Street, where Karly was last seen alive. But Sarah clarified that relationship, too.

"He's not actually my boyfriend anymore. We just broke up."

"When did you guys break up?"

"Um, two weeks ago, two or three weeks ago today."

Wells asked who was at the house when Karly stopped breathing.

"Shawn."

Wells made a couple of notes regarding Shawn, where he worked— Grempsey's Restaurant— and information about Shawn's daughter.

"Can you tell me what happened? What's been going on? I heard Karla's been sick," Wells said.

"She has really bad allergies," Sarah replied.

Someone knocked on the door. Wells excused himself and said he'd be right back after he made a phone call. He left the recorder running.

Sarah, crying harder, said, "Shelley, my baby's gone. I can't do anything, oh, Shelley."

Shelley simply could not offer Sarah any consolation. Karly was dead. What comfort was there now?

"She was supposed to grow up and be beautiful and popular and fun and funny, now she's dead," Sarah cried. "Why did this have to happen? No, no, no, God, oh, my God, I didn't do enough. What didn't I do? What could I have done?"

Shelley urged Sarah to take a drink of water.

"No," Sarah said, pushing it away. "I just want to know why she is dead. There has to be a reason. You just don't decide to die. I just can't believe, oh my God, I can't breathe."

"Take a deep breath," Shelley advised. "Hold it. You can do it."

"Oh, my God, it's all my fault," Sarah said, gasping, sobbing. "Why didn't I think of something to do? I should have known something was wrong. I should have known it was something besides allergies."

CHAPTER THIRTY

S ARAH HAD AN IDEA OF who had done this horrible, horrible thing to her daughter.

David.

At the hospital, during those early hours following Karly's death, Sarah met with Detective Wells and others from the Corvallis Police Department, and told them about the Children's Services investigation and about her jealous ex-husband.

"Karly was with David more than she was with me because I'm going back to school and working. I've always worked but David's just, you know, more established," Sarah said.

Sarah said that over the past several months Karly had been saying that her daddy hits her. "I'd asked Karly, 'Why does he hit you?' and Karly said, 'He hits me because I go pee pee.' Karly was very afraid of going to the toilet. I'd ask her again, 'Where does your daddy hit you?' and she'd point to her bottom or someplace else."

Detective Wells asked if Karly was potty-trained. Sarah replied mostly but that she was wearing a diaper that morning because Sarah hadn't done the wash and Karly didn't have any clean panties.

Sarah told Detective Wells that Karly had really loved being at

Shawn's, that she loved Kate and the cats, but that David had stirred up trouble by asking Karly, "Is Shawn going to be your new daddy? You love Shawn and not me, don't you?" According to Sarah, that's when Karly's attitude started to change, when she started pulling her hair out and hitting herself.

"Karly has been showing up with all these injuries," Sarah said. "Shawn is convinced David is harming Karly. Shawn said he put cortisone on her because it brings out bruises faster and he wanted to see what else David had done because he's convinced that David's not appropriate with Karly. He's trying to bring the bruises out so we can show what David does."

Shawn had been taking pictures to document the abuse, Sarah said. Shawn had even shown her photos that very morning of some of Karly's injuries.

"When Karly got to our house she was pretty bruised already, and then, you know, the bruises tend to get worse before they get better," Sarah said.

Sarah had noticed a bump on Karly's head earlier that week, and asked Karly what happened.

"She said her daddy hit her with a spoon. She had also said that her dad had hit her on her feet with a spoon for going potty."

Detective Wells asked if Sarah had noticed any bruising on Karly's feet.

"This morning she was crying so I was tickling her feet and it hurt her really bad. I looked at her feet; they were really swollen, and I said, 'What's wrong?' And she said, 'My daddy hit them with the spoon.' They were real tender."

Karly's feet weren't the only thing bruised that Friday morning, Sarah said. "When Karly got up this morning, it was totally shocking to see her. Her eye was swollen shut."

The more questions police asked, the more animated Sarah became, and the more convinced she was she'd better leave the hospital before David showed up. Sarah appeared so terrified of David that police considered him a real threat.

"Based on everything Sarah told us, we saw David as a threat and a potential suspect," Wells said. They began to make plans to keep David and Sarah away from each other, not only at the hospital, but also later throughout the night.

Police told Sarah and Shelley they could not return to their apartment. It had been secured by police and would be searched. No problem, Shelley said; they could stay at her parents' house in nearby Salem.

In his summary notes, Wells said Sarah had trouble keeping information straight. "Based on my training and experience, her demeanor, reactions, emotional state, and ability to recall information were consistent with victims of crimes and those who have been traumatized by events," Wells said.

The detective would later change his mind about why Sarah couldn't keep her story straight. "Interviewing Sarah was exhausting," Wells said. "She was the most draining individual I've ever interviewed. If I asked her what her address was, she'd take twenty minutes to answer. She couldn't remember anything. She was quiet, had an almost monotone voice. She never volunteered anything.

"Sarah was extremely cautious, watching her own back, always making sure she wasn't going to get tripped up and charged with anything. She is way smarter than she comes off."

Shawn Field's behavior hadn't been normal either. Emergency crews who arrived at 2652 NW Aspen Street thought it odd that the sandy-haired man, wearing nothing but athletic shorts and sunglasses shoved back on his head, kept pacing back and forth, "like a trapped animal."

Instead of offering to help the police officers and other medical personnel as they had attended to Karly, Shawn busied himself pushing a heavy wood dining room table up against a bedroom door. He then tossed the dining room chairs atop it.

Andy Louden, a battalion chief with the Corvallis Fire Department, at first thought Shawn was moving the furniture to make way for the medic crew. He'd witnessed Shawn attempt to comfort Sarah earlier. As Shawn embraced her, he rested his hands on Sarah's breasts, momentarily fondling them. It was a crass gesture that struck Louden as wildly inappropriate.

Gary Thurman, one of the emergency medical technicians, went outside to get the backboard to put Karly on. As he was going back inside the duplex, he overheard Shawn talking to Sarah.

"Don't talk to the paramedics, don't talk to the police," he urged.

Lieutenant Steve Bowen, also with the Corvallis Fire Department, heard the same thing. Bowen told Chief Louden what he and Thurman overheard. Louden offered to take both Sarah and Shawn to the hospital, but Shawn said no, he'd better not go, that his daughter Kate was due home soon. He didn't know dispatchers had already called the school and told them to keep Kate there.

Sergeant Fieman told Shawn investigators were going to need his help around the place in order to determine why Karly stopped breathing. Fieman called headquarters and told them he was pretty sure they had a homicide on their hands, that somebody needed to get some search warrants in order. The Benton County Major Crime Investigation Team had been notified. Harvey and Wells were en route.

Fieman looked around the place. The car in the driveway, a pristine white Aspire, had a child's car seat in the back and a Bush/Cheney sticker on the bumper. An empty Starbucks cup was in the console. An American flag hung motionless from the apartment's doorpost.

An assortment of tennis shoes, big ones and little ones, were lined up just inside the doorway. The child had been found lying partly on the white carpet of the living room and the cold linoleum before emergency crews had whisked her away. A child's pink coat hung from the coat rack. On the wall behind the rack was a framed copy of famous love quotes.

Pushed up against the west wall was a leather sectional, all white, draped with an orange-and-black Oregon State Beaver throw. A black-and-white cat lay asleep on the couch. A child's white rocker sat motionless in the sunrays coming through the sliding-glass door onto the south patio. Dishes were washed and stacked.

Down the hallway were several ornately framed oversize portraits of a dark-haired girl, Shawn's daughter, Kate. A Hillary Duff poster was pinned to the shut door on Fieman's right. He opened it cautiously. Bold letters spelled out the child's name on one wall: K-A-T-E. To his immediate left, a set of metal-frame bunk beds was pushed up against the wall. Red curtains hung from the window across the room.

The leopard-print bedding of the top bunk had been left unmade. There was no mattress on the bottom bunk; just a couple of small boxes, holding frames or books, and various other belongings. There were more posters pinned to the ceiling.

Missing was any sign to indicate a three-year-old lived in this home. The only photos were Kate's, the only artwork hers. The clothes in the closet were Kate's. There wasn't a bed, not even a mattress on the floor for Karly. There was an absence of anything that spoke to her life in the place, that Karly had even been a guest there. She slept on the floor where the cats prowled, with only a pink pillow and a blanket.

Fieman continued down the hallway. Just past the bathroom, he saw the pile of dining room furniture Shawn had shoved up against a door. It didn't take police officers long to figure out the reason for the barricade. Fieman noted there were six planting pots on the counter in the kitchen.

Fieman looked over at Shawn, who'd put on a t-shirt and was

pacing around the living room.

"My daughter will be home from school very soon," Shawn said. "What am I going to tell her?"

Fieman didn't answer, not at first. Then, tucking his chin down and cutting his eyes toward Shawn, Fieman offered him a bit of advice: "If it was me, I'd tell anyone who asked me the straight-out truth."

Shawn stopped pacing as Fieman continued, "I'm not going to ask you any questions about Karla at this time, but let's just say I did, or somebody else was to—if it were me, I'd tell the whole truth so everybody would know exactly what happened."

Shawn stood still.

Fieman shrugged his shoulders, lifted his chin, and looked straight into Shawn's eyes. "The police are going to find out the truth anyway; you might as well tell it to them up front."

Shawn's head dropped so low his chin was almost resting on his chest. Closing his eyes, Shawn whispered, "Oh, God."

The veteran police officer took Shawn's sigh to mean one thing: defeat.

Fieman shared his observations with Detectives Harvey and Wells when they arrived.

"Situations like this require we do an investigation," Detective Harvey said after introducing himself to Shawn.

"I understand," Shawn replied. His voice was soft, agreeable, but his demeanor was anxious. There were no tears, no outbursts of grief, but Shawn seemed nervous.

"I'd like to search the place, see if there's anything that might help us determine what happened to Karla, if that's okay with you," Harvey said. "There's not anything illegal in the house that you're worried about, is there?"

Just moments later, Shawn confided to Officer Steve Teeter: "I can't believe what I did in my bedroom. My life is over."

"What do you mean your life is over?" Teeter asked, his eyes widening.

"That guy over there will tell you all about it," Shawn said, nodding his head toward Harvey, who had walked outside to talk privately with Sergeant Fieman.

A few minutes later, when Harvey returned, Teeter told him about the exchange with Shawn.

"He's got a marijuana grow in the bedroom," Harvey said.

That explained the blockade Shawn had constructed from the dining room furniture, but it raised other questions. For starters, who worries about getting in trouble with the law for growing marijuana plants when there's a battered child lying on the floor, not breathing?

That's one of the questions Detective Harvey hoped to settle when he asked Shawn to join him at the Law Enforcement Center. Shawn Field was not under arrest.

Not yet.

Shawn said he'd be glad to go in for questioning, but first he'd have to see to his daughter. School was nearly out. Sure, go ahead, not a problem, Harvey said. But Shawn changed his mind, called Eileen Field, his ex-wife, and asked if she could pick up Kate. Something had come up that needed his undivided attention.

In the patrol car, on their way to the police station, Harvey got a call from Wells.

"The girl's dead. Beaten to death," Wells said.

"Got it," Harvey said, cutting his eyes at Shawn.

"There's more," Wells said, pausing. "The emergency room doctor said there's evidence she was sexually assaulted."

David spent a fitful Friday night at John Hogan's place. Earlier that evening, Detective Stauder and another officer had interviewed David at the hospital. The three-hour interview was grueling, particularly given that David was still in a state of shock. The detectives asked if he had anything to do with Karly's death. David replied that he hadn't seen Karly since Monday.

"What do you think happened?" Detective Stauder asked.

"I suspect Karly was over at Shawn's house—she doesn't like being over there—so Karly was acting out and Sarah couldn't deal with that. I think she overreacted," David said.

"Have you ever had any funny feelings about Shawn?" Detective Stauder asked. "Like a mother's intuition kind of thing?"

"He's a liar and a fraud," David said.

Detective Stauder warned David that his own house had been sealed off so Corvallis Police Department's evidence team could give it a thorough search. They seized the sheets from the laundry and an unlaundered Nike t-shirt that belonged to Karly. It had a red stain on the front. David told them it was from their last meal together, the pizza they had before he dropped her at Sarah's on Monday.

Wells warned investigators to be on the lookout for wooden spoons. Sarah told Wells that David used wooden spoons to discipline Karly. Every drawer, every cupboard, all closets, and all garbage cans were checked for a wooden spoon; the Corvallis Police found none. What investigators did find in David's home were toys galore, dozens of framed snapshots of Karly, and racks of the girl's clothes hanging in the closet. "It was apparent Mr. Sheehan was dedicated to Karly," the police report concluded.

Detective Wells came to the same conclusion. "Once we did the search and met David we could tell he was a victim. For most of us, David was out of the picture as a prime suspect that night."

CHAPTER THIRTY-ONE

E MMET WHITTAKER WAS IN THE south of France, two months into a
six-month trip around the world, in June 2005 when he received
a disturbing e-mail from his good friend David Sheehan.

It wasn't so much wanderlust that took Emmet away from his job at
HP as it was this nagging feeling that there had to be something more
purposeful to life than work. Emmet wasn't yet sure if he wanted to settle
in the U.S. He had come to Corvallis in 1996 along with David Sheehan
and a host of other Irish natives for training at HP's headquarters, and
he'd fallen in love with a girl named Sanna, who also worked at HP.

When Emmet's tenure on the green card was up, Emmet took
Sanna home to Dublin, where he continued to work for HP. But while
Sanna loved Emmet's Ireland, it wasn't home for her. Sanna went back
to HP in Corvallis, and Emmet took a leave of absence from work and
set out to see the world.

Keeping in touch with friends, even good friends, can be difficult
when traveling.

"Dave and I are the kind of friends who like to sit down over coffee,
breakfast or a pint and discuss life a bit," Emmet said. His distinct
Dublin accent carries a weightiness of wars fought and lost.

As he traveled, Emmet kept in touch with David primarily by e-mail and the occasional phone call, but David had not told Emmet about Karly's deteriorating condition, the state's investigation, or Sarah's new boyfriend. Nor had David discussed with Emmet his fear of deportation, although it's a common fear among immigrants.

"If you are on a green card, you are a guest of that nation," Emmet said. "If you show up on the radar for anything, even if it's unwarranted, you can be deported. It's a very real fear."

Still, Emmet knew nothing of the terror Karly had endured or the fears David left unspoken until the bright June day in 2005 when Emmet received a phone call from an HP coworker who told him Karly was dead, and shortly thereafter an e-mail from David, telling him the same. Emmet sat down before a computer screen in an Internet café in the south of France and logged into his e-mail.

"I was greatly shocked," Emmet said. "The e-mail was quite short. He said Karly was dead. I believe he said she was murdered. I was absolutely horrified."

Emmet left the café after sending David a note back, telling him if he needed anything at all that Emmet was there for him. Then Emmet when straight to the home of his goddaughter and her mother, where he'd been staying, and wept freely for David and Karly.

"I was horrified by it, thinking about Karly. It was gut-wrenching."

Emmet followed the news of Karly's murder from afar, reading the local newspaper reports in the *Gazette Times*. He called Sanna and asked her to go to David, to see if there was anything she could do to be of help.

News of Karly's death spread rapidly through the offices and hallways at Hewlett-Packard. Although Liz Sokolowski and David Sheehan worked for the same company, the two had never spoken. Still, she knew who he was, knew he was married, or had been. When she heard about Karly's murder from her friend Sanna, she was staggered by the news.

"You have this perception that those things happen, but not to anyone you know," Liz said. "There was this disbelief that it could happen at all, but that it happened to someone I'd seen around, who seemed like a very gentle and kind individual…you don't expect that."

Tragedy is the unseen sibling of every Polish child. Liz had grown up in Chicago, a member of one of the largest Polish communities outside of Warsaw. Sacrifice and suffering were common topics of discussion at the dinner table, as her parents told and retold the story of how Liz's great-grandmother had been a POW in Siberia. Soldiers had marched into the house and snatched her away from her terrified children. Twice Poland has been completely wiped from the maps, first by the Germans and then by the Russians—their daughters and mothers raped, their sons and fathers slaughtered. "I heard all those sad things growing up," Liz said.

It's a gift, knowing where you come from and who your people are. It enables a person to see a connectedness from country to country, from generation to generation, from person to person, and it keeps us from being too self-centered, too self-interested.

Liz was shocked and horribly sad for David, but she didn't know him well enough to approach him, to tell him how terribly sorry she was for his loss, to give him a hug, the way she's prone to do for anyone, any time they are hurting. The hearts of so many people at HP and in the broader community of Corvallis went out to David, but it's hard to know what to say, what to do, when a child is murdered. They wept and prayed for him, they sent hundreds of condolence cards, and they swore that from here on out they would be more watchful, for all the children's sakes.

CHAPTER THIRTY-TWO

D ISTRICT ATTORNEY SCOTT HEISER WAS buckled down writing search warrants for the Benton County Major Crime Investigation Team, per their request, and getting updates from the detectives at the scene. Two things in particular concerned Heiser: Why was Shawn Field taking photos of Karly Sheehan? And what was up with Sarah Sheehan?

"Sarah's demeanor was almost across the line," Heiser said. "She was so hysterical you had to wonder if she wasn't involved in this somehow."

Heiser drafted a warrant to seize Shawn Field's camera.

Investigators found photos of a very battered Karly on the camera's disc. Heiser wasn't yet sure about all the details of Karly's death, but by midafternoon, Heiser was certain Shawn was their guy.

And he thought the motive was the same issue that had plagued Sarah her entire adult life: money. Investigators theorized Shawn was abusing Karly and documenting the abuse with photographs for the purpose of extorting money from David.

David had not made child-support payments to Sarah because with her gambling problems, Sarah couldn't be trusted to spend the money on Karly. David paid for everything Karly needed: childcare, clothing, and medical care. In addition, David was paying off thousands in gambling debt that Sarah saddled him with in the divorce agreement.

David set up a college fund for his daughter. He had even discussed paying for Sarah to complete her college education, reasoning that the better educated Sarah was, the better a mother she'd be to Karly.

Sarah had attended college off and on for ten years, ever since she had left our house and moved to Corvallis, but in all that time, she had never completed her degree. David wanted Sarah to pursue a profession, to be a good role model to Karly. He was willing to help underwrite Sarah's education to make that happen.

From the beginning of the police intervention, Sarah and Shawn were both fingering David as the primary suspect in Karly's death, even though David hadn't even seen Karly in nearly a week.

Investigators, however, suspected Sarah was complicit in her daughter's death, theorizing that she was out to "prove" David Sheehan was beating his daughter. Then Sarah would get full custody of Karly— and the regular monthly child-support payment that went along with custody. David was making plans to move to Portland in August with Karly. Investigators learned that Sarah had borrowed $1,000 to hire an attorney to fight for custody. Sarah said she was worried that David would take Karly and move out of the country.

She saw an attorney, Hal Harding, in early 2005, and had taken along that sketchy four-day diary that she'd kept, supposedly documenting the ways in which David was abusing Karly. But she told Detective Wells that instead of using the money to hire a lawyer she had used it to pay some bills or something—she couldn't remember what she'd spent it on exactly.

Detective Harvey finished his last interview with Shawn shortly before 7 p.m. on Friday, June 3, 2005. Shawn said he was tired and asked the officer if there was some place he could lie down. He was shown to a quiet room with a sofa, where he rested until 9 p.m., when Shawn told Harvey he was ready to leave. Harvey arranged for a patrol officer to give Shawn a ride anywhere he wanted to go.

After Shawn left, Harvey informed Heiser that during his preliminary interviews, Shawn "blamed David for everything. At no time during this interview did he blame Sarah for Karla's injuries."

Heiser told Harvey to arrest Shawn—not for murder, but for manufacturing a controlled substance. At approximately 9:30 p.m. on Friday, June 3, 2005, Shawn Wesley Field was arrested as he got out of a patrol car in front of the police station. The charge was manufacturing and delivery of a controlled substance within one thousand feet of a school.

That charge was updated on Monday, June 6, 2005, when Shawn Wesley Field was charged with the murder of Karla Sheehan.

Detective Harvey had earlier read Field his Miranda rights, so he just cuffed him and booked him into custody.

CHAPTER THIRTY-THREE

GOD STOPPED THE ABUSE.

That's what Delynn had told me the day we met at the bakery. "God was the only one who could stop it," Delynn said. "We were all failing. Everybody was failing her. I know God intervened because of Karly's prayers."

The community learned about Karly's prayer from Sarah, who testified about it. Sarah said Karly had woken up complaining that her head and tummy hurt. Sarah had not been home on Thursday, June 2, 2005. The bar where she worked had a promotional event that night, and Sarah, who was scheduled to work from 4 p.m. to 7:30 p.m., had left Karly with Shawn earlier that afternoon.

Shawn was angry when Sarah drove off. Livid, Sarah recalled. They'd had a fight because she'd failed to pay the water bill and the water had been shut off. He threatened that if she didn't get over to the city water department and have the water turned back on she'd be sorry she'd ever met him. When Sarah pulled out of the drive, she looked in her rearview mirror. Shawn was holding her daughter.

"Karly looked fine, physically," Sarah recalled. "But emotionally, she just looked defeated."

Sarah paid the water bill, but didn't have enough money to pay the reconnect fee. She hurried back to her own apartment, changed for work, borrowed some money from her roommate Shelley, and then rushed back to the water department. She paid the reconnect fee and begged the city staff to *please, please* turn the water back on before closing for the day. They assured her they would.

Despite leaving her *defeated-looking* daughter in Shawn's care, Sarah did not return to Shawn's until shortly before midnight. She'd clocked out of work at Suds at 7:45 p.m., but instead of rushing back to look after Karly, she stayed for the party. She drank several beers and went to the parking lot with one of the beer distributors, where police reported the two participated in fellatio.

The jury, however, did not hear the specifics of what Sarah did on Thursday evening after her shift ended. The prosecuting attorney argued in pre-trial, "The fact that Sarah remained with a patron after clocking out is only relevant in that it shows Karly was alone, except for the defendant's nine-year-old daughter, during which time Karly was beaten severely. Evidence regarding with whom Sarah spent her time, in what activities she engaged, what she drank, what she ate, how many times she used the restroom, etc., is all irrelevant to the issue at hand."

The judge agreed, if the wider world does not.

Sarah had broken up with Shawn two weeks before Karly's death after finding gay pornography on Shawn's computer. She claimed the discovery left her feeling "really shocked and sick"—not because she thought being gay was a bad thing, but because she was worried there might be child pornography on the computer as well. Searching quickly through Shawn's files, Sarah was able to determine the sites did not involve any child porn, but she did find several e-mail exchanges between Shawn and men he met online.

Shawn's ex-wife, Eileen, testified that she had made the same sort of discovery after breaking into a safe belonging to Shawn. "I knew he was hiding something," Eileen said. What she found inside the safe shocked her. There were photos of men in various states of undress and an e-mail from a man who claimed he was having a relationship with Shawn. "He said if Shawn didn't pay him money, he was going to tell me about the relationship," Eileen said.

Like Eileen, Sarah confronted Shawn. He was incensed.

"Irate. Outraged," Sarah said, describing that moment. "He kept saying I'd ruined everything. He screamed at me to get out, to get my shit and get out. 'Leave,' he said. 'I can't believe you did this to me.' He was angry. He sat down at the computer and screamed 'NO!' and looked at me in a scary way."

After Shawn's arrest, a prominent Oregon State University employee came forward to police, worried his dalliances with Shawn would be made public. Investigators assured him he had nothing to worry about. His sexual encounters with Shawn were not deemed relevant to the murder of Karly.

As a teen, Shawn had been grossly obese, hitting over three hundred pounds. This was a point of consternation for his father Hugh, who had also struggled with his weight as a child. Hugh is a highly disciplined man, a math professional who spent a career working at Hewlett-Packard. He and his wife Ann were devastated when their eldest son, Kevin, died of a drug overdose. In the aftermath of Kevin's death, Shawn became focused on his own health. He began to exercise regularly, and switched his fare of pizza and hamburgers for low-fat buffalo and other healthy food. Shawn relished the attention his new physique brought him. He became obsessive about his hygiene, his weight, and his workout schedule.

Shawn was collecting thousands of dollars a year from his parents' estate, all part of Hugh's plan to ensure their only living child wouldn't have to pay high inheritance taxes. But had his parents known about their son's homosexual activities, they would likely have cut Shawn off financially. That alone was reason enough for Shawn to want to hide his sexual encounters with other men.

Shawn was not teaching at the university as he had claimed. In fact, even though he was thirty-three years old, he had never held down a full-time job for any consistent period of time. His primary source of income came from his mom and dad. Eileen and Sarah's accidental discovery threatened the matchstick house Shawn had so carefully constructed.

During the trial, the prosecutor attempted to portray her as a victim, a woman manipulated and so emotionally abused by the man she lived with that she couldn't possibly think rationally. The prosecutor hoped it would help explain why Sarah repeatedly left Karly with Shawn for extended periods of time, despite having promised David and others that she wouldn't.

Members of the jury I spoke with said they wholeheartedly rejected the notion of Sarah as a victim. Several stated it was likely they would have found Sarah guilty of neglect, reckless endangerment or more had the district attorney charged her.

Although she had left her daughter in obvious distress, Sarah did not check on Karly when she got back to Shawn's Thursday night. She said Shawn didn't like it when she went into the girls' room after they were asleep because he didn't want her waking them. Sarah testified that Shawn had told her Karly hurt herself that night by jumping from the top bunk and hitting her head. Still Sarah did not bother checking on Karly to make sure she was okay.

The next morning, Friday, June 3, 2005, Karly woke with her left eye swollen shut. Doctors would later declare it ruptured. Shawn reminded

Sarah about the "fall" that had happened while Sarah was at the bar Thursday night. After a prompting from Shawn, Karly reportedly gave her mother a weak "Ta-da," like an acrobat performing a circus act. Neither Shawn nor Sarah sought medical attention for Karly, even though the girl was in glaring physical distress, crying red tears—literally blood.

Once Kate left for school, Sarah gave Karly a handful of trail mix for breakfast and then joined Shawn in the bedroom. The two had sex while Karly sat on the floor of the living room, sick to her stomach, fighting a headache, watching cartoons, one eye blinded.

Afterward, Shawn left for the athletic club, and Sarah turned her attention to cleaning. She wiped down the baseboards and vacuumed, trying to rid the place of cat hair, she later explained in court.

Karly sat on the couch, or on the floor, unable to walk because the soles of her feet were badly bruised. Sarah had noticed Karly's swollen feet when Shawn brought her to Sarah earlier that morning. But when Sarah asked Karly what had happened, Shawn interrupted, "Remember? I told you she was jumping off the bunk bed last night." Sarah didn't ask any more questions.

After she finished cleaning, Sarah picked up Karly.

"She was just really clingy," Sarah said. "She wanted to be held a lot."

Sarah carried Karly into Kate's bedroom. "I was going to lie down with her for a little bit. There were some stuffed animals on the floor and Karly looked at me and said, 'Mommy, I want to go see Jesus.'"

Picking up a couple of the plush toys, Sarah tried to engage her daughter in a bit of role-playing. It was a technique a counselor had taught Sarah: a tool to get Karly to talk about things.

Sitting on the floor, stuffed animals in hand, Sarah asked Karly if she wanted to pray.

"Yes," Karly said.

Sarah prayed aloud for Jesus to come and heal her daughter, to make Karly's tummy and head feel all better.

Then Karly prayed: "I want to go be with Jesus. Amen."

Chapter Thirty-Four

I'M TYPING THIS FROM A cottage in Fairhope, Alabama. A tangerine sun is slipping into Mobile Bay. It is Father's Day, 2008. As I sat on a bench near the pier, watching the sun disappear, a little girl walked past, yelling out to anyone listening, "I like that bird! That bird there! See it!"

She pointed at a long-beaked pelican flying overhead.

The girl was wearing a blue-jean skirt, white sandals, and a pink polo top. Her white-blonde hair was shoulder-length, like Karly's had once been. Karly is frozen in time for me now—forever three, instead of the growing girl she should be.

I see her when I'm at the grocer's or when I'm out walking on the pier. I see her chasing the foamy surf at Gulf Shores, and eating ice cream at Mr. Gene Beans. I see her standing in line at Winn-Dixie, itsy-bitsy tattoo stickers spattered about her face like DayGlo freckles. I see her carrying a pink fishing pole, trailing her daddy, step for step. Wherever I see Karly, I also think of David.

David sent me a text message and said no one had wished him a Happy Father's Day today. I suppose they think it is best not to mention his loss—as if David could ever forget Karly, reminder or no.

"Karly made me laugh so much," David said, though I know he cries now.

David and I have a comfortable relationship. It's as if we walk around, slipping in and out of the same worn house slippers. He puts his grief on, I take mine off. He is the daughterless father; I am the fatherless daughter. We don't need to say anything to each other on days like this, on Father's Day.

It was Father's Day, 2001, when David first found out he was going to be a daddy. The news was a surprise, coming at a time when the marriage was threatened.

Sarah did as she pleased. When they weren't getting along, she'd move out, then back in, a trademark pattern marring Sarah's relationship with men. Sarah was back at home after a stint of being gone when she revealed she was pregnant.

David had made some off-the-cuff comment about hoping any child they might have wouldn't be burdened with his big head. David thinks he has a pumpkin head.

Sarah replied, "We'll know soon enough."

"What do you mean?" David asked, confused.

"I'm pregnant," Sarah said.

David was jubilant. Family meant everything to him. The toughest part about leaving Ireland was leaving behind the family he loved so well. Families in Ireland are less fragmented than families in the U.S. That's partly due to geography—Ireland is small, compact. Americans are more mobile but the Irish have an easier time getting together as a family for weekly gatherings, something David's family did frequently. In Ireland, family is the social network.

A child would root David in ways a job could not. There would be soccer matches in his near future—afternoons spent kicking the ball around with his very own child. A family to call his own in America.

The months that followed, the months when Sarah was pregnant with Karly, were the happiest times David and Sarah shared. Sarah quit smoking, drinking, running around at night. She settled in and nested.

Surely, this baby would tether them together and shine some love on them both.

Chapter Thirty-Five

THE TRIAL OF THE STATE vs. Shawn W. Field lasted twenty-six days: twenty-three days of testimony and three days of jury deliberation. It takes a considerable amount of taxpayer money to put on a trial, and cash-strapped counties try to avoid such lengthy trials. In fact, Heiser did offer Shawn a plea agreement: if Shawn would plead out, Heiser would make sure he only got twenty-five years in the slammer. But Shawn's defense attorney, Clark Willes, turned it down. Heiser noted in his letter to Willes that the purpose of the offer "is to save resources."

"We can have a meaningful discussion about a possible settlement of the case without wasting a great deal of time and money," Heiser suggested.

The offer was made two days after the grand jury returned a true bill on June 13, 2005. After hearing testimony from a host of people, Sarah included, the grand jury charged Shawn with five counts of aggravated murder; one count of first-degree murder; two counts of murder; three counts of murder by abuse (torture); four counts of manslaughter in the first-degree; three counts of assault in the second-degree; two counts of criminal mistreatment; one count of manufacturing a controlled substance; and two counts of endangering the welfare of a minor.

A prosecutor generally gets one shot at indictment, so they charge everything that fits. So many charges may confuse jurors and the public, but there are strategic reasons for this. It is one way to ensure that those guilty don't get away with murder.

Because Sarah testified before the grand jury, she was exempt from being charged with any crime. The decision to put her before the grand jury, to not charge her with any crime, was made solely by District Attorney Heiser.

He denies his decision was the result of being manipulated by Sarah. Heiser and police investigators said they figured out pretty quickly Sarah was a flirt who employed her wiles to try to influence them.

I tried numerous times to meet Heiser in person, but we were unable to work out our schedules. We finally agreed to a phone interview. I had one question in particular I wanted him to answer: Why did he not charge Sarah with any crime?

"There was probable cause to charge Sarah for exposing her daughter to Shawn Field," Heiser said. "At a minimum, she was reckless. She analyzed everything from her own interest first."

But Heiser said his decision to not charge Sarah was purely an emotional one.

"I chose not to charge Sarah Sheehan with anything, recklessly endangering a minor or neglect, because I weighed the cost benefit. What do we bring to the safety of the community by raking her through the coals? It was a mercy decision, based solely on empathy and grief. I felt like she had already paid a high enough price."

Besides, he noted, there wasn't enough evidence to prove Sarah had physically abused her daughter in any way. Heiser remains on the fence about whether Sarah was involved in the scheme to extort money from David.

"The question is, was she involved or did she have knowledge about the plan to frame David and to extort money from him?" Heiser said. "I don't believe she was, but she may have been. I wouldn't be shocked to find out that she was."

District attorneys make compromises. Their positions require it of them. Heiser was willing to sacrifice the wrongs committed by Sarah Sheehan against her daughter in an effort to build a stronger case against Shawn Field.

Somewhere in those first few days after Karly's death, Heiser convinced himself Sarah Sheehan's betrayal of her daughter was not sufficient to warrant a criminal conviction. He told himself Karly's death was punishment enough for this mother.

Heiser's decision not to charge Sarah with any crime wasn't all that surprising. Historically, the courts have been far more lenient toward women than men. Until recently, women were less likely to be formally charged with crime, and more often than not, when they were charged, they were likely to receive probation.

"The woman nearly always gets a lesser sentence and is viewed merely as a compliant accomplice, especially if men are handling the case," said Kathleen Ramsland. Ramsland teaches forensic psychology at DeSales University and has written numerous books on forensics and crime. "I think men are afraid of knowing women might be capable of real brutality, so they default to a softer view, mostly to preserve their own sense of insecurity. Some admit it, too."

But those views of women are changing.

The Bureau of Justice reports that between 2000 and 2008 the number of women incarcerated increased by thirty-three percent. The biggest contributing factor is drug and alcohol abuse. According to her friends, Sarah's drug of choice was alcohol and a smorgasbord of prescription drugs. Investigators had discovered what they described as a "ton of prescriptions" in Sarah's name.

"Sarah could be lot of fun," said one of her former girlfriends. "But she had mood swings. She'd be high for five minutes and then it was like she went catatonic. She'd be very flat, like she was in her own world. I pulled back after I saw too many troubling things in her personality. I didn't know how stable a person she was."

While Human Services investigators were relentless in their assumptions about David, they were disturbingly negligent in their assumptions about Sarah. If the roles of father and mother had been reversed in the death of Karly, what are the chances prosecutors would have determined the father had suffered enough already? Would the system have overlooked any contributory role David may have played in his daughter's death the way they did with Sarah?

Highly unlikely, said Eugene attorney Bill Furtick. A man who'd worked with the state's juvenile court system for decades, Furtick was called in on one of Oregon's most notorious crimes: the case of Diane Downs.

On May 19, 1983, a young woman reported she had been carjacked on a rural road in Springfield, Oregon, by an unidentified male, who, she then claimed, shot her and her children. One child, a seven-year-old girl, was killed. The two surviving children, a girl, age eight, and a boy, age three, suffered paralysis as a result of the shooting. Furtick was the court-appointed attorney for the living children.

Diane Downs, the children's mother, was later convicted of the attack, a deed she carried out as an attempt to hang on to a married boyfriend who didn't want children. Downs, a verifiable narcissist, was sentenced to life in prison.

Getting the conviction took some doing.

"The construct of the entire investigative and training paradigm for the State of Oregon is built on the idea that only men do domestic violence," Furtick said. "Men are seen as the abusers. Fathers, not mothers. Of course that's not always true."

Mothers acting alone commit the bulk of child abuse, but the judicial system has cultivated a bias toward men and allotted women preferential treatment. "There is a bias," said Dr. Debra Esernio-Jenssen, medical director for the Children Protection Team at the University of Florida. "I think society accepts that a man may not be a good caregiver. As a whole, society expects women to be nurturing caregivers."

After Karly's death, Mindy Brill, Sarah's former sister-in-law and close friend, told investigators that Sarah lacked a bond with Karly.

"Are you saying the nurturing mechanism was absent?" asked Detective Stauder.

"Yes," Mindy said. "But Carol and Sarah aren't very close. I think that has something to do with her relationship with Karly. And she gave Hillary up for adoption. I think that's affected her with Karly a lot. I think she's tried, but Sarah needs to get past that self-centeredness she has."

A former childcare provider for Karly said, "Sarah was a party mom. Everybody knew David was there to pick up the pieces."

CHAPTER THIRTY-SIX

SCOTT HEISER ASKED A DEPUTY district attorney who had turned in her resignation the week prior to take on the case. It was an unusual move. District attorneys typically handle the high-profile stuff themselves, for obvious political reasons. But it had been a hectic couple of years for Heiser and the Corvallis Police Department.

Heiser felt Joan Demarest would be the best woman for the job. He makes no bones about the fact that he appointed a woman attorney as the lead prosecutor for tactical reasons. He knew having a woman prosecutor would earn some favor with the jury in a child murder case.

Demarest grew up in Corvallis and earned her law degree from the University of Oregon. The victimization of women was a common topic of discussion in her childhood home. Joan Demarest's mother, Merry Demarest, has been a longtime member of the National Organization for Women, and has served on the organization's national board.

Demarest's father, Harry, is the former chair of the Benton County Democratic Party. The family continues to be politically active. They campaigned heavily for Hillary Clinton during the 2008 presidential election. Demarest's parents celebrated their thirty-sixth wedding anniversary by testifying before the Benton County Commissioners in support of same-sex marriage.

Demarest began her career in Corvallis as a law intern, and continued working for as a deputy district attorney for Benton County after passing the bar in 1998. But tensions around the courthouse and the birth of her first child had her rethinking her career choice. She'd already given her two-weeks notice when she stopped by Heiser's office one afternoon.

"It's too bad you're leaving," Heiser said. "I was going to assign you the Field case."

Because Demarest had been off on maternity leave in the three months prior she wasn't familiar with Shawn Field. Heiser took the next few hours to explain the case to her. Demarest asked for the weekend to consider it.

Before she could accept the job, Demarest had to come to terms with her own position on the death penalty. She had previously been an opponent. Shawn Field changed her thoughts about that.

After consulting with her husband and her parents, Demarest took the job on a contract basis.

"This was a case where I knew I could make a difference," Demarest said. "Shawn Field was a monster who needed justice and I was determined to not let Sarah Sheehan jeopardize his shot at life in prison or the death penalty."

When Demarest and I met a few times at a coffee house in Corvallis, she brought along her children. Demarest is a hands-on, attentive mom. Our meetings were scheduled to accommodate nap times and play dates.

There's no question the lady lawyer felt she was defending Sarah as much as she was prosecuting Shawn Field. "I'm convinced Sarah had nothing to do with Karly's abuse or death, aside from picking Shawn Field as a mate," Demarest said.

It was Heiser who irrevocably determined that Sarah would be a victim in a murder trial and not a co-defendant when he subpoenaed her to testify at the grand jury hearing. The Fifth Amendment ensured that Sarah would never face charges in her daughter's death.

Demarest was left to deal with the fallout of that. Under Oregon Law, Sarah was by definition a victim as the mother of a murdered child.

"Most people vilify Sarah without understanding the circumstances she was in, and without looking further," the attorney said. "I know that some of Sarah's personality traits and choices make it easy to do that. Through my work on this case I learned that emotional abuse is more effective than physical abuse at controlling other people."

But it was physical abuse that caused Karly's death.

Demarest asked the jury to weigh the evidence against Shawn and overlook any wrongdoing on Sarah's behalf. If the jurors had begun to divvy up the blame for Karly's death between Shawn and Sarah, it could have derailed the entire criminal case. The prosecution needed to keep the focus on Shawn.

"It wasn't until after I had spent hours with experts that I was able to see Sarah with a more sympathetic eye," Demarest said. "Shawn Field undermined whatever self-confidence she may have had, convinced her she knew nothing about parenting and that she was a bad mother."

Sarah said Shawn trained her to not question him. So she didn't.

Except that one time, when she confronted him about the gay pornography she found on his computer. Certainly, that took some steely-eyed gumption. So why did Sarah leave Karly with Shawn after seeing her daughter in such physical distress Friday morning? Instead of leaving Karly alone with Shawn, breaking a repeated promise to David and DHS, why didn't Sarah take Karly to daycare? David had already paid for it. If she had to go to work, why not take Karly to Delynn's on her way?

Perhaps Sarah knew Delynn would take one look at Karly's ruptured eyeball, those swollen and bruised feet, and do the thing Sarah had failed to do that morning: take Karly to the ER immediately. Sarah did not take Karly to Delynn's because she was covering for Shawn. Sarah knew Delynn was on to her and Shawn; he didn't want the state poking around anymore.

Demarest knew this, of course, which is why she had to build a case to explain away Sarah's actions. "I tried to find a way to make sense of what Sarah did and everything that happened," Demarest said. "The abuse and control made the most sense, even though it didn't explain everything."

I wondered if Demarest's upbringing didn't predispose her to see Sarah as a victim, rather than someone complicit in her daughter's death. Demarest became visibly annoyed when I told her that some community members had suggested as much. Her cheeks flushed hot, and she sat back rigidly in her chair.

"Who said that?" she asked. "Clark Willes? Did he say it?"

Clark Willes was one of Shawn's defense attorneys, although not the lead lawyer on the case. Dan Koenig, who has cultivated a reputation for getting the bad guy off, had that honor. But the contention between Demarest and Willes stretches back to the early 1800s and a religious leader by the name of Joseph Smith, founder of the Mormon Church.

At the time of Shawn Field's trial, Willes was an active Mormon bishop. Demarest told me her parents had, at their own request, been excommunicated from the Mormon Church. She said it was their way of protesting the church's stand regarding minorities in the priesthood.

Clark Willes likes to wear long-sleeve white shirts, which he rolls up on his thick forearms. His bushy dark eyebrows are prominent over his thin-framed glasses. He's a bit rumpled around the edges.

Willes is a study in contrasts. He is a Mormon bishop who helped defend a child killer, an attorney who often finds himself on the wrong side of the law. He's been brought before the Oregon Bar on disciplinary charges, and most recently was arraigned on charges of tampering with a witness.

I told Willes and Koenig I wasn't out to retry this case, that I trusted the jury had found the right person guilty. So what compelled Willes to turn over his case files on Shawn Field's defense to me? I asked Willes why he gave me access to the files during one of the several times we met. I'm not sure I ever got a satisfactory answer from him. It's an unusual move for an attorney to grant complete access to every bit of evidentiary material he amassed during the course of a trial. I was as surprised by it as anyone.

I understood why professionals like Heiser and Demarest might not like Clark Willes. As a former court reporter, I'd had intense arguments with Dennis Hachler, one of Oregon's best defense attorneys, about why he would defend some of the state's worst criminal offenders.

Hachler and I got upset with each other after he had me removed from court once to keep me from reporting on a school counselor who had sexually abused a child. Hachler told the judge he was going to call me as a witness because I had interviewed the child, and because I knew the counselor personally. Afterward, Hachler sent me flowers with an apology note and signed it, "From the Devil."

I was not amused. I sent the flowers back to the florist and told Hachler that he had overstepped his bounds. Despite the sparring, we respected each other. It was Hachler who told Willes I could be trusted—and I believe that if it had it not been for Dennis Hachler, I would never had gained access to hundreds of pages of police reports, recorded interviews, evidentiary material, photos and pretrial evidence that were critically important to this story.

District Attorney Heiser had concerns of his own about Clark Willes, but Heiser had the utmost confidence in Joan Demarest.

"Joan had considerable success with the less-than-honorable methods employed by Clark Willes," Heiser said. "And she was capable of dealing with what was often less than a level playing field in Judge Holcomb's courtroom."

It was a well-circulated rumor around the courthouse that there was no love lost between Heiser and Judge Holcomb. The two had come up through the ranks in the district attorney's office. There are some in Holcomb's camp who believe Heiser resented her success. Not so, said Heiser. It was the judge's unprofessional approach he resented.

The *Gazette-Times*, the local paper, reported that Heiser went so far as to file a motion imploring Judge Holcomb to recuse herself from the trial:

Benton County Circuit Court Judge Janet Holcomb won't step aside in the trial of Shawn Wesley Field. Holcomb is presiding over the trial of Field, who is charged with murder in the June 3, 2005, death of three-year-old Karla "Karly" Sheehan. Karly was the daughter of his then-girlfriend Sarah Brill Sheehan.

District Attorney Scott Heiser filed a motion Friday asking Holcomb to recuse herself because of evident bias against Deputy District Attorney Joan Demarest. Heiser included in his motion nine statements from the victim's family, friends and a sheriff's deputy, citing Holcomb's courtroom demeanor and expressions during pretrial hearings.

"The motion is without merit," Holcomb ruled Tuesday. "It is denied." She said firmly that the case would be tried on its merits. "It's not about the judge or lawyers," she said. "It's about Karly." The case will be tried without prejudice, fairly and impartially and in the highest judicial tradition, Holcomb promised.

She did not address complaints from Karly's father and grandparents, among others, that she did not maintain the decorum they expected in the courtroom, decorum they feel is appropriate in a case concerning the death of a three-year-old child.

Holcomb also did not address any of the specific charges in Heiser's motion. All parties declined to comment on Holcomb's ruling. Present Tuesday were Sarah Sheehan and David Sheehan, Karly's parents. Gene and Carol Brill, Karly's grandparents, were also present.

"It's tough," Gene Brill said, his voice full of emotion. "It's been a painful, painful year."

Although Judge Holcomb was dismayed by Heiser's complaint, she remained steadfast in her resolve to conduct the trial professionally and responsibly. "I didn't feel there was a legitimate reason for Heiser to make his request," Holcomb told me later. "Whatever controversy was there was his."

But Holcomb and Heiser did have a history together, and not all of it had been pleasant. Heiser had not supported Holcomb's bid for judge; he had, in fact, asked her not to enter the race. "He was upset about that, and I was surprised by how much that carried over during his tenure as district attorney," Judge Holcomb said.

The trial was difficult enough, given the trauma surrounding the murder of a three-year-old. Heiser's actions were disconcerting.

"Heiser added an extra layer of difficulty to a trial that was already difficult enough in terms of severity of emotions," Holcomb said. "It wasn't about the judge, or the lawyers. It was about Karly's murder."

Her goal as judge was to conduct the trial fairly and without prejudice.

"My rulings were meant to avoid a successful appeal later, so we didn't run the risk of trying the case all over again," Judge Holcomb said. "I believe I conducted myself with the highest degree of judicial integrity and I believe justice was served."

Chapter Thirty-Seven

NEARLY TWO WEEKS OF TRIAL testimony passed before ten-year-old Kate Field climbed into the witness box to testify against her father. She turned her shoulders so she was facing the jurors, not the defense table and the man sitting behind it: her daddy.

Kate's wide grin and expressive eyes were shrouded by her dark hair and an even darker mood. It's hard for a girl to testify against her father. It doesn't matter whether what he's done is right or wrong; what matters is that what you say may send your father to prison. Kate understood that above all else.

In those early days following Karly's death, Detective Stauder had interviewed Kate. Elisabeth Castillo from The Department of Human Services Child Welfare was there, along with Kate's mom, Eileen Field. Eileen had not yet told her young daughter that Karly was dead or that Shawn had been arrested.

"Can you remember what happened the last two days that you were in school last week, when you were at home?" Eileen Field had prompted her daughter.

Kate didn't answer.

"Can you tell me about what your dad told you about Karly's black eye or her red eye?" asked Detective Stauder.

Again, no answer.

"Are you scared? Do you want to write it down?" Eileen Field asked. Kate asked her mom what she wanted her to say.

"Just say what's true, okay? What you saw and heard."

Then Kate asked about Karly.

"Oh, Kate, I have to tell you something, okay? Karly got hurt and she's in Heaven now. Do you know what that means?"

"She got hurt and she went to Heaven?" Kate repeated, questioning.

"When people are in Heaven, will you see them anymore at home?" Detective Stauder asked.

"No," Kate said.

Detective Stauder left the room, leaving Eileen to question Kate.

"If you can remember, you need to tell us what you saw and what you heard those days," Eileen said.

"Ask me a question," Kate replied. "Not a hard one."

"Tell me what happened when you got home on Thursday after school."

"My dad had told me that Karly had a bruised eye," Kate said. "He showed me Karly's bruised eye. She didn't look good."

When Detective Stauder came back to the room, she remarked that Kate looked worried.

"I'm not worried," Kate said.

"Do you know what jail is?" Detective Stauder asked.

"Yeah," Kate said. "It's where people go when they're bad."

"Or when they get in trouble," Detective Stauder said.

"For doing what?" Kate asked.

"Well, we have laws, and sometimes people break laws, and when they break laws they have to go to jail. And I need to tell you right now, your daddy's in jail. He's in jail for hurting Karly, and I want you to know you can't be hurt at all, that you're safe."

Kate misunderstood.

"Is Karly's dad really in jail?" Kate asked.

"No," said Detective Stauder. "Your dad is in jail."

"Why?" Kate asked.

"He's in jail for hurting Karly," Detective Stauder said. "I want you to know you are safe here and that whatever you tell us, you're not going to get in trouble from us or your dad for telling what you saw or what you heard Thursday when you came home from school and Friday when you went to school."

"Is my dad really in jail?" Kate asked.

"He really is in jail. I would never lie to you about that," Stauder answered.

Kate began crying.

Joan Demarest had urged Judge Holcomb to make some exceptions for Kate in the courtroom. She requested that Kate be allowed to testify by closed-circuit TV, or that Kate be allowed to come into the courtroom incognito, with a mask or a wig, and sunglasses. Kate was understandably scared about testifying. In typical girlhood fashion, she wanted a disguise. Demarest promised Kate she would ask the judge for permission. "I was trying to keep Kate comfortable and keep a promise I made to her," Demarest said. But defense attorneys argued that allowing Kate to wear such a get-up would make a mockery of the court.

The judge denied both of Demarest's requests.

Kate had to face her father in court. The law left Judge Holcomb little other choice. It used to be that a videotaped interview of a child victim could be introduced in court instead of live testimony in a courtroom. This was particularly helpful in cases that involved sex abuse. But in 2004, the U.S. Supreme Court, in *Crawford v. Washington*, overturned a previous 1980 ruling that allowed hearsay evidence if a judge ruled such evidence was reliable and trustworthy.

The Crawford ruling bars states from using statements against a criminal defendant unless the person making the allegations is available to testify at trial. No hearsay evidence is allowed, even if the judge considers it reliable. The Crawford ruling, which wasn't drafted with child abuses cases in mind, is a terrible blow to those who work on behalf of abused children.

In California, a man previously convicted of several child sexual abuse charges involving two sisters, ages four and eight, had those charges dropped on appeal once Crawford was put into effect. It was ruled that the videotaped testimony of the oldest girl was inadmissible because it violated the Confrontation Clause of the Sixth Amendment.

So Kate was compelled to denounce her father publicly. The appearance of a child being sworn in and grilled by attorneys was wrenching for everyone present. The prosecutor was sensitive to that.

"Do you know the people sitting in that box?" Demarest began.

"No," Kate replied softly. She faced the jurors, eight men and four women. Her dark hair fell forward, giving her some privacy. In her hands, she held two stuffed bunnies.

"They are called the jury," Demarest said. "They are here today to hear what you have to tell them."

"Okay."

"Do you know who that is, sitting in the black robe?"

"Judge?"

"Yes. That's right. She's the boss of things here," Demarest replied. "Karly…"

Oops!

Demarest made a mistake, referring to Kate as Karly. She quickly corrected her error, but it's one that would be repeated. It was unsettling, hearing Karly's name called out like that, as if Karly were playing a game of hide-and-seek with the jurors.

After moving through a litany of pedestrian questions about pets and teachers, Demarest asked Kate how she was feeling.

"A little nervous," Kate admitted.

Demarest attempted to ease the girl's anxiety by asking questions Kate could answer without fear. What day of the week was it? What month was it? The sort of questions you'd expect a doctor to ask when determining if your child has a concussion. Then Demarest asked Kate if she understood the seriousness of the trial.

"When we ask you questions today, do you promise to tell the truth no matter what?"

"Yes," Kate said.

"Have you and I talked before?"

"Yes."

"Have we been in the room before?" Demarest asked.

"Yes," Kate said.

"What did we do?"

"I talked on this microphone."

"Did you sit in the judge's chair?"

"Yes."

"Did you try to get me to sing in the microphone?"

"Yes."

"Do you remember when you used to go to Hoover school?"

"Yes."

"Where did you live?" Demarest asked.

"On Aspen Street," Kate replied.

"Who lived there with you?"

"My dad."

"Did anyone else live there?"

"Um," Kate hesitated. "Uh…"

There was a long silence.

"Did you have any people who came and visited?" The attorney restated her question.

"Yes. Sarah and Karly."

"What was Karly like?" Demarest asked. It was the first mention of the slain girl.

"She was…she was adorable," Kate said.

David Sheehan looked at Kate. The little girl's answer was so frank, so guileless, so accurate, and so very brave. Whatever else anyone had been thinking up until that moment, everyone in the courtroom knew Kate had loved Karly the way big sisters do.

"Do you remember how old she was?" Demarest continued.

"Yes. Three."

"What did she look like?"

"She had blonde hair. Blue eyes."

"What did you do with her?"

"We played sometimes."

"What sort of things did you play?"

"Sometimes when she came over, um, I think we played with the cat. Um, I don't really remember," Kate said.

This stumbling over specifics continued throughout Kate's testimony. That was particularly true whenever Demarest asked Kate a question that involved her father.

"How did you feel about having Karly around?"

"Happy," Kate replied.

"How did your dad act when Sarah Sheehan was around?"

"I don't remember."

"Do you remember if he acted the same or differently?"

"I don't remember."

"Did you ever see Karly throw up when she was staying with you?"

"I don't really remember."

"Did Karly spend the night?" Demarest skirted the interrogation away from Kate's father.

"Yes."

"Where would she sleep?"

"On the bottom bunk."

"What about when there wasn't a mattress there?" Demarest asked.

"I don't remember."

Demarest warned Kate she was going to ask her some questions about the week Karly died. Kate began to cry quietly. Several of the jurors looked over at Shawn. Up until Kate's emotional testimony, the trial had moved along at an excruciatingly tedious pace.

The prosecutor had started the trial on Monday, October 2, 2006, by questioning 911 Dispatcher Andy Thompson. The 911 tape was played for the jury. The day ended with testimony from Sergeant Evan Fieman, who had performed CPR and tried to save Karly. Fieman, who knew Sarah socially, was distressed that he failed to bring Karly back to life. He felt like he'd let Sarah down.

Scheduling conflicts put the testimony on hold until the following Monday, October 9, 2006. Demarest called for testimony from Detective Harvey, along with the nurses and EMTs who had responded to the emergency that day. Demarest had painstakingly questioned these witnesses: what was Karly wearing that day, who cut off her pants, who placed them in the paper sack, who verified they'd been placed into the paper sack, on and on.

One juror, a man in his seventies, was having a difficult time staying awake. Once, he nodded off so soundly the pen and pad slipped from his hand. Out of earshot of the jury, but before the judge, the attorneys discussed whether he ought to be replaced.

But on that day, ironically, Friday, October 13, 2006, as Kate sat sniffling in the witness chair, jurors noticed that Shawn Field looked visibly pained for the first time. They could see the worry on his face, the anxiety furrowing his brow. Shawn Field had forgotten about himself.

He was honed in on his weeping daughter. He was clearly distressed that Kate had been put on the stand to testify against him.

"Do you remember the morning, the last time you saw Karly?" Demarest asked.

"Yes." Several jurors shifted in their seats, uncomfortable with the interrogation of such a young girl.

"Do you remember what kind of mood your dad was in that morning?"

"Yes."

"What kind of mood was that?"

"He seemed mad."

"Do you know why he was mad?"

"Yes. Because I had…he told me to finish my homework 'cause, well." Kate was having a difficult time fighting back the tears and talking. "Because it was almost time for me to go to school and I had to finish it."

"How could you tell he was mad?" Demarest continued.

"Um. Because he yelled."

"What did he yell?"

"I don't remember."

"Did he yell any bad words?"

"Probably a couple."

"Do you remember what they were?"

"No."

"Are you afraid to say bad words in front of people?"

"Yes."

"Would you be more comfortable writing them down?"

"No. I just know there were a couple of bad words but I don't remember what they were."

Some jurors were ready to cuss out Joan Demarest at this point. They could not figure out why the prosecutor insisted upon haranguing the poor child. What difference did it make what bad words were said? They got it—Shawn had been in a bad mood that morning. She'd made her point.

"How did they make you feel?" Demarest was relentless.

"Bad."

"Who was your dad yelling at?"

"Me."

Like children will often do, Kate took the blame upon herself. If only she had gotten her homework done, maybe her dad wouldn't have been in such a bad mood.

Kate told the court that when Karly got up that morning she had a bruise on her eye. She'd had the bruise the day before. Kate said she'd first seen the bruise when she got home from school on Thursday, and it worried her because it was a bad bruise.

"Did your dad say anything about the bruise?" Demarest asked.

"Yes, but I forgot what he said," Kate answered.

"Did he tell you about the bruise before you saw it?"

"Yes."

Kate was careful about her answers. She always stopped short of pointing the finger at her dad. When Demarest asked how Karly was acting that afternoon, Kate replied she'd forgotten.

"Did Karly seem happy or sad, excited or tired?" Demarest prodded the witness.

"She seemed…" Kate started, but stopped. She wept, then said she really couldn't remember. But it was clear from the girl's tears she likely was remembering it all too well.

"How was she acting or behaving? What was her mood?" Demarest wasn't about to let up.

"I think she asked me if she could sit down," Kate replied.

Kate said she couldn't remember if they played that night or not. She didn't remember having dinner, talking with her dad, or doing her homework. She only remembered what happened at bedtime.

"What do you remember about that?"

"I said goodnight to her when she had the bruise. My dad was holding her. I was on the top bunk. I hugged her."

"Did Karly go to bed, too?"

"No. I don't remember what she did."

Clutching a stuffed animal, she testified through tears that she'd heard slapping sounds coming from the kitchen the night before Karly was killed. She did not get out of bed to check on Karly.

"What happened after you went to bed?"

"I heard some noises."

"What kind of noises?"

"Banging noises, kind of."

"What did they sound like?"

"Um," Kate paused, and tugged at the stuffed animal in her hands. "Kind of like, I can't really sound it, but I know what it sounded like."

"Have you described those sounds before?" Demarest asked. She knew, of course, that Kate had told the forensic interviewer at the ABC (All Because of Children) House exactly what those sounds had been like.

"Yes."

"Did you use anything to describe those sounds before?"

"Yes." Kate was a defense attorney's star witness, expertly parsing her answers.

"What did you use?" Demarest was a patient prosecutor who had practiced for this moment.

"A spoon," Kate replied.

"Like a big plastic spoon?"

"I think it was plastic. I don't know," Kate replied honestly.

"Did you hear any voices?"

"Yes."

"What were those voices doing?"

"Well, they were," Kate said. She paused and thought through the question carefully. "What do you mean?"

"Were they talking, yelling, crying, anything like that?" Demarest seemed annoyed that Kate had come back at her with a question. Did she fault the child for trying to protect her father?

"Uh. Karly, she said mmmm," Kate replied, mimicking a quiet, moaning sound. "I think that was the sound."

"Did you hear your dad's voice?"

"I don't remember."

"What did you do with the spoon to make the sound?"

"Can you repeat the question?" Kate was stalling.

"Can you tell us what you did with the spoon to make the sound?"

"I hit it," Kate said. "It's hard to explain."

"Would it be helpful if you had a spoon to show the jury?" Demarest asked.

"No. Not really," Kate replied.

Demarest would not be denied. She pulled a large black plastic spoon, the sort used for ladling stews, from a paper sack.

"Have you ever seen a spoon like this before?"

"Yes. At my dad's house. Except it was, mmm…."

"Was it broken like this?"

"No."

"Kate, what would you do with a spoon like that to make the sound you heard that night?"

Kate slapped her hands together.

"How do you know it was a spoon you heard that night?" Demarest asked.

"Because I know what spoons sound like," the girl replied.

"What did you do when you heard the spanking sounds?"

"I stayed in bed."

"Did you think about going outside your bedroom to see what the sound was from?"

"No," Kate said, "because I didn't know it was..." She stopped herself. "Just no."

Kate never told the jurors or anyone else how she knew what spanking noises sounded like. If her father had ever abused her in any way, Kate never admitted to it. Her mother, Eileen Field, told the court about how abusive her ex-husband had been. How he'd once dropped-kicked a puppy in front of their young daughter. How, when angered, he'd threaten to harm Kate's beloved kittens. How he'd constantly berate her, screaming obscenities in front of Kate.

The defense team decided not to interrogate the young girl. Whether that was because it might further implicate their client or because their client begged them not to question his daughter, the jurors thought it was the right call.

Despite Demarest's belief that Kate's testimony was a critical turning point in the trial, many of the jurors said the young girl's statements really didn't change their minds one way or another. Most felt sorry for Kate—sorry that she had to be in the courtroom at all. Some were angry at Joan Demarest for putting Kate on the stand.

"Kate never made eye contact with her father," recalled one juror. "Her voice was barely audible and the answers she gave were not clear. She did meekly admit Shawn spanked Karly with a spoon, but not convincingly. It was not clear where, when, or how hard Karly was hit. The defense attorneys, to their credit, did not challenge Kate's responses, which they easily could have done."

This particular juror noted how distraught Shawn was to see his daughter on the stand. He also came away with the distinct impression Kate "knew a lot more than she revealed, but she was torn about having to testify against her father, and/or she was intimidated by the environment."

Another juror noted, "Little, if any, of Kate's testimony was useful for a juror looking at evidence. I felt it was unnecessary to have put her through it."

But Demarest remains resolute that putting Kate on the stand was the right thing to do.

"She heard Karly getting beaten the night before Karly was killed when only Kate, Karly, and Field were home. No one else could have testified to that."

Demarest did not like interrogating a child before a jury. "I had to do some very hard things in this trial in order to get an evil man behind bars. I felt badly about putting Kate on the stand then and I feel badly about it now."

By the time Kate stepped down from the stand, many of the jurors were growing increasingly agitated. They were bored to tears with tedious, seemingly useless information about Karly's clothing in an attempt to prove possible sexual abuse.

Dr. Hochfeld, the doctor who saw Karly in Good Samaritan's ER the day she died, reported that Karly had "quite a bit of bruising" along with dilation in her privates, something the doctor said "was not inconsistent with some recent sexual assault." Semen spots were found on the carpet in Karly's room but none was found in her diaper. Dr. Hochfeld conducted a sexual assault evaluation on Karly, but subsequent postmortem exams ruled the suspected sexual abuse inconclusive. In those early hours after Karly's death, both Shawn and David had provided semen specimens per investigators' requests. David asked the coroner outright if his daughter had been sexually abused, and was told that she had not been.

It had been previously determined in pre-trial hearing that the sexual assault question would not be part of the trial. But when the defense referred to in an an effort to discredit investigators, Demarest was forced to address it, lest it become an unanswered question lingering in some juror's mind later.

The tedious testimony about what Karly was wearing the day she was murdered served another purpose.

"Pounds and inches don't say much," Demarest said. "But Karly's sweatsuit gave the jury a real tangible feel for how tiny and helpless she was against the tall and muscly Field."

Demarest also brought in computer geeks to testify about the forensics of Shawn's computers in an effort to show how he planned to extort money from David, a theory that most of the jurors rejected due to lack of evidence. The jury had been led down so many rabbit trails they were getting frustrated.

If the state had proof that Shawn Field battered this child to death, they needed to ante it up, quickly. The jury was weary of all the piddling details. They needed concrete evidence, something they didn't think they had yet.

CHAPTER THIRTY-EIGHT

F AT PUMPKINS SQUATTED SIDE BY side on the doorsteps of clapboard houses throughout town. Felt spiders and cotton webs hung in the windows of bookstores and drugstores. End shelves at the corner market were stacked with bags of candy corn. The University's colors, black and orange, were even more evident during the month of October when Sarah Brill Sheehan stepped up to the witness stand in the Benton County Courthouse, raised her right hand and swore to tell the truth, the whole truth and nothing but the truth.

Joan Demarest might not have been aware of the jurors' unease regarding her decision to put Kate on the stand, but she did fear they might be harboring an increasing disdain for Sarah.

Sarah had a favorite outfit she wore to the trial: black pants with a black top. She coupled the ensemble with a selection of brightly colored scarves. Jurors wondered if she was purposefully wearing black to evoke the image of a grieving woman, or if her wardrobe was really that limited.

They didn't trust Sarah.

"You could tell she's used to flirting her way out of a lot of things," noted one juror.

Sarah wasn't the one on trial, but the jurors were forming their own judgments about her.

"She was out playing golf, drinking, while her daughter was being beaten, and she couldn't figure out anything to do about it?"

The jurors were troubled by Sarah's coy mannerisms and her seemingly blatant disregard for Karly's well-being. "We were keeping a tally of who is to blame and how much. Shawn was at the top and Sarah wasn't far behind."

Many of the jurors were having a difficult time controlling their own emotions over the testimony they were hearing and the photos they were seeing.

In the courtroom, Sarah's sexual history was off limits. But Clark Willes had managed to ask enough of the right questions that the jurors knew that while her daughter's worst nightmare was unfolding, Sarah was giving some guy a blowjob.

"We knew that she was at the bar and that at some point she disappeared into the parking lot with the beer distributor. We could read between the lines," one juror said.

While the prosecutor treated Sarah with kid gloves, the jurors felt little empathy for her. They simply could not understand how Sarah could come into the courtroom day after day and remain so detached. She didn't cry. She didn't bolt. She didn't even rage much. If anything, she seemed way too collected for the jury.

"She was either callous, which I didn't think," said one juror, "or caught up in her own world. A narcissist."

Two people in the courtroom considered Sarah a victim: Demarest and Sarah. Asked by Demarest to describe herself, Sarah said, "I have a fairly difficult time opening up to people. In my experience, it seems like when I do I get hurt."

Sarah told the jurors how she'd met Shawn Field at a bar and invited him over to her house that very same night. Within a week or two of that meeting, Sarah said she and Shawn were talking about getting married. The woman who had a hard time trusting people thought nothing of moving in with a man only a week or so into the relationship and turning over her paycheck and her tips to him.

Something wasn't adding up—not for the jurors, anyway.

"The whole theory that Shawn did this for money was a total joke," a juror recalled. "We kept expecting some grand revelation but it never came. You really had to stretch the imagination to make Joan's theory work. The case was hers to lose by going with that whole theory of motive. It was pointless."

Shawn Field may very well have been abusing Karly to extort money from David Sheehan, as the prosecution believed, but if so, they failed to provide enough evidence to convince the jury of it.

"It was way too complicated," another juror said. "The string of events didn't make that much sense. It made no sense to abuse Karly to get financial gain."

But what other motive would possibly make any sense?

Shawn Field had never worked any job for very long. He never finished those degrees in economics he kept boasting about. He'd gladly accepted money from his parents, and when they didn't give it freely, he'd lied and cheated them out of it. Investigators discovered Shawn had taken out credit cards in his father's name and, without his father's knowledge, had run those cards up thousands of dollars. It infuriated Hugh Field when he learned the extent of his son's lying, cheating ways.

Shawn knew that with his only sibling dead, he stood to inherit all the money and property his hardworking parents had cobbled together over the years. There was really no reason for him to work. He just needed to find a way to get by until that substantial inheritance was his.

The abuse of Karly began within weeks of Sarah moving in with

Shawn Field. But it was after Shawn saw David Sheehan's W-2s for 2005 in early 2006, according to Sarah, who had given them to Shawn, that he began to insist she needed to have full custody of Karly. It was Shawn's idea to blame David for the numerous injuries Karly sustained over the course of the eight months leading up to her death. At Shawn's urging, Sarah had even made an appointment with attorney Hal Harding to tell him she suspected David was abusing their daughter.

From the witness box, Sarah unraveled the tale of her relationship with Shawn. She claimed they'd broken up several weeks prior to Karly's death, after she found gay pornography on his computer—that Shawn had been extremely angry with her over it, and that Shawn had been very irate that last Thursday of Karly's life because Sarah hadn't paid the water bill and the city had shut off their water. He'd warned her if she didn't get it turned back on that very afternoon, there would be hell to pay. Sarah also recalled the look of utter devastation on Karly's face as she drove away.

David Sheehan was tense the entire time his ex-wife was testifying. He worried she would trip up, get caught in her own deceitful web. He wasn't sure what she might say. Whatever feelings he may have had for Sarah at one time had turned to an exhausted sigh of relief once they divorced. Now he was focused on one thing: making sure Shawn Field was convicted of Karly's murder. He hoped and prayed to God that Sarah wouldn't say anything to screw that up.

Sarah was soft-spoken, her words measured, alternately interrupted by the nervous gesture of her tongue clicking against the roof of her mouth, a lapse in concentration. Her testimony was littered with long pauses, or "um"s. As the day dragged on, Sarah grew increasingly more subdued, almost to the point of sounding drugged. The jurors studied her carefully, taking copious notes as Sarah explained what she remembered from those last few hours of Karly's life.

Shawn had woken up in a bad mood, angry Kate hadn't yet finished her big school project.

"He yelled at her to finish her project, asking her if she wanted to repeat third grade," Sarah said. "He yelled, 'Do you want to grow up to be a stupid bitch like your mother?'"

"Can you illustrate for the jury how he said it?" Demarest asked.

"I'll try," Sarah said. "May I stand?"

"Sure," Demarest said.

Sarah stood up from her seat in the witness box; facing the jury, she took on a decidedly intense demeanor and yelled, "DO YOU WANT TO GROW UP AND BE A STUPID BITCH LIKE YOUR MOTHER?"

One or two of the jurors flinched from the sheer volume of Sarah's voice.

While Shawn yelled at his daughter, Karly remained asleep on the floor in Kate's room, a pink blanket covering her. Sarah testified she had not seen her daughter since the day before, when she'd left her daughter in Shawn's arms, as she drove off to pay the water bill. She did not check on Karly when she got home around midnight on Thursday.

Shawn woke Karly Friday morning. He carried her past the dining room table where Sarah was helping Kate with her homework.

Sarah told the jurors that Shawn had said, "Geez, babe, her allergies must be really bad. She's been picking at her eye."

Shawn sat Karly on the countertop while he took ice out of the freezer to make her a compress. Sarah stroked her daughter's head as she held the compress to Karly's eye.

"I was trying to figure out how it got to be that swollen and trying to get her to stop rubbing it because I didn't want her to make it worse," Sarah recalled.

At some point, Sarah reached over to tickle Karly's feet, but Karly yanked them away, so Sarah turned Karly's tender feet over and saw they were swollen.

Sarah had already told the jury that Shawn and his ex-wife Eileen had once run a daycare and that Shawn had learned that sometimes people abuse a child by striking them on the bottoms of their feet so the abuse isn't readily apparent. But what Sarah didn't tell the jury was why she would leave her daughter in the care of a person who boasted about knowing how to abuse a child.

Sarah said she was shocked by Karly's appearance that morning and wanted to take her to the doctor right away, but Shawn discouraged it, saying they'd take her the next day if Karly's eye wasn't better.

Once Kate left for school, Sarah said she gave Karly some trail mix for breakfast and left her alone in the living room while she and Shawn slipped away to the bedroom to have sex.

Afterward, Shawn headed to for the gym.

"What did you do after Shawn left?" Demarest asked.

"I immediately called my father," Sarah said. She asked him about allergies but he was distracted. Sarah's mother was at Oregon Health Science Center having a heart procedure.

"Call your sister," Gene urged.

Sarah did call Kim. She told her that Karly's eye was swollen. She didn't tell either of them it looked as though Karly had been punched. Sarah would later tell detectives that her first impression of the bruising around Karly's eye was that it "looked like a fist" had done the damage.

"Because of talking with my father and my sister and the responses I got, allergies seemed reasonable," Sarah told the jury. Neither Gene nor Kim had seemed alarmed. Both her father and sister recommended Sarah give Karly Benadryl.

Sarah subtly blamed her father and sister for her own failure to take Karly to a doctor. When Shawn came home from the gym, Sarah left for work.

A short time later, Karly's morning prayer was answered—she went home to Jesus, as the child had explained her method of escaping her abuser. The law would call it murder.

•

Sarah had been on the stand since 9:45 a.m. It was now approaching 3:30 p.m. Demarest knew it was time to wrap up the day's questioning.

As sirens echoed eerily outside the courtroom window, Demarest asked, "Did you ever strike Karly besides a spanking?"

"No," Sarah answered.

"Did you ever punch her?"

"No."

"Did you kill Karly?"

"No," Sarah said.

The echo of the siren faded into the distance.

CHAPTER THIRTY-NINE

T HE NEXT DAY, DURING A fairly routine grilling by defense attorneys, Sarah was asked about the diary she kept and the statements she made to detectives following Karly's death—those statements where she had blamed David and defended Shawn, Sarah was asked about the ever-perplexing hair braid incident. Then Demarest called Sarah back to the stand.

Despite nearly two days of testimony from one of the last people to see Karly alive, her own mother, nothing critical had been introduced that would convince this jury Shawn Field was guilty. The jury hoped the prosecution was going to connect the dots for them. Thus far, the state had failed to give them anything concrete with which to convict Shawn Field. Sarah's testimony had only served to raise a lot of questions about her own role in her daughter's death.

Worried Sarah's actions, or rather her inaction, could be problematic for the prosecution, Demarest addressed that very matter with Sarah on Friday, October 20, 2006, on redirect.

"If you were free to leave [Shawn] at any time, why didn't you leave?" Demarest asked.

Sarah tried to explain. She seemed weary, or perhaps medicated, tired of being on the witness stand.

"I didn't leave because Kate was there and I felt like she really needed me. Shawn Field would lay a guilt trip on me. 'How can you leave Kate—she's attached to you. You're a good role model in her life.'

"I had grown to love Kate very much, and I still do," Sarah continued. "Shawn knew that and he would make me feel really guilty about not being involved in her life anymore. He would say, 'Then you can't see Kate anymore.' Occasionally, he would randomly say, 'I can hire somebody to track you down. I'll always know where you're at.'"

Okay. Good. Demarest moved to the next question: "Up until Karly's death and after, did you still love Mr. Field?"

"I believed I did," Sarah said.

Demarest asked Sarah to explain to the jury her mental state in the first six days following Karly's death.

"I don't know if I could exactly describe what my thought process was. If any of you get migraines…your head hurts so bad, everything is fuzzy and painful. It was really difficult to imagine that my daughter was dead. I had a hard time accepting that. I didn't even know where Shawn Field was the first few days."

Sarah paused, sighed heavily, and paused again before continuing. "So that first week was really hard to come to terms with losing my daughter, obviously. It was the most painful, but there was also the loss of other key people in my life. It just felt like one day I had a family and then I didn't. I had a hard time understanding. I just kind of shut down for a while."

Sarah may have been referring to her broken relationship with her brother. In those early days after his niece's murder, Doug Brill told investigators, "I seriously thought that Sarah was going to get arrested. I really did." Police wanted to know why he would think that. "Sarah has a really wicked temper," Doug said. He thought perhaps she had just imploded and accidentally killed Karly, or maybe she had left a bottle of Benadryl within Karly's reach. "Sarah just doesn't think about future consequences, or any sort of future. There's no thought and she kind of feels like people owe her things," he said. Doug could not forgive his sister for Karly's death.

Sarah's friendship with Shelley Freeland had been strained prior to Karly's death; now it was history, as were most of the relationships she had with coworkers and friends around town.

And despite the efforts of Gene and Carol Brill to reach out to their daughter, Sarah repeatedly pushed her parents away, turning down their invitations to join them for meals between court proceedings. Police and others, who saw the tender way the Brills treated Sarah, were annoyed when they would later hear her testify that her parents didn't support her.

Demarest asked Sarah if, when she went golfing on Wednesday night, she had any idea Shawn Field was abusing her daughter. Clark Willes jumped to his feet in objection. Field had not yet been found guilty. Judge Holcomb sustained the objection and Demarest restated her question.

"When you left for golf on Wednesday, June 1, 2005, did you have any idea Karly was being abused?"

Willes objected again and Holcomb granted the objection.

Joan Demarest was tired of playing around.

Yanking a black cloth from a huge poster-sized color photo of the dead Karly, battered and bruised, on a cold postmortem table, Demarest called out, "Sarah, did you do this to your daughter?"

Sarah began sobbing uncontrollably.

"Mrs. Sheehan, did you do this to your daughter?" Demarest fired off her question again.

"No, I did not," Sarah said through tears.

At the defense table, Clark Willes turned to Dan Koenig, and whispered, loudly enough to be heard, "That was kind of mean."

Dan Koenig answered, "It was more than mean. That's what she wanted."

Sarah continued sobbing. Demarest told Judge Holcomb she had no further questions. Demarest had issued a preemptive strike against the defense by getting Sarah to break down before they could.

"Would you like a moment?" Willes asked Sarah. When Sarah failed to answer, Willes walked back to the defense table and said to Koenig, "I've never seen anything crueler in my whole life."

Judge Holcomb recessed the jury. Some jurors were pretty distraught themselves. They were upset with Demarest.

"When she brought out that picture of Karly on the slab, it was one of the lowest moments of the trial, quite frankly," a juror said. "It was cheesy theatrics. You could tell by the looks in everyone's eyes, we were all thinking, 'What the hell was that?' What was she trying to do? Whipping out grand evidence, breaking down a witness. It's like she was saying, 'Look at me, I'm a grand lawyer.'"

Even so, the very same juror admitted, "It was one of the few times I actually pitied poor Sarah."

Koenig had it right. Demarest's actions elicited the response from the jurors that Demarest had intended. They had been provoked to pity Sarah, to see her as a victim.

It may have been the most important moment in the trial. "Showing Sarah that postmortem photo of Karly was one of the most difficult things I've done," Demarest said. "I was not proud of it. I couldn't look the jurors in the eyes for the rest of the day. But I still believe it had to happen. Sarah's reaction was the most powerful moment: pure, raw, devastated emotion."

It was a made-for-TV moment. Up until then, Sarah displayed a flat affect. She took long pauses and often seemed confused by questions.

Some observers felt she might be too heavily medicated. "Sarah had been relatively stoic. The jury needed to see her with emotion," Demarest said.

Judge Holcomb was displeased with drama unfolding in her courtroom.

"She cleared the room and yelled at me for being so heartless and cruel," Demarest said. "I felt really bad but it had to be done. The defense was trying to say Sarah had killed Karly, and her reaction made it absolutely clear she couldn't have."

CHAPTER FORTY

OVER THE COURSE OF A month, the jury heard from nearly everyone in Karly's life: father, mother, babysitter, doctors, grandparents, state child protective services, and law enforcement officials. Everyone except Shawn Field.

Shawn did not take the stand to testify, so the jury heard excerpts of tapes from the prolonged police interviews made in the early hours and days following Karly's death.

In a voice that was measured, almost imperceptibly quiet at times, Shawn explained to Detective Jason Harvey that Sarah left for work around 11:30 that morning and called him at 1:37 p.m. to say she was on her way home. Did he want her to bring home some frozen yogurt? He'd said no. Shawn said he was holding Karly during the phone call and that she was really tired. Before Sarah got home, he put her down for a nap, gave her a compress for her eye, and covered her with a blanket.

"So she was already asleep by the time Sarah got in the house?" Detective Harvey asked.

"Sarah didn't go in there right away. We were talking about her allergies and I was asking her what her dad said. I was asking about the medicine because her dad had told her to get some eye thing, I don't know what."

"What happened after that?"

"Sarah and I both walked in there, and I opened up the curtains."

"Why did you guys walk in there?"

"Cause she wanted to see her and she wanted to say goodnight, goodnight to her and so we walked in there. She was laying there and Sarah ran over to her. She didn't look right. We took the blanket away and she was not breathing. I put my hand right here and she was not breathing. And I don't even remember who called 911."

"So tell me about this injury to her eye," Harvey said. "It looked swollen to the officers."

"Ha! It's beyond swollen," Shawn said. "It's swollen shut." Shawn said it was allergies, aggravated by Karly rubbing it, poking it. "She had that damn finger up there and she wouldn't stop it."

Detective Harvey repeatedly asked Shawn what happened that day. Shawn repeated the story that Karly had allergies. That she was given a little bit of Benadryl. That he put her down for a nap and Sarah found her dead. He offered no explanation for how she ended up dead, other than that he didn't do it.

He told Detective Harvey he had been taking the photos to protect Karly, to prove David was abusing her. Shawn said Sarah had been on edge after suffering her second miscarriage, something no one knew about except Shawn and Sarah. Shawn said Sarah had sent him to get her a prescription for Vicodin. Vicodin and Percocet were Sarah's drugs of choice according to her medical charts, and Shawn said she had "drawers full of it."

"There were only two adults in this household, and there's no way that those bruises on Karly's forehead would just appear," Detective Harvey said. "So did Sarah do this? Did she snap, did she just do it by accident? What happened?"

"I haven't ever seen Sarah get mad," Shawn said. "I've seen her get frustrated and just, you know, she always told me, 'I don't know how to discipline Karly.' She would tell me this all the time. And then she'd compliment me, 'You're so good with Kate.'"

Harvey asked Shawn if he would have anything to add if he knew Sarah was across the street with other detectives, talking about Shawn.

"I don't know what she would ever say about me. I haven't done anything. I have never laid a hand on her, nothing," Shawn whined.

"Karly basically dies in your care," Harvey noted. "Something happened at your house, Shawn—it happened there. She's beaten and she dies in your home."

Repeatedly, during that first interview and subsequent ones, Detective Harvey offered Shawn an opportunity to explain who killed Karly. If not him, then who?

Only once has Shawn implicated someone else. Investigator John Chilcote asked him, "Who hit Karly with the spoons and gave her the bruises if you didn't?"

"I guess Sarah did it. She did it," Shawn said. "It's hard for me to believe that Sarah would hit Karly, but I guess Sarah did."

Karly's head injuries were such that she died within a couple of hours of sustaining them. That's what the experts, Dr. Chervenak and Dr. Lewman, told the jurors. Dr. Larry Lewman, Oregon State Medical Examiner's Office, performed the autopsy on Karly, but it was Dr. Carol Chervenak's straight-talk explanation of Lewman's findings that pulled it all together for the jurors and finally gave them the factual information they needed.

Her own explanation was aided by the Poser Model, a three-dimensional graphic of Karly revealing all of the abrasions on her body, from the bottoms of her feet to the top of her head. The computer-generated graphic allowed the jurors to study the areas in question with objectivity, a sorely needed component in a trial fraught with anger, frustration, boredom, and despair.

Oregon Law states any child abuse case will be handled in a multidisciplinary way; in other words, it will be staffed by police, child protective workers, and child abuse experts. Dr. Chervenak was the expert Matt Stark called when Karly was first referred for potential child abuse to the state's child protective services.

Karly was never seen by Dr. Carol Chervenak, the medical director of the ABC House. The photos of the injuries Karly sustained in December 2004 were never forwarded to Dr. Chervenak. That was Matt Stark's responsibility, but those photos, provided by David Sheehan, were reportedly lost or stolen, and DHS investigators never asked for replacements.

A computer graphic of Karly's injuries helped get Shawn Field convicted, but had Chervenak been provided with the same photos in 2004, photos that DHS had in their possession, Karly would probably be alive today. Well trained in all areas of child abuse, Dr. Chervenak would never have assumed Karly was injuring herself, and she would have known someone was tormenting and abusing the child. She told the jurors that had she seen the photos David provided, she would have immediately identified the cause as child abuse.

In her nine years as Medical Director of the ABC House, Chervenak said she had personally examined over 1,500 children and had testified in over 200 cases of child abuse. She attended the autopsy of Karla Isabelle Ruth Sheehan on June 5, 2005.

Using a pointer, Dr. Chervenak highlighted Karly's injuries on the graphic.

In addition to the ruptured eye and bruising on her head, there were also bruises on her arms, both where the arm bends and on the exterior surface. Her lip was cut in two places. She had bruises on her calves and her groin, and her feet were badly bruised all over: tops, bottoms, sides, and the middle of both feet.

"Once the head was shaved, more bruising was seen covering the scalp—and actually, during the autopsy, underneath, inside of the scalp, additional bruising was evident that you could not see on the skin," Dr. Chervenak said.

Demarest asked the doctor to explain how that happens.

"When there is blunt force contact to the scalp there is bruising inside the scalp, but the blood has not had a chance to migrate to the surface of the scalp so it's not seen on the surface, but during the autopsy."

Child abuse experts look for patterns. Dr. Chervenak found a pattern in the bruising on Karly's back.

"There were four bruises together, similar in size."

"What's the significance of that pattern?" Demarest asked.

"That pattern has been documented in child abuse textbooks and is consistent with an adult's fist: the knuckles of a fist," she explained.

"Is there any significance to the bruises on the underside of the arms?" Demarest asked.

"It's a location that is unusual to have accidentally injured," Chervenak said. "These are commonly known as protective wounds. They come from a person who puts up their arms when they're attacked. Particularly, children will get into a defensive posture, almost a fetal position."

Demarest scanned the graphic so jurors could see Karly had bruises on her ears. Pointing to them, Chervenak said, "Ears are very, very rarely accidentally bruised. Less than half of one percent of the time in children this age."

And then there was the eye.

"The redness in the white part of the eye indicates that there was very, very dense bleeding into the whites of the eye on the left," she said.

Chervenak told the jury children Karly's age rarely participate in self-injurious behavior. That was something more common to adolescents, not toddlers. "There's no way Karly could have done these things to herself," Chervenak said.

"What caused Karly Sheehan's death?" Demarest asked.

"Traumatic brain injury," Dr. Chervernak said.

The most damning evidence against Shawn Field came from his very own camera. He had told Detective Harvey he took photos of Karly's injuries. He'd even told Detective Harvey where to find the camera. There were two very telling photos, one taken at 7:57 p.m. on Thursday, June 2, 2005.

In the photos, Karly has a bruise on her forehead and another around her left eye. Her eyes are watery, no doubt the result of tears. Even so, she's trying to smile. The next photo is dated at 1:21 p.m. on June 3, 2005. It is the last photo of Karly alive. It was taken minutes prior to Sarah arriving home. Karly's left eye is swollen shut. There's a sheen to the skin, created by the cortisone Shawn told Detective Harvey he'd been applying. Karly's head is turned toward the camera, over her left shoulder. She has a painful smile on her face, as if her abuser told her to smile.

The reason that photo is so critical is because Karly was alive in it. Demarest showed the photo to Dr. Chervenak, who explained that Karly's death had to have happened sometime between when Shawn took that last photo at 1:22 p.m. and 2 p.m., when Sarah found her daughter dead. Dr. Chervenak explained that the fatal injury could not have occurred prior to that last photo being taken because in the photo Karly is conscious: she is responsive, she is making eye contact, she is upright, she is holding something, and she is responding emotionally. The sort of fatal injury that caused Karly's death would likely cause a child to be immediately unconscious.

"Can you tell how long Karly survived after the injury that caused her death?" Demarest asked.

"She had a short survival time after that fatal injury. Even if I didn't have that picture to look at, it would be clear that it was at least less than two hours," Chervenak said.

"Could striking a three-and-a-half-year-old who is 30 pounds, 38 inches tall with spoons have caused the fatal injury?" Demarest asked.

"Yes," Dr. Chervenak said, "if those were directed at her head with enough force. What happens is, when an impact hits the head, the head starts in motion and at some point, it stops. It either stops because it hits the chest or the child's back, or the head hits a floor, or some other object that's in the room, and it stops abruptly. All it takes is enough force generated and the head moves rapidly and stops rapidly, and the energy from the force that hits the head goes into the brain, and causes all that shearing and all that damage."

It was Defense Attorney Dan Koenig who asked the question that gave Chervenak the opportunity to make it clear for the jurors why they should find Shawn W. Field guilty.

"Did you observe any damage to the brain itself?" Koenig asked on cross-examination. Chervenak was at the autopsy, but she is not a pathologist. The lawyer was aiming to trip her up.

"No. And that's why we know she had a short survival time."

Karly did not experience massive brain swelling, a natural result of head trauma, because she didn't live long enough for her system to respond to the trauma, Chervenak explained.

"So there was no cellular damage to the brain that you observed?" Koenig asked. The very question implied Chervenak lacked expertise.

"That's right," she answered with confidence. "And no one would observe that, because Karly did not live long enough for that damage— and this is where it gets very, very confusing, and that's exactly why we *know* she had a short survival time, because a person has to live two hours to develop those cellular changes that we see on pathology. It's a vital reaction. And she did not die of massive brain swelling, either, so we know she did not have delayed deterioration. We know that her fatal injury occurred and she died shortly thereafter."

When Dr. Chervenak spoke with clarity about Karly's injuries and the time sequence in which her death had occurred, it was the evidence the jurors needed to convict Shawn Field, without a doubt, for the murder of Karly Sheehan.

"It was excellent, clear testimony," said a juror. "Looking at the pictures, it was a clear case of obvious abuse."

The evidence to convict Shawn Field, those photos, had been provided by the defendant himself. "The timeline was so specific there was only one person who could have killed Karly, and he was taking the pictures," said a juror.

Chapter Forty-One

At 10:13 a.m. on October 31, 2006, minutes after Dr. Chervenak stepped down from the witness box for the final time, Joan Demarest announced, "The State rests, Your Honor."

"Counsel for the defense, you may call your first witness," Judge Holcomb said.

"The Defense rests, Your Honor," Dan Koenig said. His voice steady and certain.

A stunned silence followed Koenig's announcement. No one had expected the defense to put Shawn Field on the stand, but to rest without having offered one bit of evidence to the contrary?

Just the day before, expert witnesses for the defense were milling around the hallway outside Courtroom Number Two of the Benton County Courthouse, waiting for their turn to offer testimony that would help persuade the jury that Shawn Field was innocent of this murder.

It was a bold, cocky move, a strategy intended to convey to the jury that the defense didn't think the state had done its job; they had not proven Shawn Field guilty. The defense was banking that the jury would agree on that.

"I was totally shocked," Joan Demarest said. "It's not uncommon for the defense to lead everyone on like that and then 'Surprise!' Sometimes it's the only strategy they have. But I didn't really expect it in this case. I thought they would have offered some expert testimony regarding their theory of Karly dying from previously inflicted injuries."

Perhaps, Demarest reasoned, the testimony offered by Dr. Chervenak was too strong to dispute. "I don't know if they just gave up or what. They had made so many promises about the evidence they were going to put on. So I was absolutely shocked."

Judge Holcomb, however, was not. "The defense is not required to put on a case, and in a lot of cases, they don't," she said.

Judge Holcomb turned toward the jurors. "Members of the jury, that concludes the testimony in the case. It's now time for lawyers to make their closing arguments. Ms. Demarest, you may address the court, the jury."

Discombobulated by the defense's move, Demarest wasn't yet ready with her closing arguments. She needed a few moments to gather her thoughts. She asked the judge for a brief recess. Demarest was hoping for two hours; Judge Holcomb gave her twenty minutes.

After the recess, but before the jury was brought back, Dan Koenig asked Judge Holcomb to dismiss all twenty-three counts against Shawn Field, from aggravated murder to torture, to the last two counts of growing the marijuana Shawn had been so panicked about hiding.

"We ask for a judgment of acquittal due to a lack of evidence," Koenig said, going through each count, one by one.

Judge Holcomb denied his repeated requests. The jury was brought back and seated around ten o'clock that last day of October, 2006. For the next hour they would listen and take notes as Joan Demarest, her voice sometimes thick with emotion, presented her closing arguments.

"You have heard a lot about what kind of child Karly Sheehan was, about how she touched a lot of people's lives," Demarest began. "She liked to play princess until the defendant entered her life. Toward the end of her life, Karly told her daddy she didn't think she was a princess anymore."

That was because as soon as Shawn Field entered her life, a marked change came over Karly, Demarest said. "She stopped wanting to spend time with her mother because when she was with her mother, Karly was exposed to the defendant."

Demarest continued, detailing the ways in which Sarah Sheehan was manipulated by Shawn Field. "She was freshly single, a single mom, who was desperate for approval, desperate for a successful relationship," Demarest said.

Sarah was neither newly single nor a single mother, given that David did the bulk of parenting, but the point Demarest was trying to make was that Shawn preyed upon the unwitting Sarah. "The defendant trained Sarah Sheehan not to question him," Demarest said.

But, the prosecutor added, it's your job as jurors to do just that: to question Shawn Field and judge his intent.

"It's one of your toughest roles as jurors, because a number of the charges you are considering require proof of intent, and there's no magical tool that allows you to see into someone's mind to determine intent. You have to determine intent by the evidence of the crime," Demarest explained.

Then, in order to emphasize the evidence one last time, Demarest put up the poster-sized photos of those pictures of Karly taken on Shawn's camera.

"What evidence showed you is that even after Karly looked like this on Thursday night, Shawn kept going. Karly ended up with sixty external injuries. She's got at least ten in these pictures. Each one, according to Dr. Chervenak's testimony, caused Karly significant harm and pain. Dr. Chervenak told you how children recoil when they are in pain to protect themselves and withdraw. Karly might have been scrambling away from the defendant on the floor, trying to get away, covering her head, trying to protect her internal organs. But the defendant kept going. Blow after blow after blow to her little body," Demarest said, pounding her hands together on the first mention of the word blow. "Shawn Field kept going. Karly was likely screaming, crying, recoiling, and even twenty minutes, before she was dead, Karly was trying to please the defendant, responding to a likely command to smile for the camera. Up until the very end, Karly Sheehan was trying to please the defendant to try and stop him from abusing her. But we know after this picture was taken, the most brutal injury of all was inflicted upon her—the injury that killed her."

Some of the jurors were weeping. Demarest, pregnant with her second child, allowed the tiniest bit of emotion to sweep over her as she envisioned Karly cowering. The prosecutor maintained her professional demeanor, but the wrongness of what Karly suffered could be heard in the slightest quiver of Demarest's voice.

"The defendant had told Sarah Sheehan that someday it's all going to come down to who lies the best," Demarest said. "Ladies and gentlemen, the defendant engaged in an ongoing pattern of abuse, mistreatment, and torture of Karly Sheehan. After the defendant entered her life, never again was there a picture showing the joy in her eyes, the smile on her face, and her carefree nature. The defendant destroyed Karly's life, and he tortured the soul out of her, and we ask that you find him guilty."

Judge Holcomb excused the jury for a short break. When court resumed it was Clark Willes, co-counsel for the defense, who stood before the jurors.

Not that Sarah Sheehan was on trial, Willes was quick to point out. She wasn't, but perhaps she should be, he suggested. Willes displayed various exhibits that included details of Shawn Field's bank statements, and what Willes considered some of the most damning evidence against Sarah Sheehan: copies of the text messages she sent during the last hours of her daughter's life.

On Thursday, June 2, 2005, David sent Sarah a text message asking how Karly was doing, and whether she'd made it back from daycare all right. David worried less when Karly was with Delynn than he did when she was with Sarah. At 10:03 a.m., only minutes after David sent that text, Sarah texted back: "Staying home. Karly much better 2day despite jumping on bed when told NO!"

That text, Willes told the jury, was a setup. Karly already had injuries. The nurses who tended to Karly on Friday, June 3, 2005, said they knew from experience that some of her injuries had to have been several days old. "Sarah knows she's going to have to deliver her daughter back to David Sheehan in two days, and she's setting up the excuses," Willes explained. Just like in December 2004, when Sarah told David, "This happened on my watch."

Sarah had gone so far as to call her boss on Thursday morning to say she wouldn't be in to work because Karly had fallen from the bunk bed and Sarah needed to take her to the doctor, Willes said. Only Sarah didn't take Karly to the doctor on Thursday, or on Friday. Instead, Sarah worked later in the day on Thursday, from 4:30 to 7:30 p.m., although she didn't get back to Shawn Field's home, and to Karly, until midnight.

"Sarah wanted to convince you that she worked off the clock during those hours," Willes said. "But when did the manager go home? Nine o'clock. The manager went home at nine because the raffle was over. Sarah wants you to believe she was working off the clock," Willes said. "And the district attorney wants you to believe that Sarah is a controlled woman, who doesn't have an independent thought or an independent mind. But when she wants to go out and play, Sarah goes out to play. When she wants to go out and drink, and party, and go to the parking lot with somebody else, she does it. Remember, she has her own place.

She lives with her child by herself sometimes. She has her own job, her own checking account, and she pays her own bills, sometimes."

Willes reminded jurors that as early as October 2004, Sarah was blaming David Sheehan for Karly's injuries, and when Karly died, Sarah blamed David for that, too.

And on that last day of Karly's life, Sarah claimed that she could not take Karly to the hospital because Shawn wouldn't let her, wouldn't give her the car—yet, Sarah received fifteen phone calls between 9:48 a.m. and 1:37 p.m.

"This is what her child looked like Friday morning when Sarah woke up," Willes said, displaying a photo of a battered Karly for the jury to see. "Sarah gets fifteen phone calls on a regular basis that day, and the district attorney wants to indicate to you that Sarah Sheehan couldn't get help, didn't have a car, couldn't take her child to the hospital. Couldn't Sarah have talked to any one of the people she spoke to that day, asked for help, including her good friend Shelley Freeland? Yet she didn't mention a word of it."

Shawn Field was not responsible for Karly Sheehan's death, Willes said. Shawn had nothing to gain from it. Sarah, on the other hand, did have a motive. "We have a little girl, Karly, who is getting in the way of her mother having some fun," Willes said.

The only reason Shawn Field was taking photos of Karly was because Sarah told him that David Sheehan was doing this to Karly, Willes said. "You couldn't miss the sixty bruises on the little girl's body. Wouldn't you take pictures?" Willes asked the jurors.

Willes offered no explanation for why it was that Shawn Field didn't take Karly to the emergency room himself. He offered no explanation for Shawn Field's behavior at all. He didn't have to, he told the jurors.

"We don't have the burden of proving who did this—the state does. We don't have to present anything. The question before you is has the state met the burden of proof beyond a reasonable doubt.

"Let me put it in different terms. If Sarah Sheehan were sitting where Shawn Field is now, and evidence had been presented like it is, would you start considering that Sarah Sheehan was guilty?" Willes asked.

Keep in mind, Willes told jurors, that when Sarah Sheehan was under oath, she answered, "I can't confirm or deny that statement" more than thirty times.

"Wow!" Willes said.

As sirens wailed by the open windows of the courtroom, Willes apologized for taking up so much of the jurors' time.

"You are parents, and that's what the state is really relying on: your gut reaction, we have to get somebody. Use the facts. Don't use your gut, because if guts were right, Susan Smith in North Carolina wouldn't be in jail today, Diane Downs in Oregon wouldn't be in jail today, Andrea Yates in Texas wouldn't be in jail today. It's because somebody followed the facts, and that's what Mr. Field is asking you to do in this case. Thank you."

Clark Willes finished his closing statements and Judge Holcomb excused the court for an afternoon recess.

"We will reconvene at 3:45 p.m.," Holcomb said.

Following the break, Joan Demarest offered a fairly direct rebuttal, when she replayed the 911 call from Friday, June 3, 2005.

Once more the jurors heard the voice of Sarah Sheehan:

"911. What's your emergency?" Thompson asked.
"OH MY GOD! OH MY GOD! OH MY GOD!" came a female voice.
"I need you to calm down. Where are you?"
Inaudible, hysterical crying.
"Hello? I need you to stop crying."
"Tww…gasp…Tww…sob. Northwest Aspen Strrrreeeeetttt!"
"I can't understand you."

"*Twenty-six-fifty-two. Twenty-six-fifty-two Northwest Aspen Street. Twenty-six-fifty-two Northwest Aspen Street. Aspen Street. Twenty-six-fifty-two Aspen Street.*"

"*Twenty-six-fifty-two Aspen?*" *Thompson repeated back.*

"*Yes. Yes. Northwest. Right across from Hoover.*"

"*What's the problem?*" *Thompson asked.*

"*Karla! Karla! Come back! Karla! Come baaaack!*"

It was nearly five o'clock when Judge Holcomb dismissed the jury. "Members of the jury, that concludes the arguments in the case. I have fourteen pages of instructions, and given the hour, and as long as the day has been, we are going to stop. I am sure you have families you'd like to get home to, and, perhaps, celebrate or give out candy for trick-or-treating."

CHAPTER FORTY-TWO

JUDGE JANET HOLCOMB GAVE THE jury instructions on Wednesday, November 1, 2006. "Members of the jury, it is your sole responsibility to make all the decisions about the facts of the case. You must evaluate the evidence to determine how reliable and how believable it is. Remember, any witness who lies in some part of their testimony is likely to lie in other parts of their testimony.

"Do not allow bias or sympathy. Do not decide on guesswork, conjecture, or speculation. When you make your decision about the facts, you must apply legal rules to those facts to reach your verdict. A defendant has the constitutional right to not testify. This cannot be considered an indication of guilt."

It took the jury three days to reach a verdict in the month-long murder trial. The jury returned their verdict on Friday, November 3, 2006. They declared Shawn Wesley Field not guilty on all five charges of aggravated murder and one count of murder, but they found him guilty of the remaining seventeen charges, including felony murder and torture. Some of the jurors wept as the verdict was read.

Consensus among the jurors did not come easily. Initially, five jurors were ready to give Shawn Field the death penalty. One juror wanted to throw out everything but the manslaughter charge. "We spent many hours talking a few fellow jurors down from what I considered an emotional, perhaps even justifiable, impulse," one juror said. "We insisted, time and again, to 'show the evidence' for intentional murder, as opposed to intentional, excessive abuse that led to death, which we'd already voted for unanimously. In the end, we voted unanimously against these charges, not because everyone was convinced Shawn was not guilty, but because we couldn't find evidence to support them."

The question they hemmed and hawed over was not whether Shawn was guilty but to what degree he was guilty. Did he intentionally murder Karly or was he "just" torturing her? Explained one juror: "I felt a little manipulated by the torture charge, as it was not something that came to mind during the trial, but was written and defined in such a way that we had to sign on, and one of the biggest traps, to me, was the total number of charges against him. We were instructed to consider each charge independently, and not pick the most severe charges, as one might think."

Intent proved to be as difficult to determine as Joan Demarest warned it would be. "We don't *know* that he intended to kill her. That's what hung us up for a long, long time," said a juror. "Was the murder the result of some other crime? Did he intend to kill her?"

Another juror recalled how fraught with emotion jury deliberations had been. "We concluded from the evidence we had that the abuse was not accidental. There had been a pattern of abuse, but there was no evidence to show that killing Karly was intentional. Shawn would have gotten rid of the marijuana plants if he'd planned to murder Karly that day. It was an afternoon of tearful exchange."

Jurors found little evidence backing up the prosecutor's claim that Shawn Field was abusing Karly for financial gain. A more likely scenario, they reasoned, was that he was abusing Karly as a means of payback at Sarah. "Who knows? Maybe Shawn became frustrated with Sarah's catting around," said one juror. "I know what he did, but I can't tell you why he did it. All I can conclude is there is barely a rational thought in the man's head. Nothing stirred him, with the exception of when his daughter testified."

The jurors had noticed how pained Shawn Field appeared when his daughter was on the stand. "It was clear that he loved her," said a juror.

Several of the jurors were upset that Joan Demarest put such a young child on the stand. "Kate was traumatized," said another juror. "I felt sorry for her."

The prosecution had taken such care to provide proof of Shawn and Karly's DNA on the two large spoons found in the trash can at Shawn's house, but the fact that the spoons were recovered from the trash was more problematic than helpful for the scientists among the group. "Anything in the trash is a mixing ground for DNA," a juror explained. "We never accepted the spoons as evidence because of that."

The evidence that ultimately persuaded the jurors that Shawn Field killed Karly Sheehan came down to the photos of the battered Karly taken on Shawn's own camera; the timeline, which included text messages from Sarah Sheehan's phone; and lastly, the expert testimony of Dr. Carol Chervenak.

"Finally, we just decided we couldn't figure out what was going on in Shawn Field's mind, it is so twisted and dark," said a juror. "There was a lot of crying but I think everyone realized, let's go with what we've got, or we'll be a hung jury, and none of us wanted that."

In regards to the defense's closing argument that Sarah Sheehan had played a part in the killing of her daughter, Karly Sheehan, many of the jurors agreed. "I don't understand why the district attorney didn't charge her with reckless endangerment at the very least," said one juror.

Sarah may not have delivered the blow that killed Karly, but she was complicit in the murder, said another. "We saw the pictures of what Karly looked like that last day of her life. I couldn't see a total stranger looking like that and not do something."

The jury was not swayed by the emotional abuse argument presented by the prosecution. "They tried to paint Sarah as being scared of Shawn, but everyone saw Sarah as a much stronger woman than that. She's not the type to put up with that, but apparently she didn't care if her child got beaten."

But ultimately, the defense attorney's closing arguments directed at Sarah Sheehan proved to be of little merit. The evidence against Shawn was too great, and, besides, the district attorney had not charged Sarah with any crime for the jurors to consider.

"We weren't there to judge Sarah. We were there to judge Shawn. Whether I thought she had fault in the crime didn't matter. Shawn Field killed that little girl. I would have been perfectly happy giving him life without parole," a juror related.

Every juror I spoke with expressed the greatest degree of compassion for David Sheehan. David was, several jurors said, a real class act. They remain distraught that the system failed Karly and David. So many people got so many things wrong, and nothing was more glaring than early suspicion by the state and the police that David Sheehan was abusing his daughter. "I think David felt hunted," said one juror.

After the verdict was read, the jurors headed over to McMenamins pub, where they drank frothy brew and freely talked about the aspects of the trial they had not been able to discuss previously. On their way out of the courthouse, they were greeted by Gene Brill. The grandfather, who had shown up in court every single day wearing a suit, wanted to thank the jurors for all their hard work on his granddaughter's behalf.

"I was amazed he was thanking me," said one juror. "I would have thought he'd be upset at us for not coming through on capital murder charges. Gene Brill is such a gentleman."

The defense responded to the verdict by moving for a mistrial. Judge Holcomb denied the motion. Sentencing began on Wednesday, November 8, 2006. The day opened with Dan Koenig asking Judge Holcomb to allow Shawn Field to be taken back to the jail and given the opportunity to dress in a suit and tie, rather than the jail jumpsuit and shackles. Koenig said that Shawn was "not dressed in appropriate attire for the proceedings in a case of this gravity." The state opposed the defense's request, noting that Shawn was a convicted murderer. Koenig responded that Shawn was not a convicted murderer until sentencing took place.

Judge Holcomb assured Koenig that the court would not be prejudiced based on what Shawn Field was wearing. "I will not allow the defendant to go back and change his clothes," Judge Holcomb ruled. Given his obsession with his looks, Shawn Field couldn't have been too happy with Judge Holcomb's decision.

Six months pregnant and stricken with a winter bug, Joan Demarest apologized for her scratchy, almost-gone voice as she asked the court to hand down the maximum sentence for Shawn Wesley Field. "This is so much more than a murder case, Your Honor, and the jury's verdict indicates that. Shawn Field tortured Karly Sheehan. The defendant intentionally inflicted intense physical pain on her."

Under the felony murder charge, Oregon Law provided that Shawn Field would receive life in prison with the possibility of parole. Demarest asked the court to consecutively apply maximum sentences for the additional guilty convictions of assault, criminal mistreatment, manufacturing a controlled substance, and endangering the welfare of minor.

"The court can impose another twenty-eight years on top of the twenty-five years before the defendant will be eligible for parole, and we are asking the court to do that," Demarest said.

Throughout the next week the court heard witness statements from dozens of people whose lives had been impacted, most often regrettably, by Shawn Wesley Field. One of the first to tesify, and one of the angriest, was Brenda Baze, Eileen Field's mother and Kate's grandmother. She spoke with such force and power that the courtroom reverberated with the electricity of her anger.

"I am appalled at what Shawn Field has put my granddaughter through," Baze said. "Kate feels guilty for being so afraid to tell anyone what she heard. Kate blames herself for not telling anyone; she blames herself for not speaking up to you; she blames herself for being scared; and most of all she blames herself for leaving Karly with you that morning. *She. Heard. You. Hitting. Karly.* She will hear you hitting Karly forever. Dads are supposed to be our protectors, our heroes, not murderers and not torturers. You have destroyed Kate's life. Every Christmas, every holiday, every birthday that her dad is not there will be a reminder of what you did to Karly. I only pray that Kate will someday realize that what happened to Karly was not her fault."

When Sarah Sheehan took the stand to give her witness impact statement she was alternatively weepy and angry, but she was the most animated she had been throughout the trial. "How can you ask your own daughter to carry the burden of a brutal murder and torture around? You are the epitome of a self-centered, narcissistic psychopath," Sarah said.

The emotional restraint that David Sheehan had displayed throughout the months leading into the death of his daughter, and over the course of the trial, was frayed. As he gave his witness impact statement, David spoke rapidly, his Irish brogue more pronounced than ever, and he paused often, sighing heavily and swallowing back tears. "In the months following Karly's death, I battled depression and lost my will to live. I still agonize over what Shawn Field did to my baby. I can't imagine what Karly felt when she was left alone with that monster," David said. "Karly is the strongest person I have ever known. I urge the court to remember and reflect on the word 'torture' when considering sentencing."

On Wednesday, November 15, 2006, Judge Holcomb did just as David Sheehan bid her to do: she remembered the suffering of Karly. "Mr. Field, this is a very sober moment in our community. When you administered that last blow on June 3, 2005, the one that finally killed Karly Sheehan, you dealt a blow to our entire community, which was saddened and horrified by that murder," Judge Holcomb said.

"You have forever changed the lives of David and Sarah Sheehan and Gene and Carol Brill. You have changed the lives of their community of friends and other family members. You have changed the lives of fifteen community members, the jurors, who sat for over five weeks, listening to evidence that was deeply troubling and viewing photos that no one should ever have to see. Finally, you have moved our community, which has closely followed the reports of this case," the judge continued.

"As a community we have to do some deep soul-searching about how, or if, we might have responded sooner. Might there have been an intervention that could have saved this child's life? I don't know, but after hearing all the evidence it seems there was a continuum of failure after the first hint that there was something terribly, terribly wrong. If we are really willing to look at ourselves, this soul-searching might be the very little bit of good that we can create from this otherwise senseless loss.

"Mr. Field, in my nearly twenty years in the criminal justice system, this is one of the worst cases of brutality I have ever seen. The jury found you to be responsible, and it is now for me to hold you responsible and accountable." With those words, Judge Holcomb handed down exactly what Joan Demarest and the state had asked for, the maximum sentence allowed under the law: more than forty-six years without possibility of time off for good behavior.

When I spoke with Judge Holcomb, she wanted to know if I had had a chance to interview the jurors. I told her I had.

"They were an incredible jury," she said.

CHAPTER FORTY-THREE

STEPHEN MEYERS, A NEW YORK native, believes in resurrections. He's been through a couple himself. Before coming to Oregon State University to work on his Ph.D. in botany, Stephen worked as an air traffic controller, then as a stonecutter.

"A stonecutter?" I asked when we met for coffee at New Morning Bakery in Corvallis in March 2008.

"Yeah," Stephen said, pushing back his shoulder-length hair. "The person who carves the headstones for graves."

I've been to hundreds of gravesites in my lifetime, and never gave a passing thought to the person with the job of carving in all those names and dates—until I met Meyers.

Stephen was one of the eight men and four women who found Shawn W. Field guilty of torturing Karly to death. The jurors' lives have been forever altered by the death of Karly Sheehan. Some still have nightmares.

Stephen's been to Karly's grave a couple of times since the trial.

"I think about Karly a lot," Stephen said. "I think about Kate, too. I wonder, does she have a chance at being okay?"

I wonder that myself.

Kate is in high school now. Driving, dating, picking out dresses for the dances, doing all the things Karly will never do.

It was obvious from the drawings Kate did for the ABC House that she witnessed far more violence than she was able to testify to. On one of her doodles, done on white paper with black bold writing, Kate wrote: Dad, kidnap, scary, kids, strangers. On another she wrote the words, perfectly spelled: Bitch. Fuck. On another she helped identify in a drawing the layout of the house. In the center of it are two stick figures. On the back she wrote, again in black bold letters: Share. Eye. Spoon. And she's blacked out the upper left corner, where she had written the words: Dad, I wanted…

I can't make out the rest of what it is Kate wanted from her dad.

In those early days of his arrest, Shawn wrote letters to Kate. I don't know if she ever saw the letters or not. In one, Shawn tells his daughter:

I know it's hard to understand why Daddy is not with you. But understand that life can sometimes be unfair to all of us. We must just do the best we can and move on. Please go give your mommy a big hug and tell her that I love the both of you.

Love always and forever, Daddy

It's obvious from his "life is unfair" remark, Shawn is trying to say he's a victim in all of this. In another letter written from jail, Shawn tells Kate:

Hello again Princess!

This is daddy again. It's about 5:30 on Monday, June 13, 2005. I was just thinking of you and wanted to write you some more. Daddy got a little sad earlier today. But I just thought of you and your wonderful smile and your big hugs and kisses and I got happy. I wonder if you are in Disneyland right now. All wet from the log ride and with a tummy full of good treats.

Remember to always keep that beautiful smile on your face and give all the love you have to others. Your (sic) such a special person and I love you with all my heart and soul.

Love, Daddy

I believe Shawn loved his daughter, however imperfectly. I believe Shawn couldn't imagine hurting Kate as he did Karly.

I spoke with Kate's maternal grandmother, Brenda Baze. She told me Kate has no contact with Shawn, or with her paternal grandparents.

Shawn's lead defense attorney, Dan Koenig, met me at Starbucks in Hermiston one winter's night. He and Shawn were hammering out an appeal on his conviction. A former Marine, Dan has a commanding presence, a head full of dark hair, and unflinching gray eyes. He's as comfortable packing a rump sack over the rough terrain of the Wallowa-Whitman National Forest as he is stringing a jury along. He can converse easily about the best places to hunt elk or about the wrongs inflicted upon Chief Joseph and his people. And he can recite with the accuracy of a history teacher every major Civil War battle and why the losers lost.

He grew up in Kelso, Washington, among loggers and green-chain gangers. He knows how to read a jury.

"My only concern is that twelve-person jury. I don't even care what the judge thinks," Dan said. His thick fingers were wrapped around a cup of bold roast coffee, a diamond ring on one finger.

Dan spent eight years as a district attorney before switching over to criminal defense. Predictably in Shawn's case, he thinks the jury flubbed up. "That Corvallis jury is different than any other I've ever had. Almost all of them had a master's degree or were working on one. Corvallis is a big town trying to be small."

Dan thought Sarah's motivation for killing Karly was better than Shawn's.

"So you don't think Shawn was trying to extort money from David?" I asked.

"Why?" Dan said. "At the time of Karly's death, Shawn was bringing in as much money as David between his parents and his school loans. Check it out," he challenged.

So I did. Shawn's parents were reportedly giving him $11,000 each, all part of keeping his inheritance tax-free for as long as possible. He worked part time at a restaurant but had only been doing that for a few weeks. His jobs at OSU were all drummed up. It's hard to know how reliable his school loans were, given that Shawn's claims about pursuing his degree were bogus.

"There's some dirty little secret behind why Heiser didn't charge Sarah," Dan said.

"What kind of secret?" I asked.

"I don't know," Dan said, shrugging. "But most courts would have charged them both and let them hang each other."

That's true. I had witnessed that time and time again during my days covering the court beat in Eastern Oregon. Prosecutors usually had no trouble getting one defendant to rat out the other one. And the quickest way to justice usually hinged on charging both people whenever a crime duet was in doubt.

"There's an hour gap between the last text message Sarah sent Shawn and when she arrived home. How do we know Sarah didn't do it? She had sent David a text message saying she had a rough night."

There was no hour gap. Demarest had proved that in court by entering Sarah's time card as evidence.

"If you have proof that Sarah killed Karly, why didn't you offer that up in court during the trial?" I asked.

"Police never even considered Sarah a suspect," Dan said. "I don't buy into that victim mentality of hers."

Sarah testified that Shawn had only hit her once, and even that was only teasingly; still, it hurt, she had said. That's why Demarest made a point to talk about all the ways in which emotional abuse can be just as debilitating as physical abuse.

"Was Sarah given immunity?" Dan asked.

"In a sense," I said. "Her testimony before the Grand Jury protected her."

I repeated to Dan a remark someone in the Par 3 crowd had made the night I visited with them: "*They got the right guy. They just haven't gotten the girl yet.*"

It was a sentiment I'd heard time and time again from Sarah's former friends, Karly's former daycare providers, lawyers and lawmen, and concerned community members.

Dan smiled. He'd love for a jury to think Sarah was responsible somehow.

"C'mon, you really believe your guy's innocent?" I asked. "You're paid to believe that."

"I don't concern myself with what I believe," Dan replied. "I worry about what I can prove or not prove. That's a different question."

CHAPTER FORTY-FOUR

KARLY'S DEATH CHANGED THE WAY Delynn Zoller interacts with her daycare children.

"There are days when you have so many children you are just going through the motions," Delynn said. "I wish I'd spent more time with Karly. I wish I hadn't been so busy."

Karly had an animal book at home her daddy used to read to her. There were four animals in it, and whenever David read it, Karly would point to each animal and name it: "That's Daddy. That's Mommy. That's Karly. And that's Delynn."

Call her paranoid, but Delynn said every mother's boyfriend is now suspect in her mind. If a child cowers behind a chair, crying, "I'm scared of him," as one tyke recently did, Delynn wastes no time in reporting it.

Shortly after Karly died, Delynn sat down and wrote a letter to the parents of the other children in her daycare:

> Dear Parents –
>
> I wrote this newsletter last week and cannot add anything new (computer problems!) but I wanted to say something about Karly before we all move on with the day-to-day life and she

fades into my memory like so many other children in my past.

Your child's friend, Karly's, full name was Karla Isabelle Ruth Sheehan. She was white-blonde with sky blue eyes. She was half Irish and looked like a pixie. She was extremely smart and could talk and think like a 5-year-old even though she was only 3. She wanted to grow up and be Princess Fiona and marry her daddy, Prince Charming.

She was easy to care for and played very well with all the kids. She could play with them and make up games regardless of their different personalities. She was quiet and talked softly to everyone. Never hit, yelled or threw any type of tantrum. She was easily one of the best-behaved children I have ever had over these many years.

She turned 3 on January 4th. She used to sing "You say potato, I say patato" and told me her daddy sang that to her. He is Irish and has an accent! She loved to eat the snap peas from my garden and wanted to even dig up the old carrots that I'd left there over the winter—to eat! She hummed while she ate her food. I would tell the kids that she was singing in her mouth!

She loved Dragon Tales and played "Dragon" with the other kids. Her favorite color was blue, "like my eyes" she would always say. Her daddy told me her favorite foods were fried onions and Shepherds pie. I always told her she was a weird kid. She would laugh and run around and get all goosey and then talk like a baby.

She asked me a lot about God and Jesus. And she wore a small silver cross around her neck that her daddy gave to her for her birthday. She told me "God protects everyone" and that Jesus was taking good care of her, and that's why she had his cross.

I loved Karly and so did all the kids. And I would like to

say that God did protect her. He was taking care of her by his dramatic rescue of her. It was an answer to many prayers for her safety. Now she is a princess in heaven.

I hope we can turn this terrible grief into a time of glory for God and His purpose on this earth.

Thank you,

Delynn

As I write this, I am sitting in a cottage not far from Mobile Bay. There's a chorus of mockingbirds heralding the morning sun. Mockingbirds are monogamous, often for life, not just for a season. Male mockingbirds are territorial, particularly during mating season.

Nesting is a chore attended by both the male and female mocks. They build their nests not far from the ground, in the forks of trees or bushes. Their nests are vulnerable to predators. But in the sacred shelter of adult mockingbirds, tiny ones thrive.

Although they aren't very big, mockingbirds are fierce about protecting their young. They will drill anyone and anything they consider a danger to their offspring, no matter the size of the predator. Mockingbirds will swoop down from the skies like kamikazes to dive-bomb snakes, cats, dogs, pigs, or people.

In a study published in the *Proceedings of the National Academy of Sciences,* researchers at the University of Florida campus in Gainesville discovered mocks are incredibly perceptive about identifying predators. In fact, mockingbirds are so keen they can pick out *exactly* which person, among thousands, poses a threat.

Volunteers who had previously touched nests where the baby birds were sheltered were repeatedly singled out. The birds seemed to bear a grudge against those who interfered. Even when the volunteers dressed in different clothing or came from different directions or in groups, the birds still knew which person had been the greatest threat. These mockingbirds could pick out from thousands of students which particular volunteer had messed with their nests, and would attack that person.

"We think our experiments reveal the mocks' underlying ability to be incredibly perceptive of everything around them, and to respond appropriately when the stakes are high," said lead researcher Doug Levey.

When their young are threatened, mockingbirds take action.

Should we do any less?

That is the question Judge Janet Holcomb asked just prior to sentencing Shawn Field.

And it is the same question that David Sheehan's father, James Sheehan, considered in the witness impact statement that he wrote from his home in Kenmare, County Kerry, Ireland.

"Six thousand miles can be a barrier at the best of times. It can be a major barrier when you're trying to get to know your granddaughter," James Sheehan said. "But get to know Karly we did quite well, largely through her two trips to Ireland. It was during the latter of these trips that she proved the old adage true: 'If I had known grandchildren could be this much fun, I would have had them first.'"

James Sheehan noted that it was his trips to Karly's hometown of Corvallis that gave him further insights into his granddaughter. "On the second of these trips, we took Karly to St. Mary's Catholic Church. It was a joyous day, with a lot of fond memories. But little did we realize that on our next trip to Corvallis, we would again be taking Karly to St. Mary's, to a little plot on the slopes of a wooded hill.

"Yes, Karly was gone, taken from us in a cruel and brutal manner. Events of that June weekend opened a wound in our hearts that no amount of retribution will ever heal, but it will stop the sopping around the moon every day for the rest of our lives," James Sheehan said.

"The one thing that impressed me about Corvallis was its community spirit," he added. "It's a town where everybody helped and cared for one another. But as in any community, whether it be Corvallis or a small town in Ireland, greed will infest the minds of some individuals, and it is made all the more sickening when that greed hurts those who are the most vulnerable in society.

"Our kids need our attention, our caring, our love—not our selfishness, our apathy, or our anger. The kids you see around every day are not just kids, they are your future engineers, teachers, police, doctors, and they should all be given the chance to achieve these goals. Nobody must be allowed to take away that chance from them by any means, and certainly not by the violent means that took that chance away from Karly. You must send out a very clear message to any budding criminal entrepreneur that you will not tolerate these actions in your society. So that you never again have to read the kind of headlines you've been reading the past four weeks. God bless you."

I am no lyricist, but I am pretty sure I can make out the mockingbird call this morning—and if I'm right, it is a call of caution: *Remember Karly. Remember Karly. Remember Karly.*

CHAPTER FORTY-FIVE

EMMET WHITTAKER HAD IN MIND for some time that David and Liz might make a good match. Emmet was eager to see David happy, given all the heartache. It took some scheming, but along with some help from his wife, Sanna, Emmet finally managed to set David and Liz up. Emmet and Sanna had talked about it ahead of time, of course: how they could get these two together.

Liz Sokolowski is a lithe classic beauty: Audrey Hepburn with fair hair and shockingly blue eyes. She moves with grace and embodies that *katharos* Jesus spoke of when he said, "Blessed are the pure in heart for they shall see God" (Matt.5:8).

David couldn't help but notice her. "I'd always thought she was cute," he said. Their first few encounters in early 2008 were sporadic. David would meet Emmet after work on Fridays for a beer. Liz would join Sanna for a glass of wine. David had had surgery on his shoulder and couldn't drive, so Emmet would pick him up, and because Liz lived closer to him, she would give David a ride home. Their conversations were clumsy. Mostly, David would talk to Emmet and Liz would talk to Sanna.

One evening, a large group of HP professionals got together for dinner and to attend a friend's play. David decided to ratchet things up a notch. "I made sure to sit across from Liz at dinner and next to her at the play," David said. "But another friend was talking to Liz about a handsome friend of hers. She wanted to set Liz up on a date. I was thinking, 'How handsome can this guy be? Maybe he's not!'"

Fortunately, nothing ever came of that, thanks to Emmet and Sanna, who had finally devised a plan to get David and Liz alone. "You want to meet Sanna and me for breakfast Sunday?" Emmet asked David.

"Sure," David said.

"Liz might join us," Emmet added.

Splendid! Breakfast with Liz was something David had been yearning for. On those Friday nights when Liz would give David the occasional ride home, he found himself entranced. "I often wanted to reach across and plant a big kiss on her face," David said.

Liz, however, didn't have a clue David was crushing on her. "He was so quiet," she said. "We usually sat in different spots, so the only time we talked was on those rides home. I didn't get the idea he was interested in me."

And David didn't know that Liz was already in love. "I loved David right off the bat," Liz said. "I know that sounds crazy, but I feel like I did."

The foursome met for Sunday breakfast at a neighborhood bakery. But when Sanna had to leave for an appointment (or so she claimed), Emmet suggested everyone else head over to The Beanery for some coffee. The three of them found a table and had just gotten their mugs of coffee when Emmet stood up abruptly and announced he had somewhere else to be. It was so obvious to both David and Liz they were being set up that they laughed.

"Emmet thought we were a good match from a personality stand-point," Liz said. "He was trying to get us in the same place at the same time. He wanted David to be happy."

In my almost weekly phone conversations with David during the spring of 2008, he told me about the pretty, smart chick from Chicago. He sent me e-mails, reassuring me that he intended to be extra careful this time around. In May, he sent me this note:

> Hey Elly May (his pet name for me),
>
> I will keep doing this group thing for a while and see where it goes. Anyway, Liz might have no interest in me, so it could be a moot point. But I hope she is interested; she's a sweetheart. She e-mailed me on Tuesday to acknowledge Karly's anniversary and she offered to help with the playground on Wednesday.

That had been a big point of concern for me. David knows I disapprove of the silent treatment when it comes to grief of any sort. A loving mate doesn't tell their partner, "I don't want to hear about all that." Initially, I held my tongue (a first for me) because I loved David and, like Emmet, wanted so badly for him to be happy. When he told me Liz had sent him an e-mail acknowledging the anniversary of Karly's death, he knew it would score big points with me. He was right. It softened my heart toward Liz right away.

Liz has the gift of mercy, the result of having grown up hearing all those tragic tales of the Polish people. "I'm drawn to people who have suffered," she said—part of why she was drawn to David. "I had a huge amount of compassion and empathy for him. I couldn't imagine what it was like to lose Karly. David was so kind. From the start, I got this sense that he was a good, good person. I didn't know if we would wind up getting married or not, but I thought that we might."

Falling in love with the father of a murdered child isn't the hard part; figuring out how to talk to him about his child is what takes some skill. Liz wanted David to know that he could talk about Karly with her anytime.

"David can be hard to read. He's very reserved. He was concerned; he didn't want all this to be the focus of our relationship."

One of their first dates was a trip to Karly's grave. It was Memorial Day weekend, this one marking the third anniversary of Karly's death. David debated whether to ask Liz to go to the cemetery with him. There was a lot of complicated history to consider.

"He was pretty cautious," Liz said. "He thought maybe I didn't want to hear about it, maybe I didn't want to go with him—but he told me he was going and asked if I could come along."

Karly is buried on a gentle hillside at St. Mary's Cemetery. Not surprisingly, David picked the spot and planned the funeral without any help from Sarah. He didn't want her input. He waited for his family from Ireland to arrive before burying Karly, so although Karly was killed on Friday, June 3, 2005, Karly's services didn't take place until the following Thursday.

When she saw Sarah Sheehan across the room at the funeral home, Noreen Sheehan hesitated. Should she speak to her former daughter-in-law? Could she speak to her? It was a question Andrea debated as well. Andrea was so angry she had no intention of speaking to Sarah, but when David implored his sister to be mannerly, Andrea walked up to Sarah and said, "I'm sorry."

"I'm sorry, too," Sarah replied.

Those were the only words the former sisters-in-law exchanged.

But that was more than Noreen received. "This was the mother of my granddaughter," Noreen said, "so I did approach her. I put my arm around her and asked, 'Sarah, what happened to our little girl?'"

Sarah never said anything, not then or the next day at the graveside. The two women sat side by side, and when the time came for them to put flowers on Karly's grave, Noreen asked, "Sarah, are you ready to do this?"

Silence was all that Sarah offered Noreen Sheehan. Karly's graveside service was the last time the two saw each other.

Noreen Sheehan struggles with the passage of time. "I could picture what Karly would have been like at four, maybe, but not what kind of nine-year-old little girl she would be."

Karly's grandmother thinks about all the plans she had for Karly and mourns for what might have been. "We are left with the sadness, our own and the sadness of our son losing his only child."

It's the memories that strengthen Noreen: "The memories of talking to her on the phone. She sang happy birthday to me only two weeks before she died and asked if I would love a cupcake."

Even now the recollection of that brings a smile to Noreen's face. "These are the memories of a little girl I will love forever and never forget, and so life goes on."

Andrea has her memories, too.

"I think of Karly every day, mostly of the beautiful little girl who came to visit, who wanted to visit the chippy fry store for 'chocolate moatshakes.' I think of all the goodness she brought to our lives. But it's hard not to think of how she suffered at the hands of that monster, and to this day I cannot understand how her mother didn't protect her. I know it's wrong but I hate what Sarah did to my brother and to my family. She took away a treasured child, grandchild, niece, and cousin, and for that I cannot forgive her."

Burying Karly violently tore David from the arms of all he held precious. While he can't cuddle her, suds up her hair, or kick a soccer ball between the two of them, or awaken his sleeping princess with the perfect kiss, David feels her presence when he's sitting with her under the tree on that knoll, watching the deer and squirrels romp like storybook animals. Karly would love that.

•

A year after Karly's death, Andrea's son, who is only seven weeks older than Karly, asked his mother to take him to town to buy some wings.

"What do you need wings for?" Andrea asked.

"So I can fly straight to Heaven and bring Karly home in my arms," he replied.

When it grows dark in Ireland, Andrea's children ask their mother, "Why did Karly turn off the lights?" And when it rains in County Kerry, as it so often does, Karly's cousins ask their mother, "Is Karly splashing in the bathwater again?"

These are the ways Karly's cousins keep her memory alive, through stories of tricks they imagine Karly playing on them.

David and Liz parked on a slope near Karly's plot. The air smelled of wet bark. A bright mixture of fresh and artificial flowers were scattered about the graves like mismatched colored socks. A spinning flower garden ornament marked Karly's headstone.

St. Mary's is a pioneer cemetery, with graves dating back to the mid-1800s. Catholic families paid $50 for the two-and-half-acre cemetery in 1873. Some of the graves' inscriptions have eroded with the passing of time and the soft rub of gentle rain. Although located by some of the city's most well-traveled streets, the cemetery is shrouded with trees: tall ones and short ones, thin ones and thick ones, a protective shoulder-to-shoulder watch. Sometimes, most often in the spring, OSU students will bring their books and study under the oaks.

David led Liz over to Karly's plot. They had brought carnations— something the deer wouldn't eat. David knelt in the damp soil, wiped wet leaves from the headstone, and traced his fingers over Karly's name.

Karly had been baptized at St. Mary's on Easter, Resurrection Sunday. She wore her daddy's baptismal gown. It all seemed fitting now, almost poetic. This child who so willfully kept rising above the darkness. She was joyful and merry, curious and cute, and so very independent.

David had taken her to Avery Park one late summer afternoon to play. When it came time to leave, Karly put up a fuss—she was not ready to go, not yet. "Hold my hand," David said, holding out his open palm. Karly reached up to take her daddy's hand, then, pausing briefly, she grasped his wrist instead. It was a technical defiance, one that had David laughing to himself as they walked off into the golden sunshine.

One night David was in the kitchen preparing dinner, but Karly didn't want to wait for supper; she was hungry now. She walked toward the refrigerator. "Karly, do not touch that fridge," her father instructed. The impetuous child put out her hand and touched it ever so slightly with her index finger. She then looked up sweetly, assuredly at her father. Score! Another technicality. David had to fight to keep from laughing at Karly's willful ways.

These joyful memories break his heart. The times he had to stifle his laughter in order to teach his daughter to do better. That impish personality that was all bubbles, and brightness, and boldness, all Karly—that is what David misses most. It is not the memory of her death that haunts him; it is the memory of her living.

David began to sob as grief pitched through him. Standing behind him, Liz reached out and placed a hand on his shoulder. It was a simple gesture, but the sentiment was not.

"I'd never seen him like that before," she said. "The only thing I can do is be there to support him, whatever grieving he needs to do, now and forever. I want to be there."

Karly had done that once: touched her daddy's shoulder in that very same way. It was the Saturday night after her death. David was lying face down in the bed. He'd been inconsolable then, too. All of a sudden, he felt Karly's little hands rubbing his shoulders. She didn't say anything, and neither did he, but his breathing relaxed and he fell into a deep and restful sleep.

A visitation from the child of Resurrection.

"I know that was Karly saying goodbye to me before she went to Heaven," David said.

EPILOGUE

INMATE 16002306 HAS REFUSED ALL my requests for an interview. One law enforcement official offered that perhaps the reason Shawn Field will not meet with me is that it gives him a certain amount of control. The causes of child abuse are multidimensional: drug abuse, mental illness, domestic violence, or an abusive childhood, to name a few. Some abusers do it simply to exercise power and control.

Perhaps the theory that Shawn Field wanted to extort money from David is true. But it could also be true that Shawn Field tortured Karly because he is a sick bully. He liked the power it gave him. David believes this and so do I. It certainly helps explain why Shawn began to torture Karly almost as soon he struck up a relationship with Sarah.

I have no relationship with Sarah. We have not spoken to each other in the past few years. I cannot tell you what she thinks. I can only tell you she continues to act as if life is one big party thrown in her honor. Her Facebook is full of photos of her all dolled up, or scantily clad, at one party or another. She's usually snuggled up to some new groovy guy—often several of them—although they are getting older and older.

On what would have been Karly's ninth birthday, Sarah made a trip to Corvallis and, while she made no mention of Karly, Sarah did put up this post on her Facebook: "Status update: traffic in Seattle to be expected. Traffic in Corvallis, OR? Effing annoying. I've been at the same gd traffic light for twenty minutes. Gah, I LOATHE this town!!!" (Emphasis Sarah's).

People who know this story often ask me, what do you make of Sarah? It is a difficult question to answer. I am conflicted. I love and adore the girl that I met in that Helix classroom all those years ago. But the Sarah who repeatedly placed Karly in the hands of her killer, and lied about it as she was doing it, evokes grief and sadness. Not only is Karly lost to us forever, so is the Sarah I once regarded as a daughter.

The most telling moment of this entire story for me came the day I visited the Oregon Court of Appeals. Because Shawn Field was appealing his conviction—an appeal he lost—the evidentiary files were being stored at the Judicial Department's building in Salem. I spent a few days going through the documents, word by word, photograph by photograph. When I came across a video investigators had made at Shawn's place the day Karly died, I asked if I could view that tape.

Having already been screened by security, I was escorted to a room with a television. It was while watching, and re-watching, the tape that I realized that when Karly was at Shawn's house she slept on the floor. While there were bunk beds in the tidy bedroom, there was only one mattress: the one for Kate. Sarah testified that Shawn was fanatical about the all-white couch in the living room, yelling at her if she so much as let Karly sit on the couch, worried that she might accidentally tinkle on it.

So on the last night of her life, Karly slept on a folded-up blanket on the floor in Kate's room. Seeing that pallet on the floor in a room that sang Kate's name with its leopard-print décor, Hilary Duff poster, and cat toys, I realized how diminished Karly must have felt, sleeping on the floor like a servant girl, not even allowed to sit on the sofa.

I sometimes wonder whose betrayal hurt Karly most: Shawn or Sarah's? Every child expects their parent to be their protector, their defender, their safe shelter. It must have been very confusing for Karly to have her mother choose her own wants over her daughter's needs.

The public might find it startling, but the people who work on the front lines of child abuse assessment centers routinely encounter mothers, who for a host of complex reasons, put their children in harm's way. Or, more commonly, inflict the abuse themselves. Even after all these years of diligent research, I struggle to understand why Sarah repeatedly left Karly alone with Shawn. As a mother and a grandmother, my heart breaks for the neglected and abused children among us. We can and we must do better by them.

David sued the Oregon Department of Human Services for negligence in Karly's death. The lawsuit maintained the state did not conduct appropriate follow-up on abuse complaints, lost photographic evidence, failed to properly train workers, and failed to have Karly examined by a medical examiner. The state's attorneys were aggressive in their response, putting the blame where the state had always put the blame: on David. "The damages alleged by (David Sheehan) were the direct and proximate result of his own negligence in failing to report to the state facts he knew about Karly Sheehan's condition."

The case was settled out of court with a non-disclosure clause. David has established an endowment through the Benton County Foundation in Karly's honor. "I think every kid should have an equal shot at life," David said. "I think it's a pretty sad reflection on our society that there are fundamentals that kids just don't have. I wanted to try and do a little bit to level that playing field."

Once the community learned of Karly's death, David received a deluge of condolences, cards and donations. He used the money gifts along with Karly's college fund to build a playground at Avery Park in memory of Karly. For locals, Avery Park represents the best of Corvallis. There are kites flying, bicyclists pedaling, joggers running, dogs fetching, families picnicking, people visiting, and children laughing. David spent a lot of time with Karly at Avery Park.

In September 2007, I stopped by the memorial playground and called David to tell him I was there. A toddler in a red t-shirt and blue jeans was scooching down the slide as his mama held onto his dimpled hand. Nearby, a copper-headed girl squealed in laughter as her mother gave her a push in the swing. David told me there was a plaque inscribed with Karly's name on the wooden structure attached to the slide.

David and the good people of Corvallis built the memorial to Karly in a grassy sanctuary, surrounded by lichen-covered trees. This is the place where children kick their way to the sun and back without ever leaving their swings, where wind speaks in whispers and laughter hollers as loud as it wants.

When David and Liz have children, if they are so blessed, they will take Karly's brothers and sisters to that playground and speak to them of the sister who died. One day, when those children are old enough to understand, David will tell them of the whole story of Karly. David and Liz will remind their children that evil is always threatened by goodness and that the only way we can truly honor Karly is to be good and joyful like she was.

Six months into his third term, and only a couple of weeks after the sentencing of Shawn W. Field, Scott Heiser resigned his position as Benton County District Attorney. He cited Judge Janet Holcomb's conduct in the trial as the reason for his departure. Justified or not, his feud with Holcomb was legendary. He had filed motions to have her disqualified in nine high-profile cases. Heiser said he would ask the Commission of Judicial Fitness and Disability to assess Holcomb's conduct in the trial of Karly Sheehan.

Heiser now works with the Animal Legal Defense Fund on behalf of those who can't defend themselves.

Dr. deSoyza left her job, too. I asked her if she left her practice behind because of Karly's case. She marked up her departure to issues with administration. Specifically, Dr. deSoyza said she wanted to take unpaid leave to go visit family in Sri Lanka, but the administration wasn't keen on the idea.

When a job at the Oregon State University campus opened up, she thought it was the perfect position, from a mother's standpoint. She gets vacations and most of her summer off. There are no rounds or weekend rotations.

There's also no chance she's ever going to deal with the nightmare of child abuse again. "Most of my patients are younger and middle-aged women," she said. "It's interesting to work with college students, but I miss my babies. Pediatrics was a pretty large part of my practice."

She still thinks about Sarah Sheehan, about the "what ifs" of Karly's death. "Sometimes I wonder if Sarah had not been my patient, whether I would have been more suspicious. Having had a relationship with her the way I did, she didn't seem like the kind of person who would put their child at risk."

Officer Dave Cox resigned from the Corvallis Police Department in 2007 amidst allegations that he was arresting sober motorists on DUI charges. Cox averaged twenty-plus arrests a month for drunken driving charges. Eight citations was the average for most city police officers.

The Oregon State Bar disciplined Clark Willes, the defense attorney who opened up his case files to me, in 2008 for fraudulent behavior. Willes had his client sit in the gallery and put another person at the counsel table in an attempt to keep the state's witness from positively identifying the defendant. Willes disclosed the ruse himself following the testimony of the state's witness.

Detective Mike Wells left the Corvallis Police Department after a distinguished career. He now works as a special agent with the Oregon Department of Justice. In 2007, he received DOJ's Officer of the Year award. He has traveled around the nation, telling Karly's story and instructing others in the field how to avoid the pitfalls that led to her death. Throughout the investigation of Karly's murder, Detective Wells was disturbed by Sarah Sheehan's actions. "I have never lost one hour of sleep over whether Shawn Field killed Karly, but I have lost sleep over what role Sarah Sheehan played in Karly's death. Rightly or wrongly, the decision not to charge Sarah with anything was made early on."

On the first anniversary of Karly's death, most of the jurors gathered together to remember the little girl for whom they'd rendered justice. They thought it would be an annual event but it hasn't been.

One juror wrote recently to say that he had thought the trauma of the trial was all behind him, until he was called to serve on yet another jury. "It wasn't at all emotionally charged, simply awarding financial damages, but once I sat in the same courtroom, in the same jury box, looking out of the same windows and seeing the similar fall colors in the leaves, I teared up and had such an anxiety attack that I asked to be removed, which was quickly granted after they learned I was a juror for the Karly trial," he said. "It kind of surprised me, since I rarely think about the trial or any of the key players."

Flashback moments like this juror experienced are referred to in military circles as post-traumatic stress disorder, or PTSD. You don't have to go to war to suffer from it.

Karly was one of eighteen children who died in Oregon in 2005 because of child abuse. Two years after Karly's death, and due in part to the tireless efforts of Representative Sara Gelser of Corvallis, the Oregon State Legislature unanimously passed a bill in support of child-abuse victims.

Karly's Law mandates that if a caseworker or law enforcement officer interviews a child with suspicious injuries, they must take photos of those injuries and the pictures have to be shared with the Child Abuse Response Team. Additionally, a previously designated medical professional with specialized training in child abuse must see that child within forty-eight hours.

These safeguards were put in place as a direct result of what were deemed the failures in Karly's case. While Matthew Stark conferred by phone with Dr. Carol Chervenak on Karly's case, the doctor never examined Karly herself. Instead, Karly was seen by her family physician, who did not have the tools necessary to make the correct diagnosis.

Joan Demarest has opened her own practice, focusing on criminal defense, victim advocacy, and family law. Additionally, she devotes time each week to helping OSU students with legal problems. She also worked alongside Representative Gelser in the push to get Karly's Law passed. "Gelser approached me after Karly's trial and wanted help drafting meaningful legislation that would make it less likely that this could happen again," Demarest said.

"Rep. Gelser had been told by DHS that the real problem was that they weren't able to access people's criminal histories," Demarest explained. "I told Gelser that was nonsense. Shawn Field had no record of note." Demarest told Gelser that the failure was that Karly was never seen or treated by a trained child abuse specialist like Dr. Chervenak. "As you may recall, we had a patrol officer concluding that Shawn Field's explanations of Karly's injuries were valid," Demarest said. "Representative Gelser did an amazing job working with different factions and getting Karly's Law passed. David Sheehan and I testified at the hearing."

Rep. Gelser says that Demarest came to those hearings with a baby in arms.

"Most prosecutors move on to the next thing after a case is done, Joan did not.

"Her willingness to come to the capitol multiple times with a newborn didn't go without notice. I specifically remember checking before the hearing on where there would be a comfortable place for breast-feeding while Joan was in the building, because her son must have been only about three or four weeks old at the first hearing. She came not only for the hearings, but she sat in the gallery when the bill was voted for on the floor."

Putting Shawn Field away was not enough for Joan Demarest. She continues in her efforts in helping improve the lives of children.

"Over the years since the case, I've watched as Joan continues to talk about ABC House," Gelser said. "Joan encourages people to make contributions or to serve on their board. I've seen her urge contributions to child abuse-related causes instead of gifts to her children on their birthdays."

A few months following the Karly Sheehan trial, Joan Demarest gave birth to a healthy baby boy. She is now the mother to four children —three boys and a girl. Joan Demarest loves being a mother.

I asked Representative Gelser why, of all the issues brought before her, she latched onto Karly's Law and has fought so diligently for it. A mother of four, Gelser followed the news reports on Karly's death closely. She was mortified that such a tragedy happened right in her own backyard.

"The right thing to do is often a hard thing to do," Representative Gelser said. "Child abuse is grossly underreported." Too often people see children as property and parents as owners of that property, Gelser said. Onlookers are reluctant to interfere. "I can't imagine how many people have seen something and wondered but failed to take the difficult step of reporting it." As is too often the case, people do not get involved until child abuse affects them personally, and even then they remain reticent.

Gelser has been fielding phone calls from officials in other states, wondering how they might also implement Karly's Law. It should be a federal law that any child with injuries be photographed and seen within forty-eight hours by a medical professional trained in child abuse. But most doctors lack the training to correctly make such an assessment.

"On average a medical provider gets less than fifteen hours of training concerning child abuse issues in medical school. That is not enough," said Karen Scheler, director of ABC House. If Karly's case had been handled correctly, as Dr. Chervenak testified, she would have identified Karly's injuries as classic signs of abuse. A doctor with specialized training in child abuse is twice as likely to correctly diagnose abuse as one who hasn't received the appropriate training.

"Karly's Law is making a difference," Representative Gelser said. "It's been quite effective at getting these kids identified a lot earlier."

Abuse centers throughout the state are seeing a jump in the number of children they assess. The first year Karly's Law went into effect, ABC House saw a jump of 150 additional child abuse referrals. Dr. Chervenak was called in on each of those. On average, the ABC House serves 350 children in-house and an additional 150 through consultation.

Rarely does a law receive the support of the full legislature the way Karly's Law did. Representative Gelser was elated that the bill passed unanimously—understandably so, since she had put her formidable shoulder to pushing it through.

But passing a law is easy enough for any legislative body. The real struggle is funding such mandates. The budget for the ABC House is cobbled together from a variety of sources, including grants, medical billing, specialty funding from the state, and private donors. Rep. Gelser worked hard to find funding to support the impact of Karly's Law on centers like the ABC House. At her urging, Oregon legislators dedicated a million dollars toward funding Karly's Law. But then the recession hit and that money went to help backfill harsh cuts made to the Child Abuse Multidisciplinary Intervention (CAMI) funds.

Karly's Law brought an additional workload to ABC House and other child abuse centers throughout the state. "We in Oregon are dedicated to doing better and Karly has been the inspiration for that," said Karen Scheler. "But it is a struggle every day. This year our agency had 160 consults for physical abuse alone."

Finding the resources to meet the needs is difficult. Taxpayers will pay to lock people like Shawn Field away for life, but when it comes to funding the people who are working "boots on the ground," our state's Child Abuse Response teams or Child Abuse Intervention Centers, those positions are considered expendable. Just another strike-through on a line-item budget.

Rep. Gelser agrees that the funding issue remains a problem for cash-strapped states. But Oregon's legislators took the bold move of dedicating funds to Karly's Law, even when they could least afford to do so. "It was a good-faith effort on their behalf," said Rep. Gelser.

Funding issues aren't the only problems that arise during a recession. Domestic abuse and child abuse rates rise during times of economic hardships. Twenty-two children died in Oregon in 2010 as a result of child abuse—nearly twice the number of children who died in 2009. Most of those children had never been reported as potential victims or evaluated at a Child Abuse Intervention Center, like the ABC House.

Nobody was issuing a cry for help on their behalf. There was only the silence of people who suspected but never spoke up.

Dr. Chervenak serves Linn and Benton counties—one doctor to assess all those cases, all those children. And when she is on vacation or sick, she reviews cases via the Internet.

The medical assessment component of Karly's Law has been a huge challenge. "When the law was envisioned, we thought a lot more doctors would advocate for this. But they don't like to be involved in these cases. It can take up a lot of time—all the training, plus the possibility of having to appear in court," Representative Gelser said.

Every five hours, a child in the U.S. dies from abuse or neglect, according to a 2011 investigation by the BBC journalist Natalia Antelava. The U.S. has the highest child abuse record in the industrialized world. America's child abuse death rate is triple Canada's and eleven times that of Italy. High rates of teen pregnancy, high school dropout rates, violent crime, imprisonment, and poverty are some of the contributing factors, said Michael Petit, president of Every Child Matters.

Here in America, a report of child abuse is made every ten seconds. Here in the land of the free, an estimated 906,000 children are victims of abuse and neglect every single year. That's nearly a million children. Here in the home of the brave, 1,500 abused children die annually, usually from injuries sustained in their own homes.

In Oregon alone, there were 11,090 confirmed victims of child abuse during the most recent reporting year. That's more than thirty a day—and those are just the confirmed cases.

What we are doing for abused children in this nation isn't nearly enough.

In 2011, Miami-Dade county law enforcement officials found Nubia Docter's ten-year-old body in the back of a truck, doused with chemicals. Her twin brother, his body also badly burned by chemicals, was convulsing in the front seat of the truck. "Systematic failure," the term Heiser used for Karly's case, was the same excuse offered by Florida state officials to explain how years of repeated complaints to the Department of Children & Families (DCF) were ignored, even when those complaints came from reliable sources: teachers and principals. Nubia told her teacher herself that her father was touching her inappropriately.

Nubia's adoptive parents dismissed the laundry list of complaints— hair loss, sexual abuse, starvation, obvious bruises, reports of torture, all of it. Nubia's adoptive mother worked at a pediatric clinic. Perhaps that affiliation made it easier for Florida's DCF workers to conclude that Nubia's problems were a result of her "hyper" personality.

Instead of spending the money necessary to protect the children, the state is now shelling out considerable funds to incarcerate the offenders. Prosecutors are seeking the death penalty against the man and woman who adopted these twins and tortured them.

Yet getting people to put the dollars on the front end to prevent child abuse is a lot harder to do. "I find it disturbing that we don't have designated funding for child abuse," Karen Scheler said. "Kids like Karly do slip through the cracks. No one wants that to happen—no one. But it's hard when there's no funding. I think that funding should come on a national level. I find it appalling that our federal budget includes $28 million in designated funds to sponsor NASCAR as a recruiting tool for our military but we do not adequately fund child abuse to help intervene, support and protect our children."

Note to Readers

PLEASE JOIN THE EFFORTS TO put an end to the epidemic of child abuse in our nation. Contact your state representatives and urge them to pass Karly's Law in your state. Educate others by giving a copy of this book to every elected official, every childcare worker, every teacher, every doctor, every law enforcement official, every pastor, every social worker who comes in contact with children.

Learn the signs of child abuse. If you have a *feeling* something isn't quite right with a child, don't be so quick to rationalize it away. Don't wait to ask yourself, "What more could I have done?" Instead ask, "What will I regret not having done if this child turns up dead?" Then, whatever that thing is, *do it.* Don't wait on someone else to intervene, because chances are, you are the only one who can save that child.

To see photos & videos of Karly, visit:
www.patheos.com/blogs/karenspearszacharias/

To contact the author: karenzach.com
Twitter: @karenzach.com
zachauthor@gmail.com

For more information on Karly's Law:

www.saragelser.com/karly

Child Abuse in America

- The U.S. has more child abuse and neglect deaths than any other industrialized nation, ranking highest in both the total number of deaths and deaths on a per capita basis.
- Nearly five children die every day in America from abuse and neglect.
- In 2009, an estimated 1,770 children died from abuse in the United States.
- Over 40% of all child abuse is inflicted by the mother acting alone. Eighteen percent of child abuse is the father acting alone. Neglect makes up for over 75% of all reported abuse.
- In 2009, approximately 3.3 million child abuse reports and allegations were made involving an estimated 6 million children.
- In 2010 Children's Advocacy Centers around the country served over 266,000 child victims of abuse.
- Nearly 80% of children who die from abuse are under the age of 4.

Signs of Child Abuse

(PreventChildAbuse.org)

- Has unexplained burns, bites, bruises, broken bones, or black eyes.
- Has fading bruises or other marks noticeable after an absence from school.
- Seems frightened of their parents or others and protests or cries in their presence.
- Reports injury by a parent or another caregiver.
- School attendance is sporadic.
- Begs or steals food or money from classmates.
- Lacks needed medical or dental care, immunizations, or glasses.

- Is consistently dirty and has severe body odor.
- Lacks sufficient clothing for the weather.
- States there is no one at home to provide care.

Signs of Sexual Abuse

- Has difficulty walking or sitting.
- Suddenly refuses to change for gym or to participate in physical activities.
- Demonstrates sophisticated or unusual sexual knowledge or behavior.
- Becomes pregnant or contracts a venereal disease, particularly if under age fourteen.
- Runs away.
- Attempts suicide, or expresses a desire to die.

For More Information:

NationalChildrensAlliance.org
ChildHelp.com
EveryChildMatters.org
ChildWelfare.gov

With special thanks to these musicians for ministering to me as I wrote:

THE BAND PERRY
If I Die Young

ALLISON KRAUSE
Jewels
Jesus Help me to Stand

AQUALUNG
Brighter than Sunshine

JOHNNY CASH
Jackson
Ring of Fire
Belshazzar

CELTIC WOMAN
Away in a Manager

CHRIS RICE
Come to Jesus

CIVIL WAR
My Father's Father

DAVE BARNES
Carry Me Through

DIXIE CHICKS
I Believe in Love
Top of the World

EVA CASSIDY
Fields of Gold

HILLSONG
From the Inside Out

FERNANDO ORTEGO
Come Thou Fount of Every Blessing

JEFF BUCKLEY
Hallelujiah

MERLE HAGGARD
Folsom Prison Blues

MERCYME
Finally Home

NEEDTOBREATHE
Girl Named Tennessee
The Heat

NORAH JONES
Seven Years

NICKEL CREEK
Sweet Afton

NICHOLE NORDAMAN
How Deep the Father's Love

REGINA SPEKTOR
The Calculation

Author's Note

ANN RULE TOLD ME THAT I should write this story. "It is your Ted Bundy story," Ann said. But she also warned me that few publishers would have courage enough to print such a book. David Poindexter at MacAdam/Cage did. I am indebted. Thank you, David.

Dorothy Carico Smith took Karly's story and translated it into the stunning artwork that is the cover and the heart of this book. Thank you, Dorothy.

If it is possible for someone to believe in a book more than the writer, my agent, Alanna Ramirez at Trident Media, did that. Alanna took the first manuscript of this story and told me to rewrite the entire thing. I was terrified, but I did as she suggested. What you are now holding in your hands is the result of Alanna's vision and insight. Thank you, Alanna.

It can be difficult to pass a book off to an editor, when you know that editor is going to take Solomon's sword to your baby. I knew I had chosen the right editor, though, when Sonny Brewer called me one afternoon in September 2011 to talk about the story. Only he couldn't; he was too overcome at the first mention of Karly. I knew then that

Sonny *got* this story, and *got* what I was trying to do as a writer. This book is not the one I gave to Sonny. It is a much better book. Thank you, Sonny.

Michelle Dotter also added her keen insights and kept me from stumbling along. Thank you, Michelle.

Thank you, David Sheehan, for entrusting Karly's story to me. You know how you tell me you just want to live a life that honors Karly? My hope is that I've written a story that honors you, the way you honor her. You have taught me more about what it means to live a life of faith than I ever learned in Sunday School. I hope Karly's story stirs up the waters between Oregon and Ireland. I hope and pray we save another child's life.

While this book is memoir, I did not rely on memory alone. Shawn Field's defense attorney, Clark Willes, shared his files with me. Additionally, I did further research, conducted dozens of interviews, and had generous assistance from the staff at the Benton County Courthouse and the Oregon Department of Justice, as well as articles from the Corvallis *Gazette Times*, who reported the story with diligence. I have taken the liberties to alter five names: Jack, who remains in touch with Shawn Field, and Kate and Hillary, who are minors, and Chuck and Missy McDonald, Hillary's parents, who are trying to protect her.

Thank you to Mike Wells, Joan Demarest, Judge Janet Holcomb, Scott Heiser, DeLynn Zoller, Dr. Shanilka deSoyza, the jury of fifteen, the staff at the Benton County Courthouse, the staff at the Oregon Department of Justice, the Corvallis Police Department, Dan Koenig, Clark Willes, Karen Scheler and Albany's ABC House, Representative Sara Gelser, Emmet Whittaker, Liz Sokolowski, Bill Furtick, Rick Wallace, Noreen Sheehan, Andrea Sheehan, and the countless others who contributed to this story.

These people read early versions of this book and offered valuable feedback: Debbie Johnson, John Cole, Rick Wallace, Bob Welch, Peg Willis, Rebekah Sanderlin, Kathy Richards, Andy Meisenheimer, Shellie Rushing Tomlinson, Eleanor Lucas, and Konnie Handschuch. Thank you.

Shelby Zacharias read the manuscript countless times, paying careful attention to all the litter I'd left behind. She cleaned up after me without complaint. Thank you, Shelby. Ashley Sinner took my idea and Sonny's idea and came up the perfect title. Thank you, Ashley, and also for giving me and Daddy a precious "Sinner" to adore.

And to my circle of writer friends—your stories kept me laughing through the tears. Thank you to Patti Callahan Henry, Michael Morris, Marjorie Wentworth, Mary Alice Monroe, River Jordan, Shellie Rushing Tomlinson, Gary Nelson, Kerry Madden, Renea Winchester, Robert Dugoni, Bob Welch, Amy Sorrells, Billy Coffey and all you other Luddites committed to the craft.

Thank you to Communications Department at Central Washington University for giving me the opportunity to share my love of writing and journalism with the writers and journalists of tomorrow. I'll always be a Beaver Believer but I'm honored to be counted among the Wildcats.

Big hugs to all my Facebook and Twitter friends. You keep the lonelies away when I'm writing. Thank you for the prayers and the one-liners.

Thank you to Thom Chambliss of the Pacific Northwest Booksellers Association and Wanda Jewell of the Southeast Independent Booksellers Association for all your tireless efforts on behalf of writers, readers and booksellers. And a huge thank you to all you indie booksellers.

These friends listened and encouraged me as I talked my way through the Karly story. Thank you Karin Wilson, Peggy Wright, John B. and Stacey Howell, Skip and Nancy Jones, Linda Barnes, Lynn Wilkes, Gary Nelson, Lois Breedlove, Debbie Johnson, Rick Wallace, Becky Philpott, the ladies at Wednesday morning Bible study, and my care group buddies.

Tim, honey, thank you for being my faithful sponsor all these years. I hope I can return the hospitality someday soon. And Mama, thank you for all the ways you kept me safe.